Environmental Quality and Society

ENVIRONMENTAL QUALITY AND SOCIETY,

Edited by Richard A. Tybout

Ohio State University Press

"Early Education and the Conservation of Sanative Environments," by
Paul F. Brandwein, is adapted from "Origins of Public Policy and Practice
in Conservation: Early Education and the Conservation of Sanative
Environments," from FUTURE ENVIRONMENTS OF NORTH AMERI-
CA, edited by F. Fraser Darling and John P. Milton. Copyright © 1966
by The Conservation Foundation. Reprinted by permission of Doubleday
& Company, Inc.

The adapted version appearing in this volume first appeared in *Theory
into Practice*, Vol. 4, No. 3 (June 1970).

"Reorganizing the Federal Environmental Effort," by Michael McCloskey,
originally appeared in the *Duquesne Law Review*, Vol. XI (1972–73).

Library of Congress Cataloguing in Publication Data
Conference on Quality of the Environment, Ohio State University, 1970
    Environmental quality and society.

    Conference sponsored by the College of Agriculture and Home Eco-
nomics, College of Biological Sciences, College of Education, College of
Engineering, and College of Social and Behavioral Sciences of Ohio State
University.
    Includes index.
    1. Environmental policy—United States—Congresses. 2. Environ-
mental protection—United States—Congresses. 3. Human ecology—
Congresses. I. Tybout, Richard Alton, 1920–   ed. II. Ohio. State Uni-
versity, Columbus. College of Agriculture and Home Economics. III. Title
HC110.E5C664 1970   301.31   75-2244
ISBN 0-8142-0214-4

TABLE OF CONTENTS

NOTES ON THE CONTRIBUTORS

Durward L. Allen is professor of wildlife ecology, Purdue University, former president of the Wildlife Society, and recipient of numerous conservation awards. His published books and other works include over 170 titles in conservation.

Arthur A. Atkisson, Jr. is president, Institute of Urban Ecology and Public Affairs, Inc., and consultant to the Institute of Environmental Health, School of Public Health, The University of Texas. He has been professor of urban health and administrative sciences at the School of Public Health; adjunct professor of urban design at Rice University; executive director of the Institute of Urban Ecology at the University of Southern California, and deputy director of the Los Angeles County Air Pollution Control District. He has participated as member or chairman of a wide range of public service committees, and is the author of many works in the field of urban environmental quality.

Robert Bierstedt is professor of sociology, University of Virginia, former president of the Eastern Sociological Society, and former vice-president, American Sociological Association. He has published extensively in general sociology.

Paul F. Brandwein is adjunct professor, University of Pittsburgh, a member of the National Humanities Faculty, senior vice-president, Harcourt Brace Jovanovich, Inc., and editor-in-chief of the School Department. Recently he has been curricular designer and senior author of three programs of instruction and learning in the elementary schools: *Concepts in Science; The Social Sciences: Concepts and Values;* and *Self Expression and Conduct: The Humanities.* He is author and coauthor of some 45 books and numerous research articles in science and education.

Adolf Ciborowski was deputy director for research and development, Center for Housing, Building and Planning, United Nations. A Polish citizen, he headed the United Nations task forces for assistance in the postwar reconstruction of Warsaw, Poland; Skopje, Yugoslavia; and other cities destroyed by war and natural disasters.

W. Wesley Eckenfelder is Distinguished Professor of Environmental and Water Resources Engineering, Vanderbilt University, and private consultant for industrial waste treatment. He is the author of a large number of books and articles in the fields of sewage treatment, water quality, and environmental health.

Morton Gorden is president of Development Sciences, Inc., and former associate professor of political science, University of Pennsylvania. His interests and publications deal with systems analysis of political affairs and environmental policy.

S. Smith Griswold (deceased) was president, S. Smith Griswold Associates; formerly: president, Seversky Dynamics Research Associates; associate director, Abatement and Control, National Center for Air Pollution Control, Department of Health, Education and Welfare; and for approximately twelve years, air pollution control officer, Air Pollution Control District, County of Los Angeles. He was the author of a number of publications and the contributor of services to many public agencies.

Orris C. Herfindahl (deceased) was senior research associate, Resources for the Future, Inc. He was the author of many books and articles on natural resource economics and pollution control. A memorial volume, titled "Resource Economics: Selected Works of Orris C. Herfindahl," in honor of Dr. Herfindahl is in preparation by the staff of Resources for the Future, Inc.

Charles L. Hosler is dean of the College of Earth and Mineral Sciences, Pennsylvania State University, and fellow, American Meteorological Society. He serves on a large number of public committees, panels, and other bodies dealing with meteorological problems, and has published extensively in the field.

G. Evelyn Hutchinson is Sterling Professor of Zoology, Yale University; Hon. D.H.L., Lawrence College; Hon. D.Sc., Princeton University, Niagara University, and Washington University, Saint Louis. He has worked and published extensively on all aspects of freshwater biology, but also on ecological theory and a number of miscellaneous aspects of natural history and archaeology. Celebratory issues of *Limnology and Oceanography* (March 1971) and of the *Proceedings of the Connecticut Academy of Arts and Sciences* (December 1972) were published in his honor.

Justin W. Leonard is professor of natural resources and of zoology and senior research scientist, Museum of Zoology, University of Michigan. He has served on a number of public bodies, and is the author of many works on natural resources, fishery biology, and aquatic entomology.

Michael McCloskey is executive director of the Sierra Club. B.A. Harvard University, Magna Cum Laude; J.D. University of Oregon. He is the author and editor of numerous articles on conservation policy.

Gaylord Nelson is United States senator from the State of Wisconsin. He is a member of the Senate Committee on Labor and Public Welfare, and chairman of the Subcommittee on Employment, Poverty, and Migratory Labor. In this capacity he has authored poverty legislation such as the Legal Services Act, manpower legislation, and economic opportunity amendments that extend and expand such programs as Head Start. He is also on the Senate Finance Committee, and chairman of its Subcommittee on Private Pension Plans, and on the Senate Interior Committee, where he has done much of his work in the field of conservation and protection of Indians' rights. Nelson is also chairman of the Monopoly Subcommittee of the Select Committee on Small Business, and has conducted his well-known investigations of the drug industry and its pricing practices. He served two terms as governor of Wisconsin, the first Democratic governor to be elected in this century.

Edward Stainbrook is professor and chairman, Department of Human Behavior, University of Southern California School of Medicine; past president, Southern California Psychiatric Society; and a fellow in both the American College of Physicians and the American Psychiatric Association. He has written extensively in the field.

Richard A. Tybout is professor of economics, Ohio State University. He is the author of many books and articles on pricing and public investment policy, especially as related to energy resources.

Richard A. Tybout

chapter one

INTRODUCTION

Modern man in the late twentieth century is probably close to his zenith in quality of life attainable through existing social institutions. Annual gains of GNP, in the Western world and elsewhere, are accompanied by annual losses of our natural heritage in unspoiled land, clean air, clean water, wildlife, and open space; for man is engaged in a one-way replacement of his natural environment by the wastes of civilization. The replacement is, of course, sought not for its own sake but for the material gains and comforts created in the process. It is nonetheless a replacement, and has reached proportions that now reduce the enjoyment of the material welfare it has produced. Over the decades ahead, and in the absence of institutional renovation, environmental degradation can be expected more and more to offset the satisfactions from real goods consumption and to render still less effective attempts to improve the lot of humanity by means that ignore environmental effects.

At some extreme level of environmental deprivation, life itself is threatened. Even this level has been experienced today. Use of the environment as a receptor for waste has led to a wide range of pulmonary diseases, to lead poisoning, mercury poisoning, and other afflictions. At less extreme levels, the quality of life is reduced, and a range of human reactions, personal and social, render unimportant the answer to the biological question of whether we are living. It is the humanistic question of the significance of life that counts.

I

The present anthology places environmental issues in a social context. This is the context in which they enter human affairs and in which they will be resolved, if they are resolved. It is through the effect of each man's activities on his neighbors that our seemingly relentless march into oblivion is being perpetrated. It is through changes in social institutions, or the rules by which men live in society, that our collective destiny can be salvaged.

Never before in human history has it been so important that men in collectives behave rationally, not only to avoid the holocaust of global war, but, beyond war, to achieve a quality of life worthy of peace. The question is whether humanity can organize itself to realize the goals that distinguish humane from other life objectives. Twentieth-century man is forging an answer.

The essays that appear in this volume were drawn from the Conference on Quality of the Environment conducted at the Ohio State University in November 1970 as part of the university's centenary commemoration.[1] The Conference was sponsored jointly by five colleges: College of

1. There are two exceptions. The Brandwein essay is reproduced from another source, but carries the same message as given by its author at the conference. The Tybout essay was written after the conference. The McCloskey essay, on the other hand, is the same (with limited updating) as presented at the conference, though it was published in the Duquesne Law Review before the present volume appeared.

Agriculture and Home Economics, College of Biological Sciences, College of Education, College of Engineering, and College of Social and Behavioral Sciences.

The present collection, and the Conference on which it is based, were designed to maximize insight produced by juxtaposition of the individual views of experts in as many different disciplines as represented by the sponsoring colleges. Some of the authors deal in concepts, some in facts. Some are philosophical, others pragmatic. Some state problems, others cast them in an operational frame and intimate directions in which politico-economic solutions may be found. The approach is eclectic. The emphasis is on basic understanding, and the content is explicitly interdisciplinary.

A grand synthesis is not at hand, nor is it likely soon to be discovered. Environmental problems are as diverse as man's contacts with his physical universe and as pervasive as his social institutions. Individual scholars have long held deep understanding of a wide range of separate aspects of the environment. But effective integration of their knowledge has been lacking, effective communication difficult, and effective public understanding inadequate. This volume seeks to lay a foundation that will remedy these deficiencies, to find common ground for discourse among specialists, common understanding among generalists, and to set forth a structure of knowledge for further pursuit of the same ends.

The spirit of the present work is very much in the utilitarian tradition of American higher education, though the need for environmental studies exceeds the pace and magnitude of higher education's response. Lesser needs a century ago gave rise to the establishment of land grant colleges for agriculture and the mechanical arts. Public health programs subsequently received attention. Problem-focused interdisciplinary education and research in these areas, persisting over fifty to a hundred years, have

brought impressive results, so much so that a reordering
of priorities is now called for. As our material welfare
advances, our quality of life declines, in large part as
a result of the means by which gains have been made
in material welfare. The need is current for a review of
time-honored priorities and for a commitment of intellectual resources commensurate with the magnitude of environmental problems.

Unfortunately, we do not have fifty to a hundred years
to solve our newly discovered environmental problems.
The time horizon is more like a few decades, and the
penalty for a late start is a late finish. The doubling times
of today's degradations are at least as short as the doubling
times of the American GNP and world population. Technology may permit us to accommodate more people on
this earth in relative comfort. But only social change can
restructure our relationships to the natural environment
and bring population control, redistribution of income and
the preservation of natural havens—for human refuge.

Social change is important, first and foremost, in higher
education and the closed circles that surround it. If we
are ever to face up to the imperatives of the man-nature
confrontation, we must study them, seriously and comprehensively, in our colleges and universities. If we are to
honor our obligation to the next generation, which is
already among us; if we are to establish a new integrity
of social decision-making in a more complex world; if we
are to strike a balance with nature for the first time in
human history—if we intend to do those things, then we
must give them the attention they deserve in our centers
of learning.

II

The contributors to the Conference on Quality of the
Environment were each asked to submit papers in writing

or, as an alternative, to permit their remarks to be transcribed for editing and publication. The great majority submitted prepared papers, though the lead contributor, G. E. Hutchinson, spoke spontaneously, without manuscript or notes. His simple, straightforward discussion of ultimates from a biologist's point of view sets the context for the discussion of ecology and human affairs.

Allen applies the lessons of ecology to man's predicament. Perhaps the most characteristic feature of the human adventure is its ecological disequilibrium. Man has substituted learned for geneticly determined behavior but has not directed his technology to replicate nature's cycles or substitute for them other stabilizing mechanisms. Humane values have abridged natural selection with ecological consequences as yet unclear.

Leonard and Gorden, one an ecologist, the other a political scientist, evaluate in different ways and with different conclusions the ability of contemporary man to grasp the significance of ecological matters and, through social processes, to act on his own long-run behalf. The lessons of the past are not encouraging, particularly in view of the need for worldwide cooperation. Additional insights on the same problem appear in other essays, particularly that by Herfindahl, an economist.

The establishment of self-renewing processes, whether nature's original processes or man's substitutes, would provide long-term assurance of the viability of the human species, hopefully in conditions of life consistent with a high degree of self-realization. The astonishing thing is that humanity has progressed as far as it has in the absence of man's participation in a stable ecosystem. The observation is most relevant in the industrial world of the last two centuries, and the explanation is, of course, that economic man has found ways of circumventing the limitations of his natural environment. Whether preindustrial agrarian societies were in equilibrium with the natural environment in all respects is not as important a question for present purposes. If isolated from world trade, they tended to reach maximum population levels.

Science may continue to remove the major limitational effects of natural resources on man's population growth, but probably with increasing destruction of natural landscapes as lower-grade mineral resources are exploited. Interdependencies in society can be expected to increase as the ability of any man to strike off on his own is reduced. The social problems of future worlds in which scarcity is overcome by close-knit organization offer a number-one priority for study and more than a few opportunities for nightmares.

Two aspects of the subject are covered in the present volume. Hosler discusses meteorological consequences of increased fuel consumption. Others discuss recycling, either to complete nature's cycles, as Gorden puts it, or to minimize new defacements of nature from exploitation of virgin materials. The point of view in these recommendations is that man should restore and preserve nature for his own well-being, because he is a part of nature and needs the psychic qualities it offers. Preservation is justified by nature for nature's sake and does not depend on the use of natural resources as inputs to any present or future production process. Nature's processes become a value to be preserved in their own right.

III

The environmental problem is exacerbated in all aspects by population growth. Sheer numbers of human beings can create environmental stress, even at low standards of living, and, in addition, produce crowding effects that reduce the quality of the social environment. The incidence of our most serious social problems in densely populated urban areas attests to some of the consequences of crowding.

Worldwide humanity is now experiencing the most rapid population growth in its history, and there is every prospect that growth rates will hold in the decades ahead. Means of achieving the necessary birth control practices, if not realized through improvement in the standard of living, will necessitate other adjustments in social customs, as discussed by Bierstedt. It will be ironic if human freedom to multiply eventually brings a decline in other freedoms and forces far more drastic changes in life patterns.

Man in a crowd is impersonal, detached, more concerned for his individual welfare than for that of the community. Paradoxically, a sense of community diminishes at the very time that environmental problems create the need for empathic collectivism. This is part of the significance of Atkisson's population implosion, though his patterns of migration also suggest a behavioral recognition of optimal size of urban centers.

Ciborowski's experiences with the reconstruction of destroyed cities provide a number of insights into the possibilities of reconciling environmental amenities and urban functionalism, also on the importance of participation by the prospective occupants in the design of whatever local environments they are expected to occupy. Atkisson's Venetian experience speaks to the same and a number of related points in the conceptualization of local urban environments.

If we are concerned to protect the natural environment, we must protect the living conditions, sociological as well as physical, in which men develop their self-images. The origins of delinquency can be traced to deficiencies in the home environment. Following Brandwein, conservation begins in early childhood. If we do not practice human conservation of the children, they will vandalize the environment. Examples are apparent in all walks of life and all ages of yesterday's children.

Western man is experiencing accelerated dehumanization and denaturalization in the technocratic regime to which he continues to adapt his life. Stainbrook analyzes the psychological nature of human conservation. Physical design in the cities of the future can provide more avenues for personal gratification. To a greater extent, human conservation requires social relationships that keep man compassionately related to man in the larger framework of his natural origins. The case for protecting both the psychological and the physical environments is based on a concern for human welfare. If that concern is not strong enough, then we shall fail to protect either of them, for lack of a sense of community.

IV

Our unprecedented and continuously rising standard of living is both a remedy and a cause of our difficulties. It is a remedy in that we cannot hope to satisfy the need for material improvement of urban and rural poverty without the products of an affluent society. It is a cause in the wastage of resources that comes from not taking account of the damages that arise from our narrow view of production processes. In our present scheme of things, natural resources are valued primarily as inputs to production processes, which in turn derive their significance from their material outputs. Exceptions, of limited scope in comparison with our total natural resource endowment, appear in reclamation laws, parks, wilderness areas, and the like. A more comprehensive approach may evolve over the coming decades through national land-use zoning or other instruments for wider recognition of our stake in natural amenities, but these are not yet with us.

At the other end of the production process are pollution waste products. Again, public policies for taking account of the damages and offenses these create are yet to be built into social decision-making. To do so is the heart of the pollution control problem as seen by Herfindahl and Tybout. The need for social renovation takes an immediate form in the qualifications implied for traditional market processes and property rights.

The damaging effects of pollution are properly viewed as a cost imposed on some—those who lose health, natural amenities, and property value—for the benefit of others—producers and consumers of the products whose production gives rise to by-product pollution. A full social costing would require compensation of the former by the latter, with the resulting adjustments of price providing a deterrent to consumption and an incentive to reduce pollution.

Our political systems and social institutions have not yet come to grips with this most conspicuous of environmental problems. We persist in defining pollution control in a way that makes it very difficult for the public to take effective action. The use of standards and approaches that require public officials to confront private plant managers on the question of whether a given method of control is "technically feasible and economically reasonable" typically results in frustration of the public interest and occasional inequity to private interests. The widespread practice of giving tax benefits for add-on pollution control devices is still less conducive to long-run solutions. The subversion of the public interest in the latter case and its obfuscation in the former persist despite their obvious shortcomings, while scant attention is given to implementing an effective effluent tax system. Other challenges to institutional renovation are found in Herfindahl's survey.

At the technological level, the evidence is that a great deal can be accomplished to control pollution without much adverse effect on conventional output. Eckenfelder takes the first steps in analyzing pollution control costs. A high degree of further improvement, it would appear from his graphs, can be achieved at costs that are no more than two to four times those required for the modest goals set in present federal standards. Moreover, it should be remembered that we are at the beginning of our efforts to develop efficient pollution control techniques. The history of technological progress suggests that rapid improvements can be expected in the early stages of development of new technologies. Accordingly, there is every reason to think that abatement costs will rapidly decline in the years ahead as more attention is given to pollution control. Technology responds to the lodestone of economic utility and can be expected to produce the necessary adjustments better the more thoroughly environmental preservation is built into our economic calculus.

Federal policy in the United States is still being developed, and federal organization for environmental protection is in a state of flux. Senator Nelson speaks from his vantage point to the multiplying needs for environmental protection in a large number of specific areas. Griswold confirms the need for institutional renovation. McCloskey reviews recent changes in federal organization and sets an agenda for the future, culminating in his "Environmental Bill of Rights."

As a general proposition, whether in the Western world, Eastern world, or Third world, political power tends to be very much associated with economic power. Unfortunately, economic power is, in turn, often produced by environmental exploitation. The validity of the implied syllogism is apparent to every casual observer. Whether we shall have the political courage, wisdom, and inventiveness to shift the facts of the situation remains to be seen. If Nelson's and McCloskey's agendas for the future are to become realities and, beyond these, if the reasoning found in this volume is to be effective in government decision-making, environmental protection must be represented in public decisions at least as strongly as is its antithesis.

V

The Age of Man has brought environmental manipulation, some deliberate, some coincidental. Nature's patterns have been changed, often with adverse consequences for the well-being of man himself. Now we face the need to adjust man's patterns. The need is immediate and compelling. It is reflected in the current doubling of real American GNP every seventeen years and of world population every thirty-six years. For how many centuries can we stand the unmitigated environmental effects of these growth rates? At stake in our response is nothing less than the ability of man to master his own destiny.

part one

ECOLIBRIUM

G. Evelyn Hutchinson

chapter two

FOR WHAT SORT OF LIFE
SHOULD MANKIND AIM?

I want to start as if we were all paramecia or water fleas or something of the sort, with nice, simple populations that are amenable to study in the laboratory over many generations, or what, from a human point of view, are very long periods of time. I think it is important for ecologists to appreciate the idea that different organisms have very different sorts of time scale even though they are all living on the same earth, which goes around on its own axis once every 24 hours and goes round the sun once every 365 and a quarter days. The time that nature provides is imposed onto a good many different kinds of life history, and sometimes it is convenient to be able to look at a system in the laboratory, behaving as human populations conceivably might behave over a period of tens or hundreds of thousands of years. The kind of model I want to use is the one to which biologists naturally turn.

The biologist draws an S-shaped curve (figure 1), and

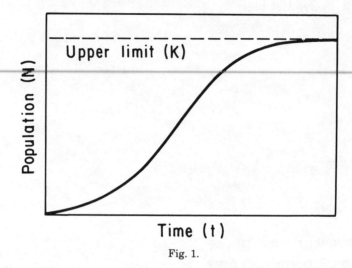

Fig. 1.

then he writes down a differential equation of this form:

$$\frac{dN}{dt} = rN\left(\frac{K-N}{K}\right)$$

dN/dt may be read as the rate of change of the population with respect to time, or, more simply, its rate of growth. At the beginning, the birthrate is r, sometimes called the Malthusian parameter, for obvious reasons. N is the number of members of the population at any given moment; when N is very small, the quantity in parentheses is almost unity and the population starts growing at a rate proportional to N, as Malthus said it would. The expression in brackets is essentially the relative number of vacant spaces that are left in the system that you are dealing with, the ratio of the difference between saturation and the actual number, to the saturation value. So there are two constants, r, which is the initial birth rate unmodified, and K, which is the upper limit, so that when N reaches, or practically reaches, K, the term in brackets becomes zero and nothing happens.

It is not at all difficult to make a system of this sort in the laboratory with water fleas or paramecia. When you get anywhere near K, life becomes very uncomfortable, and this discomfort is expressed in the fact that under starvation conditions practically no reproduction takes place. The value that K reaches can be set in a number of different ways, and one of the ways, of course, is to have a constant food supply coming in from outside. In the case of a theoretical biological system, this is essentially sunlight producing the growth of a plant and hence the growth of a population that eats of the plant, and so on, at a rate that will finally bring the population up to saturation at a level corresponding to the rate of input of energy. At that point, if a member of the population is to reproduce, another member has got to die. Actually you can see this occurring in water flea populations very easily. Practically no individuals are carrying even a single egg at saturation, but occasionally an egg appears that will probably correspond to the random death of an individual. This is the sort of system that makes people thinking in human terms shiver, a society consisting mainly of starving adults. When one dies, an occasional birth is allowed.

We also could limit the population, and do in some cases in experiments, by allowing the excretory products of the organism to accumulate. With yeast, for instance, the accumulation is of alcohol, and finally that puts the yeast into a somewhat somnolent condition. The yeast does not reproduce any more but remains for a long time viable, so if you dilute the alcohol, it will start growing again.

The curve shown in figure 1 was first developed by a man named Verhulst in 1838 for human populations, but human populations behave much more irregularly. The reason for this undoubtedly is that we have various tricks by which we make K bigger and bigger. If one starts thinking of the whole of human reproduction and population growth largely in these terms, I think it becomes a little bit clearer what we are doing.

We try to increase K in all sorts of different ways. For one thing, we do not regard ourselves as all one population. We regard ourselves as little subpopulations; each one of them is trying to make K bigger, and one way of doing it is to take somebody else's K. This has been probably the favorite method in the past. It is becoming so dangerous that we can only hope that when we stop our involvements in such processes in Southeast Asia, we will stop doing it for good. That is, perhaps, a rather dim hope, but it is one that we must entertain.

Among the more legitimate tricks, we can increase our productivity, of food or other goods that might be limiting population at any given time. This is, in fact, what we have done on a large scale by scientific agriculture, and it is what underdeveloped countries in general want to do. There are, however, certain problems that can arise here that should warn us of possible difficulties ahead. Though it has been rather generally felt that food supply would set an upper value to the human population in the relatively near future, producing, at best, the unhappy situation of the equilibrium *Daphnia* population, it seems not impossible that in some areas various kinds of pollution may begin to operate before the limitation by food becomes threatening. Moreover, at the present time, given the tendency of expanding human populations into ever-growing cities, it seems likely that a quite complicated effect of crowding and general environmental deprivation, leading to ennui, drug addition, and crime could come to have significant demographic effects. An excessive preoccupation with increasing productivity may be most unwise.

There is also a specific aspect of the matter that needs investigation. Most economists believe foreign trade to be a good thing. However, when trade is between a highly developed country making special demands for non-renew-able raw materials, and a less-developed country needing industrial products, the effect of trade may be to prejudice the future of the underdeveloped country, which is left high and dry when the supply of the raw materials runs out. This happened in Peru after the palmy days of the guano trade, and could happen in many oil-producing but otherwise potentially barren states today. I feel very strongly that the most-developed countries, particularly the United States, should exercise more restraint in their demands on global resources of uneven distribution.

In dealing with any of these problems, we very easily find ourselves passing from the simplicity of the logistic growth curve to the problem of what we can do with its theoretical formulation to produce desirable ends. We have, indeed, to pass from the mathematics of the growth curve to what are essentially ethical considerations.

The first ethical question that I feel we should ask is, "What do we mean by a desirable population?" What is it we want in a population? My feeling, looking at the thing as a biologist, is that ideally somewhere about one-third of the way up the curve to a constant K things would go very satisfactorily. There is plenty for everybody; in human terms, there are enough people around to have adequate types of social interrelations. If we could have a stationary population in a system that was about one-third saturated, we should probably be doing very well. I do not know whether there is any possibility of stabilizing at that kind of level, the significance of which depends very largely on what is setting the K value.

It must be remembered that in the original case we considered K as defined by a constantly renewable resource. If it were determined by a non-renewable resource such as petroleum, the population might approach an upper limit where the maximum possible exploitation rate just balanced consumption at a given time; but then as the reserve began to dry up, the population would have to turn to other resources or perish. Most economists in the past have assumed that human ingenuity will always provide the other source, but in a limited world with a finite if large number of geochemical possibilities, this is not entirely obvious. Whatever level we set as desirable, if the general growth rate is determined by biological considerations interacting with a non-renewable resource, we finally have to face either a radical change in that resource or disaster.

Even if the upper limit is something like food, which in essence is renewable, it still seems to me very unwise to regard a nearly saturated system as desirable. The consequences of living close to an equilibrium are obviously too unpleasant. There is also another very important aspect of the matter. Since the adjustments of a population to its resources cannot be instantaneous, there is a distinct possibility of oscillations being generated, as the value of N may overshoot K, producing more offspring than can be maintained in equilibrium. There is then a decline below equilibrium. If the time lag adjustment is short, the oscillations may damp out; but if it is longer, a very marked limit cycle may be generated. This can be realized experimentally in fast-breeding animals such as water fleas. In human populations living in a markedly modifiable environment, a regular oscillation would be most unlikely; but the unpleasant aspects of the decline after K is surpassed might be, in some circumstances, very great indeed. We should be much better off in every way if we kept away from saturation.

The energy consumption, for instance, of the average inhabitant of the United States is about 10,000 watts per day; whereas the energy required to stay alive is closer to 100 watts per day,[1] and the average consumption elsewhere in the world is more like 1,000 watts per day.

1. S. F. Singer, *Scientific American*, September, 1970, p. 175.

The political and moral aspects of discrepancies of this kind—and there are many of them—involve appalling difficulties. Some may be solved by the Third world catching up with the first and second; but in many cases the resources are not enough to go round, and the only solution is great restraint on over-consumption.

We can ask ourselves what a population set at a reasonably desirable level really demands, and, of course, it demands food. It demands, in all temperate and arctic regions, a good deal of fuel, fundamentally as a necessity for remaining alive. There are people in Berkeley, California, who apparently can live most of the year on the pavement; and there are people in Bombay and Calcutta who are forced to live the entire year out in the streets, all functions being performed in the open air among mass groups of people. This seems to me to be comparable to the *Daphnia* culture that has reached its limit and is doing a mild amount of reproducing to fill the spaces produced by dying *Daphnia.* But the comparison is only partial because the area of the city can extend and the pavement slums move out with it. This example is something we ought to bear in mind in showing what human populations are capable of, not what they ought to do.

So we need, for biological necessities, food and in all temperate regions some way of keeping warm in winter and sufficient space just to move around in, and, presumably, also some natural amenities like a stream or rain running down to wash away excretory products. This, then, does not give one very great room for what we regard as human values. We should be much better off being chimpanzees or birds with low intellects, leading fairly free emotional lives. We obviously want a great many more things than that.

First, we presumably want methods by which the backbreaking aspects of human life are ameliorated. In nearly all parts of the world that we inhabit, the natural conditions of the environment impose a great deal of work if we are going to live even at the simplest kind of human level. Even in the paleolithic age, hunting was presumably a fairly strenuous occupation, though paleolithic man doubtless also enjoyed the chase, because this kind of activity has gone on long after it has lost any significance for actual food production. As soon as agriculture became invented, which permitted a much greater value of K for any given area, the amount of work that had to be done in some ways increased; in other ways, the food supply became much more constant, much less dependent on all kinds of external contingents. As a good deal more work had to be done, there were doubtless ways by which some people put that work over onto other people. Much of the food production presumably passed from men to women when agriculture was first invented. All this kind of activity, which permits the colonization of slightly less favorable environments than the tropical savannah country that we presumably evolved in, meant more and more work as less and less favorable areas were colonized, more and more incentives to find ways of reducing that work, and, of course, finally led to the industrial revolution.

This means then that one of our major preoccupations is with what may be called labor-saving devices, such as fire and the wheel and the domestication of animals and the invention of the steam engine and the use of electricity and the development of aviation and all the other things that we regard as an essential part of modern civilization. These are clearly the prerequisites to a large extent of modern human life, and they are also the major causes of difficulties that we have with the environment. They have been developed without any consideration of material and energetic balances, and this is really what we are having to face up to.

In addition to this, as human beings we obviously require a great many things that we regard as values, and some of these things involve also material objects that go along with them. Status is frequently expressed by the possession of valuable objects. When very few people had status and the valuable objects were mainly valuable because they were rare things like gold or precious stones, it did not provide any great threat to the environment. When many people want status, and they can buy it from an automobile dealer, then it does begin to pose a considerable threat to the environment. A new car uses iron and a number of other things that are not recycled at all easily. Then status begins to be overexpensive.

We need, obviously, all the kinds of satisfaction that go along with our condition as a human social organism. This involves merely being in groups in the strictest sense of the social organism; it involves sexuality, and it involves the parent-child relationship. Now there is no difficulty about being in groups at the present time. The only trouble there is that perhaps the groups are much too big. In any kind of group interaction, you can legitimately expect the difficulties to rise by the square of the number of the people because the number of interactions will be proportional to their square rather than to their number. When you reach a certain size, mere bigness is not an advantage at all.

Sexuality is something that we talk a lot about at the moment. I am inclined to think that it probably will take care of itself. It is not something that we need to worry too much about in the present context. The question of the child-parent relationship is probably a much more significant thing to think about. Both sexuality and the other kinds of social interaction all are involved here. It is reasonably certain phylogenetically that our position as a social animal is based fundamentally on the parent-child relationship, that nearly all social interaction of a positive kind that brings people more closely together is phylogenetically based on the attitude of parents to their children. And I say parents because it is quite clear that in the primates, and probably in the primates alone, right from the beginning the male may take interest in grooming the baby. We do know this can happen in both of the major groups in the prosimians, which suggests that it is quite fundamental.

One of our difficulties, and this is something that is very important at the present time, is the very simple one that people like having children. The hopeful movement to get zero population growth is probably a prerequisite of any kind of solution, although it raises its own difficulties, very major ones. I think a decline in the population might not be at all a bad thing. Against this we have all the economic difficulties, all the difficulties that are inherent in having an age structure where promotion from assistant to associate professor becomes a near impossibility, where most of the people when they really learn how to do anything have to retire because otherwise no one else is ever going to get a chance. All that kind of difficulty is added to the problem of unemployment if you do not have economic growth. This does not mean that even in a stationary population there is not an enormous amount of work to do improving the place in which we live. When people say there is no work to do, they really mean there is no money to pay for the work.

Finally, I feel that one of the things we have to do is try to see how far all the values that we hope to follow can be satisfied by a minimum demand on the environment. The main way of doing this, provided that we have a reasonable amount of food for everybody and in temperate regions a method of keeping people warm, is to attempt to substitute for all the kinds of activity that are material- and energy-consuming others that are less so. This presumably can only be done by an enormous increase in the satisfactions that can be derived from purely mental activities (I mean here both intellectual and emotional) and will involve education being changed from something that enables you to get a front-office job in a big industry to something that enables you to take pleasure in a large number of things that can be just held in the head. The amount of paper that is needed to print all the great literature, all the great music of the world must be very very small compared with the amount of paper that is needed to print the daily delivery of junk mail, for instance. If we could only get people to read and appreciate and go about their business, as they walk down the street, thinking about Sappho's Odes or a Bach fugue, then we would probably produce something that was really saving the environment quite a lot of strain.

I know this sounds absurdly utopian, and I have expressed it in the most extreme form that I can; but I feel quite certain that if we do not project our desires—what we aim for—as far as we can see, we have no guarantee that we are going in the right direction at all. It is only if we can see the light at the end of the road that we know that we are going in the right direction. This light may be a very long way off, and it may appear to some people to be, in the current term, totally irrelevant. But in some ways, I would say the most important thing to do in education is to introduce an adequate supply of irrelevancy along with all the other things that we need in order to save the environment.

Durward L. Allen

chapter three

MAN AND THE ENVIRONMENTAL ETHIC

Among better-informed people of the world, a great debate
is flourishing. In halls of government, in the public press,
at scientific meetings, and in mány another forum, the
works of man on earth are both praised and deplored.
On the one hand, there is authoritative alarm over the
state of our environment and the possibilities for survival.
On the other, we have expert opinions that there is little
to worry about. The wide divergence of views makes one
conclusion, at least, seem fairly reliable: there is a great
deal in human affairs of which we have little understanding.

Our modern ignorance is not so much in detail as in
using what we know. Recently a sociologist pointed out
the imbalance between the large-scale collection of facts
in public programs and the study and analysis that would
convert masses of raw data into useful policy-making. He
said that ours is "a national perspective which is often
well-informed about the specifics but lacks a comprehensive overview."[1]

Certainly no realm of discourse illustrates this better

1. Amitai Etzioni, "Fact-crazy, Theory-shy?", *Science* 170:391.

than our human environmental relationships. Yet a hard look at the disagreements suggests that they are a matter of interpretation common between specialists and generalists, those who fractionate and those who integrate the human problem. An expert in the mechanics of a resource program may be quite inexpert in deciding on its social significance. Each subject-matter professional tends to see the salvation of humanity as a function of his particular skills and accomplishment. Thereby he is optimistic or pessimistic. In some critical fields, little has been done because the unkowns lie between disciplines. Few are interested or trained to handle them.

Semantics is much involved in man-environment misunderstandings. How many can agree on what a living standard should be? An optimum population? As the saying goes, how clean is a clean world? Still another failure in the meeting of minds concerns the time factor. It is especially true of economic theory that little attempt has been made to develop guidelines for the future. Only a few economists have been interested in problems of stability as opposed to year-by-year expansion. Far out on the other extreme is the view of man on the geological time scale, his development of culture over at least a million years, and the fateful challenges of the next millenium. One may well ask: How responsible can we be?

No doubt we are building a body of knowledge that eventually could resolve much of the confusion. But events are marching double-time, and there is a premium on deriving and applying what policies we can. Extracting principles and conceptualizing dynamics and variables is basically an ecological job. This is not to say the ecologist is qualified; but his outlook is the proper kind, and among today's environmental work force he is getting delayed recognition. Commonly an ecologist is some kind of specialist who has greatly broadened his interests and purview. Often he can see significant trends and influences, but he is not particularly good at selling his product through scientifically respectable quantification. His services have seldom been sought in government advisory functions, and this is understandable. He is little comfort to the political pragmatist, who must hold himself accountable to a poorly informed constituency and make choices between demands of the present and obligations of the future. Characteristically the ecologist is concerned with a complex of problems not amenable to simple and popular remedies. His goals are likely to be decades, even centuries, ahead.

Despite these present complications, it is unquestionable that we must develop a concept of man and his future through the application of interdisciplinary eco-logic. We must go further and promulgate a set of mores that most people can accept on faith.

How reliably this can be done at present is indeed open to differing viewpoints; but there probably are basic criteria for, at least, a generalized problem analysis. We know approximately where we have been, and perhaps we can decide about where we would like to be. Somewhere along the line the present is a point in time—exactly where is another issue. The most tenuous unknown of all is what to do now and next. If this exploration of ideas is crude, it may be constructively stimulating; and certainly it is only a beginning. Despite any proximate reasons for pessimism, it is proper strategy to set high ideals and assume that, perhaps by excruciating effort, we the people can muddle our way through to a better world. There seems to be no convincing reason for accepting lesser goals; we won't be here to witness the outcome. If we are right, they will say we were wise; if we are wrong, they will say we meant well.

Creature Origins and Natural Order

Many have been philosophically charmed by the question of man's place in nature. A recent book by a clergyman is addressed especially to those who still consider their own kind as something arbitrarily separate from the rest of the biological world.[2] For a biologist, this question is not likely to arise, but man's primitive beginnings have great significance in understanding his present status.

It may be said of all the surviving organisms of this earth that each fits into some kind of life community. No doubt this was true also of Pliocene hominids in our own line of descent more than two million years ago. Probably these were forest- or savanna-inhabiting creatures that, over a long time period, had developed a mutualistic role among their associated species of plants and animals in certain habitats of tropical Africa. Perhaps the ecological niche of the early hominid could be described as that of a social, ground-dwelling, omnivorous primate.

Our point of principal interest is that this primate must have played some kind of role contributing to the survival of its ecosystem. In turn, it received services essential to its continued existence. It had a life-support system that required only a knowledgeable gathering of food. It had automatic population controls—quite likely both behavioral and ecological—that prevented over-use and over-contamination of its range. Certainly, all its products, including the remains of individuals, were biodegradable.

No doubt a major part of the functional adaptations of early prehumans were genetically determined. This situation changed to a predominance of learned behavior as the human stage was approached. The enlarging brain, the long childhood, the improvement of communications led to the use of tools and then of fire. In witness are the primitive pebble tools of the australopithecines and later the hearths of *Homo erectus*. The latter species, by any preferred name, appears to have been distributed from

2. Frederick Elder, *Crisis in Eden* (New York: Abingdon Press, 1970).

Europe to China by somewhere around a million years ago.

By all logic, it was the development of culture that permitted man to spread out from the ecosystems to which he was endemic. Glacial periods of the Pleistocene put new ways of life to the test and probably stimulated refinement. The process continued as primitive man penetrated to every corner of the habitable world. Culture went through a sequence of stages from gathering, to gathering and hunting, to agriculture, to modern technology. Today the human species is using, or has left its sign, in every habitat of the biosphere, and even beyond.

The Global Ecosystem

Conceptually it is true that man abandoned his place in nature and preempted the entire earth as his ecosystem. It came about because a totally unnatural culture permitted survival rates to out-gain death rates and brought about an unprecedented adaptability to environmental conditions. It has been stated with assurance that the proper study of man is man himself. Yet it is evident that the humanistic disciplines do not do the entire job. To understand the status of our kind on this globe involves a consideration of prehuman adjustments, an appraisal of our physical and behaviorial inheritance, and the study of many analogies in communities of living things.

Man is now on his own to design, worldwide and for vastly more people, something comparable to the life support mechanisms and survival insurance that were built into the automatic operation of that primordial ecosystem. This includes the control of population and the preservation of environmental quality. It is the test of an ecosystem that it have the characteristics for renewal. Natural life communities improve and protect their sites and reach interspecies adjustments that make the whole self-perpetuating.

Man has never created an ecosystem capable of independent survival. Probably we know enough to protect those that we have inherited and that produce for us through natural processes—forests and estuaries being good examples. We depend on many intensively used sites, especially agricultural croplands, whose quality for future production must be guarded through continuing study. These are clear-cut issues technically amenable to control. There are many other aspects of present resource use that definitely cannot be sustained or are poorly understood. We are in a sorting-out process in which those factors and conditions that do not contribute to durability will inevitably be eliminated.

Authorities on many aspects of our society are making surveys to learn what people want, what they do, and how our system works. This scholarly enterprise has many applications. But in the long view, what is being studied does not work; we have no system because it is not self-renewing. Man's relationship to the earth and its resources is today an unstable and unpredictable pseudo-system. There has been no time for the development of stability mechanisms, and the entire world is one vast disturbance community that cannot and will not replace itself.

The Course of Speciation

Evolutionary change has operated at the level of individual organisms, in animal societies, and in the structure and dynamics of the community. In abdicating his position in a natural ecosystem, man undoubtedly interrupted the direction of his own speciation. The primordial rules of order were geared to preservation of the species at the cost of individuals. Indeed, adaptation to altering environments through geological time depended on the routine overproduction and selective elimination of major segments of populations—those least suited to meet social competition and the limitations of habitat. The victims were part of the energy-transfer dynamics of the community, a food supply for something. It is an inscrutable, impartial process that many humanitarians with a keen "reverence for life" find difficult to acknowledge. Through his intelligence and perception, man is a tragic figure in the organic world; for in trials that beset the individual, he is the only triple sufferer. He imagines how it is going to be, he finds out how it is, and sometimes he lives to remember how it was.

It seems beyond doubt that senility and death are built into the life pattern of all "higher" animals, including man. This is the clearing-out of expended breeders and mistakes of variability. Thus a part of the adaptation of any species to its environment includes mechanisms for minimizing the allocation of resources to useless or low-value members of animal society.

Man has done his best to disavow this system. He has asserted the "rights" of the individual as against the primitive pattern of race preeminence. At the cost of society, he keeps alive, with encouragement to breed, the genetically weak and afflicted, the aberrant and disruptive elements that under the original biological rules would be eliminated.

Within the humane context of what we call civilization, this process will need reexamination. What society can do for the individual is a major concern in rational management of the environment. But the individual enjoys short-term privileges. In the standards they set for themselves, men will need to acknowledge an obligatory concern for racial quality and cultural improvement. This is a law of nature that must become part of the ethical outlook of humans responsible for their future.

Numbers and Order

The development of cultural efficiency had its most significant effect in the growth of human numbers. Population density is integral with problems of environment, since any resource must be appraised in terms of the number of people who use it and the level of living they require.

The history of human increase has been so much discussed that it is becoming trite to review it. For present purposes, we need point out only that we are confronted with a geometric progression that has reached the irruptive stage. Ehrlich estimated the successive doubling times of world population to be 1,000,000 years, 1,000 years, 200 years, 80 years, and 35 years.[3] This would bring us to the year 2000, at which time some have predicted a doubling in 23 years. Figures of the Population Reference Bureau indicate that in mid-1970 world population was 3.63 billion. The gain this year will be 72.6 million, as a result of 123.4 million births and 50.8 million deaths.

Any student of animal populations regards a build-up in this pattern as inevitably setting the stage for habitat degradation and a catastrophic decline of numbers. Commonly this involves the onset of such density-dependent ills as social stress, disease, habitat pollution, and resource depletion. A population that exceeds an optimum threshold becomes progressively more unstable, needing only an effective disruption to bring it crashing down. In the human population, medical technology that has contributed to geometric increase continues to guard us against the onset of pandemics (e.g., cholera, typhus) that effectively reduced our numbers in centuries past. It is a matter of simple logic that the population can not continue to irrupt; but what combination of environmental and social factors will bring it to a halt is subject to varying opinions. To allow food shortage, habitat pollution, or the behavioral ills of crowding to reach the critically effective stage is a prospect

3. Paul L. Ehrlich, *The Population Bomb,* Ballantine Books ed. (New York: Random House, 1968).

best appreciated by those who have seen similar things happen in natural communities—commonly these are situations disrupted by human interference.

Probably least understood are the relationships of population density to the behavioral and social requirements of man. How much is left of the genetic code that governed the relatively small societies of the early hominid? For many higher vertebrates, as numbers increase the growth of social stress and competition appears to be on some kind of exponential scale, and the same can be said for the sheer complexity of relationships among humans.[4] In concentrations of population, the ecological problem is not the sum but a multiple of its parts.

Obviously, the challenges of mass living in cities are not just social; a great many of them are economic and concerned with the day-to-day services needed by people who cannot pump water, grow food, cut wood, or dig their own sewers. Taken together, all the public measures required to mitigate the effects of crowding involve costs that increase in the same manner as the problems. Thus it is literally true that the preservation of a high, or even decent, living standard becomes more costly the larger human aggregations grow. This is an immediate dollar cost with implications in the field of taxation. A longer-range cost is the additional drain on resources that is required to serve people in concentrations who have in many ways lost the means of serving themselves.

In a recent statement applying generally to the man-resources problem, the president of the National Academy of Sciences, Philip Handler, observed that "if the projected doubling of the world's population is realized, and if political order is to be maintained, it is not unreasonable

4. Durward L. Allen, "Population, Resources, and the Great Complexity," in *Transactions of the Thirty-fourth North American Wildlife and Natural Resources Conference* (1969), pp. 449–61.

to expect that the demands on the biosphere by the end of the century will be three or four times those of the present."[5] This is a neglected but completely realistic concept.

The interaction of human density with social, economic, and political problems is an almost untouched area of research, and some specific questions suggest themselves. If the populations of our metropolitan centers are growing, and if increasing densities develop problems at accelerating rates, then there is little difficulty in understanding the inability of cities to collect enough taxes to render needed service in such fields as public health, education, and pollution abatement. Further, if the federal government cannot collect taxes sufficient to provide aid to localities, then the national debt must be directly related to overpopulation. There are questions about labor surpluses, automation, unemployment, and the devaluation of currency that could logically be made a part of such investigations.

We may only speculate as to how a better knowledge of these relationships might benefit policy-making in the future. But the possibilities cannot be ignored as irrelevant until they are studied. The need for facts is rapidly reaching emergency proportions as government at all levels bogs down in a welter of complexity. There are hopeful signs in educational and research institutions that the teams are assembling and that the essential skills in many fields will be available.

Although such research needs are real, we should not wait for anything more than we have for constructive action. We may safely conclude that the population increase is basic to an onrush of events that is leading to a crisis in decades immediately ahead. Also, if our only recourse

5. Philip Handler, "Biology and the Future of Man," Natural Academy of Sciences, *News Report* 20 (1970): 4–5.

was to cure our environmental ills by technological means—as one way of looking at it, by the sheer weight of dollar expenditures, while numbers continue to expand—then our problem would have no solution.[6]

We have, of course, the obvious alternative of reducing the population by applying all socially acceptable methods of birth control. What is required is an orderly reduction of the birth rate well below the death rate to achieve a declining population. We cannot regard this as a cure-all, panacea, or quick and easy solution. But it would reduce an almost universal pressure that exacerbates practically every kind of social and environmental difficulty.

The many obstacles to such a worldwide program are as well known as any aspect of our ecological confusion. The question of lead time required for reducing human numbers helps to account for a widespread tendency to discount its practical relationship to resource management programs. It becomes easier, in particular, to disregard implications that there might be reasons for curbing the developmental onslaught that aims to make everything within sight available for immediate use.

In an address to the board of governors of the World Bank, Robert S. McNamara stated that if the developed countries reached the point where couples only replaced themselves in the year 2000 and the underdeveloped countries accomplished this fifty years later, it would still, as of 1970, require 150 years to stabilize the world population. In the meantime, human numbers would have grown from 3.5 billion to 15 billion.[7]

What this might mean to living standards and conditions

6. See Garrett Hardin, "The Tragedy of the Commons," *Science* 162:1243–48; and Paul R. Ehrlich and John P. Holdren, "Population and Panaceas, a Technological Perspective," *Bio Science* 19 (1969): 1065–71.

7. Address by Robert S. McNamara to the Board of Governors, World Bank Group, Copenhagen, Denmark, 1970.

of the biosphere is implied in H. R. Hulett's estimate based on the present agricultural and industrial system of the world.[8] At our level of consumption, the world could support a maximum of a billion people. We may surmise that if space resources and other more elusive components of life style were plugged into this, or if we adopt as an objective the kind of existence one could wish for in the future, the maximum number of people would be considerably less.

It is evident that, at best, any population control program is going to have a built-in lag during which our social and environmental penalties will continue to grow. For several decades, at least, we will be depending largely on technological means of surviving in decency and preserving whatever the present inhabitants of the earth can be persuaded to leave for someone else. This has been referred to realistically as a "buying of time," and the most hopeful accompanying development would be a snowballing of interest in problems of human numbers among the young generations who are most concerned. It is beyond doubt that the development of a new ethic toward the environment can take place only among the young.

Growth and Quality

Probably the most important block to what must be done with our population and environment is the particularly American assumption that we can go on increasing our numbers and demands on the resource base. This came naturally when a few people were populating and exploiting by any available means a largely vacant and surpassingly rich continent. The result was the concept of the open-ended economy in which expansion is a built-in feature.

8. H. R. Hulett, "Optimum World Population," *Bio Science* 20 (1970): 160–61.

It should be evident by now that the limits of the earth are in sight and that we are well behind in planning for a stable eco-social adjustment to the space and the resources that support us. It is a moot question how rapidly Americans can do this about-face in their ideology. The nation has no population policy, and our "planning" still is for the satisfaction of immediate "needs."

Illustrative of this is the most recent large-scale effort to develop guidelines for the use of public lands. In its report to the president and Congress, the Public Land Law Review Commission made a basic assumption that in the last 35 years of this century the population of the United States will grow by another 100 million people. The report states that, since this is going to happen, we must meet the demand by expanding present cities and building new ones in our open spaces to absorb the additional people.[9]

In effect, this is the time-worn assumption that populations grow in thin air, rather than in reference to a resource base—which is the biological reality. It is a continuation of open-ended development and exploitation that foreclose options to people of the future. By bringing new water to old deserts, and by other drafts on the tax returns from productive lands, we are to buy more habitat where human numbers can continue to build.

On the other hand, it is evident that we are being called upon to make huge, and necessary, investments in the quality of our built-up habitats. To neglect this obligation in favor of further costly adventures in populating open spaces is asking for more trouble than our children and grandchildren will be able to handle. The open spaces themselves have a value that seems strangely obscure. Behind every concentration of people, there must be a

9. Public Land Law Review Commission, "One Third of the Nation's Land," Report to the President and Congress, 1970.

great hinterland producing food and fiber—and, indeed, serving the "recreational" function that is becoming steadily more visible as a requirement of life.

The thrust of technology has not been such as to improve the estate of man and ensure his future. It has obeyed the challenge of immediate gain for the present proprietors of earth. This is not a characteristic of our science and technology; it is a result of the use we have made of it. On the basis of various indices, Price concluded that technology is doubling in fifteen years. Since the population is doubling in about thirty-four years, this has given rise to the abstraction that "technology is more important than population" as a source of environmental problems.[10] This is a misleading exercise in logic, since neither rate can be sustained and the combination is intolerable. The short-term doubling of many industrial aspects of technology—such as power generation and the production of motor vehicles—plus the similarly increasing components of global air, water, and land pollution, create a situation that will be controlled by policy and effort or it will be controlled by catastrophe.

In making and implementing public policies, there is sometimes a fuzzy line between ignorance and cynicism. It might be said of our people-environment syndrome that we have a scattered and truly outstanding leadership supported by a poor following.

This appears to call for understanding, and a vigorous information effort that will reach enough people to make the right thing right on its face value. In such a program, we have a growing liability. The human species has been so domesticated that great populations are produced and acculturated in isolation from the natural world. Their lives involve little or no experience with the origins of

10. Derek J. deSolla Price, *Little Science, Big Science* (New York: Columbia University Press, 1963).

the earthly produce they consume and no schooling in biological science.

As a result, the world of nature is commonly regarded as a chaotic and by-chance mixture of conditions and living things. If one perceives no natural order, he is not likely to be alarmed or stimulated to action by a world of disorder. In fact, he is without a measuring stick by which to judge what is taking place in populations and environments. Human life is too short to encompass much of the past, and change becomes the status quo.

Under such conditions, how do we administer a strange remedy fast enough to cure humanity's ills—and slow enough so that people can swallow it?

There is no question that technology will continue to be refined and that industrial response will be, literally, unending. This can be profitable for all humanity if our emphasis is changed from quantity to quality. These are difficult to separate, and a critical test lies in the social effects of our enterprise. It can be considered right when the satisfactions of people can be met while at the same time their environment is improved. If this outlook seems visionary, we can reflect that resource overdrafts and environmental despoliation are necessarily a temporary condition.

Time and the Human Continuum

The characteristics of a desirable human habitat must inevitably be defined more clearly as the future unfolds. Yet reliable principles can sometimes be recognized. We may take as an example what has been called "diversity" in the habitats of both animals and men.

For men, the preservation of existing forms of life and every kind of habitat is a way of keeping open the possibilities for further research and learning. More broadly, a diversity of environment is essential for people needing challenge and swath—a means of developing character and individuality through enriching experience. In such light, there is urgent need to retard in every feasible way the disruption of natural communities and homogenizing of the earth's fauna and flora that are taking place as a result of man's heedlessness and excellent transportation facilities. By this and other means, we could easily bring about a monotone of sameness in what is left of the natural world, in human works, and indeed, in man himself.

This is to recognize also that the subcultures of ethnic groups and ways of life that provide future options are worth preserving. Looking well beyond the Pennsylvania German cookbook or carvings of the Eskimo, we may affirm that the rights of minorities to existence are in keeping with good management for mankind at large. There are reasons for apprehension over whether we are getting into an era of congestion and competition such that only those effectively organized into dominant pressure groups can expect a satisfying measure of social and economic justice.

Technical and philosophical decisions are largely for informed leadership. For most of society, the difference between right and wrong is largely a matter of ethical standard—an ethic being a set of moral rules accepted as guiding principles.

Simpson delineates three conditions that must be met for an ethic to have meaning: "(a) There are alternative modes of action; (b) man is capable of judging the alternatives in ethical terms; and (c) he is free to choose what he judges to be ethically good." He states further, "A system of naturalistic ethics then demands acceptance of individual responsibility for those results, and this in fact is the basis for the origin and function of the moral sense."[11]

To be a socially useful attitude toward environmental

11. George G. Simpson, *Biology and Man* (New York: Harcourt, Brace & World, 1969), p. 146.

problems, an ethic must govern what a given generation will do with the earth and its resources, recognizing that this will decide what a later generation has to work with. In effect, it regards humanity as a continuum in time and the earth as a commons that must be used for all time. Thus people yet to be born become equal shareholders in the common freehold.

As part of a respectable ethic, it seems in keeping with human dignity that the quality of life should not be sacrificed to support greater numbers. At present our numbers are at odds with our living standard. Since the potential for more people is without end, setting the limit at one point or another can hardly be done on any but a qualitative basis. One might say that with proper strategy we have all of time to produce more and better people. In this sense, the ethic includes acceptance of birth control measures and what Wolfers called "the small family norm."[12] The usual family size will be two, varying below or above to suit the need for declining or stable numbers. Looking well into the future at a kind of world that is possible for intelligent human beings, we may suppose that population status will not be a great issue. It is evident that well-off, well-educated people commonly achieve low birth rates as part of their cultural pattern.

In the context of global problems, any effective ethic must be a way of life for every cultural segment of the human race—perhaps by varying courses of abstraction, but achieving the same essential purposes. In the industrialized nations of today, its development will need a deliberately planned beginning in the early grades of our educational system. It is no cynicism, but only reality, to say that it will not be effective guidance for the bulk of adults now alive.

The recruitment of primary-grade humans to a provident

12. D. Wolfers, "Problems of Expanding Populations," *Nature* 225:593–97.

philosophy toward the earth and the quality of life must involve every kind of truthful logic. Yet it would be a delusion to suppose that all the converts will become authorities on relationships and reasons why. It is the distinctive quality of an ethic that people know what they should do because it is right and socially acceptable. The endless defense of position, now imposed upon anyone with a conservative view toward human numbers and resource use should not go on forever—not, indeed, beyond the next generation.

Justin W. Leonard

chapter four

ETHICS AND REALITIES

What do we really want, and do we want it badly enough? If by some fortunate chance we escape the imminent fate of making ourselves the shortest-lived species in the span of earthly evolution, our descendants may find it diverting and possibly instructive to inquire into why we stood so long tottering on the brink. Because, for a moment borrowing Heilbroner's device of viewing the future as history, later generations seem certain to conclude that we possessed sufficient science, technology, and institutions to cope with environmentally damaging aspects of industrialization. And it is tempting to speculate on what this putative posterity may view as the negative, divisive, and obstructionist traits that brought their twentieth century ancestors so close to self-extinction.

Those who may study us from some later point in our space-time continuum may see that we inherited an ability to comfort ourselves in the face of misery and danger. "This is the best of all possible worlds." So did Candide doggedly repeat to himself the sovereign formula of his tutor, Dr. Pangloss. Never very angry, sometimes disillusioned, but mainly whimsical and bemused, he wandered over the eighteenth-century world to see what it was like. Plunder and destruction battered at his awareness and tugged at his innocence. The instinct for self-preservation finally prevailed, and he found his way home, where, joined by his varied household, he settled down to cultivate his garden. Moderately useful, nondisruptive, only occasionally quibbling over life's meaning, he basked in moderate well-being with no further evidence to change his conclusion that it was, after all, the best of all possible worlds.

If it isn't, why not? The earth is productive. Some five billion years ago, if the cosmologists read the signs correctly, it came into being, a tiny part of the awesome stroke of creation that sent our galaxy and its millions of sister galaxies reeling through the incomprehensible reaches of space. Despite long periods of calm, the earth's crust has been dynamic—heaved up into mountains, reduced to level plain by the grinding of glaciers and the gentle action of rain, flooded by intruding seas, piled up into mountains again. For over half of its existence, the earth has supported life, infinitely varied, but resting ultimately on the photosynthetic process that fixes solar energy in the carbohydrate molecule.

So, we may ask, if life could successfully survive the natural vicissitudes of the past three and a half billion years, why is the environmentalist needed? Why should he exist?

The answer clearly lies in our new attitude toward the earth. And I say *new* advisedly; for even though hominids and humanoids may have existed for two million years or more, it is only within the last ten thousand years that man learned agriculture—that he domesticated plants and animals, and exchanged his long span as a nomadic hunter and food-gatherer for the settled life of village, town, city, and megalopolis. And it is only about this long ago that his numbers and practices enabled him to impress his permanent mark on the landscape.

Studies of fossil pollen in Europe show that there is little land there that is "natural" in the sense of lacking signs of human occupancy. Slash-and-burn agriculture seems to have swept Europe as the Pleistocene glaciers receded. Signs of man are abundant where conditions permit their preservation: signs of the men who occupied the caves of Jarmo, of the members of the sophisticated Harappa civilization of the Indus Valley, of the much more ancient hunters coming to light in the Olduvai Gorge. As Lynn White has pointed out, all forms of life modify their context (earthworms are a ubiquitous example), and man is no exception. Although it is not proved, it is plausible to believe that fire-drive methods of hunting may have created the world's great grasslands. Because of early attempts to till the soil and to store and direct water, Babylon and Ur suffocated in rich silt eroding from the fields of Mesopotamia. The axmen who felled the Cedars of Lebanon to build fleets for Phoenicians and a temple for Solomon left a desolation that persists today.

What is "new" in our attitude stems from the fact that only in the most recent moments of our history have we commanded enough energy and technology to ride over Earth roughshod, forcing her to our will rather than trying to win her consent. In ancient times, man worshiped Earth as the Great Mother of the Gods under as many names as there were tongues: Gaea, Rhea, Demeter, Persephone, Isis, Astarte, Ishtar. He had learned that though Earth was a bountiful mother, her punishment was prompt and inexorable when her laws were flouted. We tend to assume today that earlier peoples could escape the results of ecologically damaging practices by moving on. True, there were new lands awaiting the adventuresome. But while conquerors took them, the conquered were crowded into hostile and impoverished regions, thus balancing the earth's accounts. Instead of new worlds, we have found new sources of energy. And we are still so exhilarated by the inanimate power awaiting the touch of our fingertips that the foolhardy exuberance with which we now approach our planet seems somehow inevitable.

Philosophers and students of literature still debate Voltaire's intent in having his hero constantly reiterate the reassuring refrain "best of all possible worlds." But there is here the portrait of an idea, and that is the twofold problem man has in apprehending the world as it is: first, in the ability to accumulate enough material images to provide accurate perspective; and second, a persistent blindness in recognizing why he himself thinks, reacts, and operates as he does.

Ethics is the fruit of intellectual exercise performed among the high peaks of human aspiration. Reality exists when men like us conceive and direct their share of the world's work in the abysses of the mind, guided by emotion, prejudice, impulse, and habit, informed by pragmatism, and only rarely and distantly illuminated by the glow from the heights.

Yet it is this occasional flash of illumination that has made us what we are by showing us that we might become something better. That we still share this desire to improve is more important than our differences over how to improve. It may be the trait to save us from being the shortest-lived species in the history of earthly evolution.

This persistent blindness to the consequences of our own actions was captured before the turn of the century by Kipling, whom no one reads, much less quotes, any more, when he had his spokesman for the Neolithic complain,

> I ate my fill of a whale that died
> And stranded after a month at sea.
> There is a pain in my inside.
> Why have the gods afflicted me?

And later, without any notable progress in the race's ability to relate cause and effect, his spokesman for the Middle Ages grouses,

> My privy and well drain into each other
> After the custom of Christendie.
> Fever and fluxes are wasting my mother.
> Why has the Lord afflicted me?

We try, of course, to attain insight. It has long been recognized that man's success as a species, a success that early allowed him to live almost anywhere on the earth's surface, is due less to his biological evolution than to the cultural evolution that enabled him to take his own critical environment with him as he traveled, whereas less-favored organisms can occupy new territory only if it already fits their needs. It seems supremely ironical that this ability to modify the environment, the crux of man's evolutionary success, now haunts him with threats of doom.

Even at a time when our pleasures so often are made possible by our technological expertise in manipulating materials, we gain much of our aesthetic satisfaction from our natural environment. Yet in the midst of this awareness and effort there is a growing momentum of habits, influences, and even militant, aggressive stupidity that poses an immediate threat not only to the aesthetic quality of the environment but to the safety with which we can merely occupy it. What is there about us that makes us disregard facts, contradict or negate our own best efforts, and overlook our better judgment?

First, perhaps there is something in our heritage. When we speak of "quality of the environment" today, many of us assume a fairly liberal proportion of "wilderness" in that environment. And several writers, including Roderick Nash, have noted that the idea of wilderness as a desirable place in which to seek spiritual refreshment is a concept relatively new to our Western culture. Those of us who share this particular heritage look back to ancestors whose fears peopled the forests with werewolves and hobgoblins and who taught terror to their children. Think for a moment of the real menace that undergirds our innocent versions of "Red Riding Hood" or "Rumpelstiltskin." The "wetlands" we seek to preserve from dredging and filling were the haunt of Grendel, fearsome man-eating monster of the Beowulf legend, and a real enough threat in the absence of malaria control. Our progenitors saw it as a holy mission to take the new continent God had entrusted to them and reduce its wilderness to well-ordered fields, orchards, and vineyards.

A second consideration that deters us from applying all our existing knowledge and skills to improvement of environmental quality is our sense of individuality. As our forebears moved west, their independence grew. Only the independent and self-reliant could survive, because there was little or no community to offer protection, strength, or advice. A man's property was his to do with as he chose. It is still hard for us to adjust to close neighbors, to the fact that smoke from steak broiling in our backyard becomes smoke over the neighbor's yard, smoke over the city. There is deep-seated conflict between actions we have always regarded as individual rights and results that have effects reaching far beyond the individual. The individual does not like to think of his actions affecting anyone but himself. Our response to the problem is ignorant and naïve at best, callous and belligerent at worst. In fact, our sense of community responsibility lags far behind the extent to which we *are* a community and live as a community.

Those seeking catalogues of recent environmental devastation can find them ready to hand among many of the paperbacks that have flooded out since 22 April 1970 and the Environmental Teach-in. All of these deplorable things do happen; and a third factor, possibly strongest of all in restraint of real effort to curb them, may lie in the question of our own basic desires. Traditionally, we have looked to see if smoke was coming from the stack of the factory on the hill. We profess to deplore what we know is now unnecessarily ugly. The economy can live and grow without it. But leaf through any major magazine today and sample the ads. See how many of them, while urging us toward progress and holding out to us the tantalizing reward of security, depend on the old stereotype. From the full color ad a man with silver at the temples (but no bald spot) gazes at you very earnestly (but with no middle-aged paunch in evidence) and exhorts you to be part of a growing, progressive, proud America. Through the window behind him you can see a row of billowing industrial smokestacks. He may be selling insurance, or whiskey, or automobiles. Much of what has been said about subliminal advertising by association reflects personal values of which we are hardly aware but which we would give up only with great reluctance. If smoke means progress, prosperity, and ambition, who would willingly make it invisible?

Many of us would, apparently, if only we could shift the blame and the expense to others. It is a basic human characteristic, when threatened by catastrophe, to resort to immediate, often violent, action, whether well considered or not. To aid this action, we band together—but not in too large bands. We suffer from the bark beetle syndrome: we are unhappy, even vaguely frightened, if we cannot feel our fellows jostling us on all sides; we are positively thigmotactic; we crave "togetherness." But we are comfortable only with our own species of bark beetle. And ever since we first sought ways to cope with the consequences of earlier rapacity, we have been spawning an amazing number of agencies, societies, organizations, and other institutional tools to channel, but also regrettably to fragment, our efforts in environmental matters. A quick survey reveals that in the United States there are twenty-two major federal agencies of the department level or equivalent and about three hundred state agencies (figuring out at an average of about six for each of the 50 states) that are concerned with natural resource use and management, and therefore able to be of considerable influence on environmental matters.

These are, in many cases, political necessities in a democracy. But in other ways, we reveal our certainty that only ourselves and a faithful few have perceived the path to true salvation. In the United States and Canada, international, national, regional, and interstate or interprovincial lay organizations and professional societies oriented toward natural resources number 239, according to my count. Most of them have represented single-minded devotion to a single purpose. How comparatively easy we have found it to develop a lofty and sonorous statement of an ethic when we grouped together in pursuit of a specific, circumscribed objective and ignored or shrugged off onto another group the unwanted side effects of our practices.

Most of us have been so preoccupied with producing, digesting, and, hopefully, assimilating the fruits of our own intellectual fields that we have had no stomach for those of others. So we may yet succumb to an unbalanced conceptual diet, and, like a northern white-tailed deer wintering at a haystack, be found dead with a full paunch, the food edible but inadequate.

The ecosystem approach to problems of environmental quality may speed the revision of single-purpose ethical positions into acceptance of broader responsibilities. Not, let me hasten to add, that ecology has a monopoly on the systems approach: poets and philosophers have always concerned themselves more with relationships than with things. But here I believe we are coming to some of the most plausible but least palatable explanations of why both our environmental policy and the ethic from which it grows have so far proved inadequate. Despite the plethora of conferences and the information explosion generally, faulty communications earn a sizeable share of the blame.

Predictability is the essence of policy. Perhaps this is why proposals for environmental policy are notorious for their negative tone. With a few demographic projections and a hasty trial balance of resource reserves, one can be in the Cassandra business overnight. However, our past has made it abundantly clear that we do not respond meekly or obediently to "no-no's." Pundits seeking to explain the colossal nationwide noncompliance with the post–World War I Volstead Act, the "Noble Experiment," opined that it was foredoomed to failure once it became generally known as "Prohibition."

Furthermore, in the democratic process, a course of action is anything but assured when all the available scientific information has been gathered and analyzed. As any elected politician or any professional resource administrator understands, at this juncture the decision-making process is not ended, it is just beginning. Many other factors will enter the equation: emotions, vested interests, cultural influences, even conflicting facts and scientific evidence.

The foregoing is by way of preparing for my comment that after the first flush of enthusiasm for environmental quality subsides, muttered recriminations begin to be heard. The momentum of the forward thrust begins to be dissipated as people insist on behaving like people and start to polarize—old hands versus newcomers, professionals versus amateurs, federal versus state and local government, agency versus academia. Some of the trouble stems from such obvious emotions as impatience on one side and injured pride on the other. It is a human enough trait, for example, when one of us steps into another disciplinary cabbage patch and discovers that "cabbages is beautiful," to think that we are the first to stumble upon this profound truth. And our blissful conceit is sure to grate on the sensibilities of those who have spent their lives working to perfect this beauty. An art critic once wrote that a certain painter had aroused hostility among fellow artists because "he painted young women's posteriors as though he were the first artist ever to perceive that young women's posteriors are attractive."

Part of the lack of total rapport between academic sages and resource administrators covered with scar tissue hinges on the latters' conviction that the former fail to recognize the extent of gains already achieved in environmental affairs by these people—at the cost of heavy casualties to their own ranks. And part of the tendency of the new generation of environmental activists to ignore what has gone before makes some of their philosophy and demands seem retrogressive to professionals, who see old fields being respaded when the need is to break new ground.

Another divisive factor hinges on semantics or the creation of straw men. Aid and comfort for the anti-ecology backlash was given in a guest editorial in *Science* by a leading sociologist when he wrote recently, "We should continue to give top priority to unfashionable human problems. Fighting hunger, malnutrition, and rats should be given priority over saving wildlife." Here I am sure is a good man and true. But not many ecologists would share his position that malnutrition and rats somehow are not part of the environment and that both the environment and wildlife exist exclusively in some remote, never-never land where, by inference, man never penetrates.

It is regrettable that social scientists and ecologists have often met in essentially adversary situations. Neither can solve our problems alone. In point of fact, encouraging examples are emerging in almost every discipline that concerns itself with the environment—anthropology, archeology, geography, geology, public health—even the law has developed a new and aggressively growing branch concerned with environmental quality. Such examples give hope that a truly healthy involvement by any of these groups will lead to an increasing search for cross-disciplinary and interdisciplinary contacts and inputs.

Just as fragmentation of responsibilities has placed governmental agencies in embarrassingly conflicting positions—I think particularly of the conflicts between those who shape policies governing the use of pesticides—so many professional leaders are engaging in deep and obviously traumatic introspection as to the kind of training their new recruits should receive. And the word *training* may serve as a pivotal point. Increasingly, spokesmen call for education, *not* training. Such calls more often than not may sink into a semantic morass. But many in education today see an increasing interest in curricula that minimize "how to do it" in favor of "why."

No sensible scholar or professional would seek to evade responsibility for "maintaining the purity of the discipline." Really, there is no need for this to become a point at issue. A major obstacle to development of a truly eclectic curriculum has been the mulish tendency toward "either-or" rather than "and-and." The situation is well illustrated by my own field of biology, where university programs during the last two decades moved preponderantly to the cellular and molecular approach—certainly challenging and intellectually exciting—and in the process all but abandoned as hopelessly old-fashioned the field-oriented studies that are at the heart of ecology. The wholly unforeseen upsurge of current interest in the environment shows that both are right and either one alone is wrong.

Our problem, as usual, is the race against time. We have practiced agriculture for ten thousand years out of two million. In the span of a single lifetime, we have moved from the sickle to the self-propelled combine, from muscle power to the energy of fossil fuels. Indeed, we are slow learners. And with the energy of the atom in our grasp, we have won the power of the gods while still clinging to the instincts of the jungle.

Granted that increasing commonality of viewpoint and approach may help us move from fragmenting to synthesizing ethics, we may be able to define our objectives and bring them closer to reality. And after what I have said, any attempt to list or catalogue desirable objectives for environmental policy would probably be to retrogress to the narrower and more limited goals I have deplored. One man's list of desirable objectives would sound too much like one small boy's letter to Santa Claus. It would be difficult, in fact, to criticize the statements in the National Environmental Policy Act of 1969 and their recent discussion in a broader context by Richard Carpenter (1970).

The requirements for physical health may be set by physiological requirements. But beyond that is the everpresent threat of the regimentation of tastes. Attitudes toward the environment are emotional and hence fiercely personal. Which particular Utopia do we want? More than a generation ago, in *Men Like Gods,* H. G. Wells created a utopia that was, in essence a worldwide exurbia. The population was very low. The individual members were unbelievably creative people whose homes were scattered sparsely throughout a pleasant countryside that resembled, as noted, a worldwide exurbia. Another, more recent writer who sought to capture the imagination with his own particular utopia was Arthur C. Clark, who in his book *The City and the Stars* created the city of Diaspar to represent all that would exist of earth a billion years in the future. Here was a very densely populated city, so contrived that it was completely free of outside influences and proof against any semblance of a natural environment. The reader is confronted with a completely artificial environment in the utopia of one author, with a wholly natural world in the other. The limitless variety of our tastes, even when they are in conflict, is responsible for much of the zest of living. It is terrifying to contemplate establishment of policies which would regiment them and force them into a narrow mold.

A few years ago, when the economy still supported rising employment, the back pages of scientific and technical journals were filled with advertisements of various corporations competing with each other for recent college graduates. These notices usually followed the line of offering so much for a B.S., a bit more for an M.S., still more for the new-fledged Ph.D. One firm, however, took a different approach. Their quarter-page ad was bordered by a montage of photographs of sailing, golfing, fishing, and swimming. In the middle was a photograph of a delightful home set in a rolling, sylvan countryside, with no other house in view. Beneath the picture, instead of a listing of salary and fringe benefits, was the simple statement, "A Blank Corporation engineer lives here." This employer was imaginative enough to sell a way of life. The stress was on variety.

If pressed for a commitment, most of us would share the belief that an ever increasing income means little unless it will buy us the way of life we want. But tastes differ. More importantly, they change. Many of the attributes of environmental quality that we regard as essential parts of the standard of living vary in our esteem with time and place. All of us can adduce examples of environment-dependent, environment-affecting activities and uses that passed with time. Others surely lie ahead of us, unimagined.

The need is for policies that will allow the development of objectives in a way that will not foreclose other options. Most men will continue to take the environment for granted with little or no curiosity about its composition—just as an actor takes for granted the stage on which he displays his artistry: he is an actor, not a carpenter.

And for that matter, outside the Western world who will share our concern? The late J. D. Williams once observed that if a worldwide referendum were to be held on the proposition that the earth is flat, it would win, hands down. He offered the further diverting statistic that there are alive in the world today more headhunters than astronomers. And it may be hard to awaken a meaningful interest in maintenance or improvement of environmental quality among those who live on the edge of starvation. Population control is still an impatient challenge. Even such studies as the International Biological Program's integrated research in human adaptability, no matter how high their yield of practical knowledge enabling us to occupy marginal parts of the earth, can provide only a short-term palliative before more brutal methods of population control intervene.

Our needs, succinctly stated, are for a resource base that will meet our growing material demands and for maintenance of environmental attributes that will nourish man's spirit. Two such attributes, clearly, are elbow room and pleasing surroundings.

Our demands for both material things and inspirational surroundings are sure to change. Learning to predict these changes and devising means for meeting them shape our ultimate challenge.

Continuing to provide the material resources for our material needs is by far the lesser segment of the challenge. Wider application of existing technologies and incorporation in technology of existing knowledge could give us an extended period of grace.

The imperative need is to ensure that this grace period be utilized to provide an environment that will liberate, rather than regiment, the creative imagination.

Broad spaces and scenic vistas may not continue to serve these needs. Other generations are sure to respond to other stimuli. But it is hard for us to accept the organization of the hive or political and economic authoritarianism as man's ultimate achievement.

Development of a comprehensive ethic for environmental

policy has been hampered by the circumscribed ethical positions of tightly focused disciplines and organizations. Attempts to broaden both ethical positions and the training of individuals for environmental missions are handicapped by sectarian thinking and by entrenched interests, both academic and administrative, that see in synthesis a threat to their security.

If we can work together regardless of disciplinary boundaries to develop a new and comprehensive ethic for environmental policy, definition and realization of objectives will be readier—and safer—than at any time in history.

References

Carpenter, Richard A. 1970. Information for decisions in environmental policy. *Science* 168:1316–22.

Leonard, Justin W. 1965. Moral, ethical, and fiscal aspects of wildlife management. *Trans. Thirtieth North American Wildlife Conference,* pp. 422–25.

Nash, Roderick. 1967. *Wilderness and the American mind.* New Haven, Conn.: Yale University Press.

Wagar, J. Alan. 1970. Growth versus the quality of life. *Science* 168:1179–84.

White, Lynn Jr. 1967. The historical roots of our ecological crisis. *Science* 155:1203–7.

Morton Gorden

chapter five

ECOLOGY AS IDEOLOGY

Since the French Revolution, and, if we insist, since the American Revolution, policies for the future have often been derived from ideology. Ideologies help us set priorities, help us allocate resources, and help give us confidence to tread on new ground. Ideologies are important in human intellectual experience, and as the ecology movement begins to grow, the question arises as to whether it is becoming an ideology.

Three aspects of this process are worthy of consideration. The first is an evaluation of ecology as an ideology. Does it, in fact, satisfy the requirements of an ideology? The second is the role of ecology in public policy formation. The public is ready to move from the will to do something to defining necessary skills in which ecology, instead of being an ideology, becomes in fact the new dismal science. Some economists will be happy to know that economics has lost that title to a new dismal science, ecology. The third aspect of the growth of ecological thinking contributes to the problem of how to get rich, without getting poor.

Ideology

There are a number of prerequisites of a bona fide, good, useful ideology. The first one is that it has to be grand, indeed, it has to be cosmic; it has to show in some way, as did communism, as did the French Revolution, that the reverberations of what is said are very important to mankind. The second characteristic of a good viable ideology is to be predictive, to be able to handle the future, indeed, to be able to explain the present in terms of some sort of inevitable and inexorable path to the future, and, therefore, to illustrate that the present conforms to certain rules. Another attribute needed for a good ideology is some sense of certainty, preferably, in our day, to be scientific. In addition to being grand, predictive, and certain, an ideology has to get rid of abstractions and find some way to tie policies for the future to individual lives, to give meaning to an individual life through cosmic vision. Lastly, an ideology needs the potential to organize large segments of the population. These are prerequisites for a viable ideology.

Initially, it appeared that ecology had most all of these characteristics. However, this was superficial. First, ecology is not necessarily grand. It is grand in the way global commentators practice it, indeed, it is cosmic. But many ecologists have been suggesting that our choice is not life or death, but something less, perhaps learning to deal with wastes from our life style. In some ways, the public problem of ecology has boiled down to sewerage systems and waste disposal problems. It is hard to be grand and cosmic about those kinds of problems.

Secondly, ecology is not so predictive, unfortunately. It raises the question of where is K, to use Dr. Hutchinson's analysis.[1] His question was where is that population level

---

1. See chapter 2 of this volume.

at which we can live some kind of decent life? Ecology is not very predictive in terms of our capacity to say where K is for human population; also, unfortunately, it is not so certain.

We have not been able to get reliable damage functions to be able to predict what will happen if we insult the environment. Usually when you deal with insults to people, you know what the reaction will be; but the feedback from the environment has been less clear, and the certainty that we are being given by some of the predictions is not very good. For example, ecologists are now issuing warnings about variations in climate. Their experiences with microclimates lead them to think in terms of instabilities and climatic fragility. On the other hand, astrophysicists, who are accustomed to dealing with large masses and eons of time, see climate as essentially stable, beyond our poor power to add to, or to detract from. The ensuing debate, based in part on the psychic experience of the astrophysicist versus the ecologist renders ecology unfit for an ideology, just because the certainty level is not good enough. Lenin would never have tolerated that kind of debate among his ideologists.

The fourth thing that ideology needs is some way to give meaning to individual lives. Initially, it appeared that ecology was satisfying for this. It gave youth some sense that individual behavior was meaningful. This, however, is an illusion. The problems that we have in the environment are such that individual behaviors are not a sufficient target for correction—a lot of people have to do a lot of different things. Unless enough people go along—indeed, a whole culture—individual activity of well-intentioned citizens is insufficient, leading to frustration rather than meaning.

The last thing needed by a good ideology is potential for organizing, or mobilizing, the population. Once again, ecology looked very good. Youth looked as though it would play the role reserved by Marx for the proletariat, but youth is no more stable as a political base for this problem than was the proletariat. Young people are forced to sell out when it comes time to make a living. They are faced with the problem of moral man in an immoral society (economy), which means that there is too much pressure and structure for anybody to live an ecologically sane life. There is a limited number of communes available. Others will have to commute to work.

It is also very bad strategy for anyone who wants zero population growth to rely on the youth as the basis for a movement. There is a self-defeating expectation that the only people who can vivify a dead society are the youth. That argument sits poorly with the age pyramid of a zero-growth population. All in all, ecology is not a good candidate for an ideology.

Perhaps this should have been anticipated, because the last time biology made a bid for an ideology, it also failed. If we look at Social Darwinism of the late nineteenth century as an outgrowth of applying biology to order human affairs, we can see that a great deal is left out by the law of the survival of the fittest as a law for human interactions. Ideology is made of more human stuff.

The New Dismal Science

Yet, we must find some way to make ecology help us relate man to nature. This is truly a more difficult problem than we have had in the past. If we look at primitive societies and note how man used to regulate his relations to nature, we would find that magic or religion was a very useful tool to provide taboos to order these relations, to keep some kind of limits on population, and to give some sort of stability, both psychic and economic, to the way men lived. But in this century the secular requirements on ideas exclude these taboos, and we are left with

the problem of regulating man's relation to man in order
to relate man to nature. That makes the situation especially
difficult. I would like to call attention to three different
problems that are associated here that make it difficult
for man to relate to man in order that he can successfully
relate to nature.

The first is the problem of the commons, which nowadays
is known as the tragedy of the commons. I hope that in
going from "problem" to "tragedy" we have not lost our
interest in being able to solve the problem. Essentially,
the problem of the commons is that it does not pay an
individual to behave in a socially responsible way. Individual behavior on its own may well not be good for the
society, but it can be good for the individual: so if farmers
are trying to raise cows on a fixed acreage and there
are too many cows on the acreage to sustain the yield,
it still pays each individual farmer to put one more cow
on to try and get what he can. But for all farmers as
a whole, it is a self-defeating idea.

There are other ways to express the problem of the
commons, but it is an essential problem because we are
dealing with cultures that tend to reward individuals and
a structure and a system in which individual calculations
of benefit are primary. We run into this problem in the
competitive production of oil from a common pool, in the
congestion of vehicles on a common roadway, in fisheries
exploitation, and in many other situations where there
is no charge levied for the use of common property or
where a charge, if levied, is less than the scarcity value
of the use of the property. The basic problem is that of
restraining men's behavior when individuals themselves
can gain from overusing the commons, though they will
do great damage to mankind if they do so. It may well
pay an Indian farmer in need of labor insurance to have
another child. It may be a very good rational calculation
for him, but a bad calculation for use of the world resources,

when we talk about being on the commons.

Incidentally, if historians would like to illustrate this problem of the commons and note how it was solved, they should look into the Enclosure Movement in England, often analyzed as essentially a social conflict. In fact, there is a lot of ecology in it and a lot of real interest in how the commons was regulated at that time. That was the first time in industrializing society that the problem of the commons became very important and that institutions had to respond to it. When the industrial revolution grew to the point where interdependencies of food and labor and urban and rural demands became significant, the Enclosure Movement was a necessary step. Perhaps there is something to be learned in that. It required from England a lot of effort to do it, and it is going to require from us a lot to solve the problem of the commons.

Second, ecological quality is pluralistic. We are exceedingly arrogant when we talk about the use of the commons from the standpoint of our own values. There is a great deal of narrow-minded middle-class chauvinism involved in trying to apply our values to resource allocation in the environment. Moreover, there is the highly personal question of risk. What kind of risk are we willing to take with our environment in order to maintain our values? Furthermore, quality requires, not an individual act only, but a social solution. Anybody from the United States in an underdeveloped country who implies that a man's need is less important than a tree is doomed to failure. At some point man is worth less than a tree if letting that tree stand means that some man cannot live. But we do not know where that line is crossed, and until we have very good evidence on the risks, we will not convince somebody in an underdeveloped country that he should organize the economy to avoid cutting down that tree.

Consider other cultural differences that have to do with quality. A Japanese needs a lot less space than an American to have a high-quality environment. Similarly, Americans at different ages and different income levels have different environmental quality aspirations. The Boy Scout hiker has a view of the environment similar to that of many conservationists. The high-rise-apartment dweller may have a different view, and the ghetto resident still another. At the beginning of married life, income levels and space aspirations are different from those that exist at middle age, and these in turn are different at old age. The point is that environmental quality is pluralistic in many respects within our own country and more so throughout the world.

One approach is to fall back on authoritarian solutions, or maybe I should say Olympian, which is a middle-class way of defining authoritarianism. This approach is, of course, morally reprehensible in terms of the value system in which most of us have been socialized. Second, it has not prevented Soviet commissars from shooting polar bears against the laws of the Soviet Union, just as our hunters do. Moreover, there is a theoretical reason why authoritarianism or Olympianism will not work. If we are considering questions of values, risk assessment, and social solutions, we are talking about a cybernetic system that needs feedback, because there is a great deal of diversity on these issues. If we want to keep a healthy human environment, diversity is useful for survival. The feedback system that has to deal with all this diversity has to be good, and no authoritarian system has a good feedback system or one that is sufficient to deal with the kind of diversity that these issues provide.

An obvious alternative is the democratic process. The ability of democracy to sustain radical change has been amply demonstrated in the last 20 to 25 years, and this is a small time period compared with the 300 years, 200 years, or 70 years that biologists and ecologists talk about. In fact, the shift of concern toward ecology has been tremendous in the last few years, as indicated by bibliographical dates in books on ecology. Books on water resources gave the basic message by 1962. By 1968 or 1969, the important books were directed to masses of people instead of just water-quality specialists. That is a matter of about six to eight years since the first good indicator. A climate of opinion conducive to environmental improvement has developed in less than a decade.

A final ingredient is science. We have to get knowledge and understanding and the capacity to deal with the environmental problem because the democratic process by itself, if it is misled, will make foolish decisions. We have to get scientific evidence and get it rapidly, and in a way that can be understood. The major task now is not simply to define the will to act; I think a good number of people have the will to act. The task now is to move from will to skill and to upgrade the predictive power of ecology in the process. That leaves ecology as the new dismal science because it is the best candidate as a science for dealing with the problem of the destruction of the environment.

How to Get Rich without Getting Poor

There are three basic requirements to solve this dilemma. First, we have to define the problem. We have to define the problem in a way to specify the level of attack for politicians, who worry about values and risk and the social solutions necessary. It does not do any good to tell a politician that there is a catastrophe over the horizon. He cannot get any reins on a catastrophe; it will take him over the hill long before he can ever do anything about it. So the level of the problem has to be disaggregated, with intellectual handles of less than catastrophic size. It also has to be defined as more than funding tertiary sewage treatment plants all over the United States. This level also is not sufficient.

One candidate for a useful conceptual level of attack is to know what constitutes a closed materials cycle. We could almost define pollution as unclosed natural and man-made cycles, and the amount of pollution in a society would be that amount of material that is not recycled to the economy or to nature. If we could know that, we would also derive one more important fact. We could calculate what the "net return" is on the payment of nature to man. That is, what man can use from nature's bounty before natural cycles are seriously disrupted.

We need to know what the net return is on the capital of the natural resources of the globe. If we knew what the net return was, we could live on the maximum sustained yield over a long period of time. That might be enough for many men, but there is a lot of basic science that is not yet able to calculate the "net return" on natural resources. Maybe with technology we can make it high and be able to sustain a large K in comfort.[2] If we were able to answer that question, we could tell just how dismal ecology would be as a science.

Whatever the standard of living implied by a materials balance with nature, there is no implication that this is the level society will choose. The point here is only that defining the balance provides useful data for any decision requiring a trade-off between unbridled materialism and closed cycles. The level of "exploitation" (depletion) at which we decide to operate must evolve from social goal formulation processes.

The second requirement for a useful level of attack is to deal with the problem of the commons. It is a competitive, aggressive American soul that we have, but the competition has to be fair. If someone is using the commons more cheaply, we can say he is enjoying an advantage over us; and that is not fair. The rule of first

2. Ibid.

access is not enough. I think Americans can understand that one person should not be allowed to use the commons for individual gain when it prevents others from getting ahead. That is a good value anchor. To help us define our problem, ecologists should give us some levels of the carrying capacity of the commons.

Third, if ecology is to be a useful science, we are going to have to write it in a language that can be communicated to the people who make decisions, to the listeners who are most relevant. These listeners have certain criteria that have to be met.

It will be necessary, though not sufficient, to have an ecological early warning system of some reliability. If ecologists are going to be effective in helping politicians, then they are going to have to design an early warning system that will allow us to prevent difficulties rather than trying to undo them. It is very costly, both economically and politically, to try to correct a misplaced investment, and that is why we have to get to the problems before investments are made. Before an investment is put in the ground, we have to simulate its effects. Proposals for science funding should have this in mind.

A second part of the early warning system has to be able to identify incremental damage. It is a fact of life that our pollution problems are the sum of many small problems. Each individual demand on the environment must be evaluated: Yes, you can do that; yes, you can do this; no, you can't do that. But we can say "yes" six times in a row and the effect is additive, so that we approach limits without trading off incremental changes against each other. In some way we are going to have to show politicians that there is only a limited space to grow in, and we ought to maximize the return for incremental change. That allows us, then, to assess damages for the person responsible for incremental change and also allows us to know how much the commons can tolerate. Then we can allocate resources with priorities.

To summarize, there are three criteria for performance of the ecological sciences: (1) Define the level of attack with reliable priorities of criticality. (2) Stress the problem of the commons, which has good prospects of solution, at least in the culture of the United States. (3) Communicate these in the format of the listener–decision-maker in a way that can identify incremental change and is preventive in that it is based on an early warning system. The successful formula should try to solve the paradox of how to get rich without impoverishing nature, and therefore impoverishing ourselves.

There is an agenda. In it ecology does not play the role of an ideology. We can apply ecology to our problems by assessing and understanding nature's cycles. Natural imbalance gives men adequate warning that they are using the commons inefficiently. We can then manage our resources and ourselves, with an understanding of the value plurality of the world, to allocate priorities for new incremental demands on the supply that nature and technology give us. These are your tasks and your agenda and they are mine, and I hope we can do them well because the stakes for which we are playing are high indeed.

Charles L. Hosler

chapter six

MAN'S IMPACT UPON THE ATMOSPHERE

I

We are fortunate to live in a country that still retains
much of its pristine beauty, but signs of environmental
change are apparent everwhere. Even the skies are not
sacred; we now see many days a year with artificial clouds.
In Pennsylvania, on the airway between New York and
Chicago, hundreds of jet flights pass over each day. About
one day out of three now is overcast with artificial clouds,
as shown now beginning to form in figure 1. The sun
is sometimes cut to from one-third to one-half of its
intensity by artificial cirrus clouds. Not only is the sunlight
prevented from reaching the ground, but the jets disgorge
their tens of thousands of pounds of water vapor and
unburned hydrocarbons into the low temperatures of the
upper troposphere. There the air is already either saturated
or slightly supersaturated with respect to ice but not with
respect to water, and the additional water vapor provides
additional supersaturation and nucleates the ice phase;
and we get spreading and growing of the clouds that,

from a single jet, can cause an overcast of the entire sky.

As also shown in figure 1, snow trails fall down and can have a severe impact on days when there are lower clouds. When ice is introduced into the lower clouds, they may freeze, releasing latent heat of fusion and resulting in additional growth. The release of the latent heat of fusion in localized areas causes convection, which intensifies precipitation in these areas and suppresses it in others; and this is the way nature indeed produces the bands and lines and the variations in intensity of precipitation within a larger-scale storm system.

Very often, cumulus clouds in our part of the world are suppressed by a weak inversion, a layer of warm air above them, and they can only grow to a very limited height. But if they contain super-cooled liquid water, as they usually do, and the ice crystals fall into the cloud, turning supersaturated drops to ice, the latent heat of fusion is released, the cloud has additional buoyancy, can break through the inversion, and giant showers and thunderstorms can result. Again, this is what nature does. We are helping nature do it in localities where the jets fly. And, of course, we can deliberately inject materials into the atmosphere that will do the same thing where we want it to happen, as indeed we do in overt weather modification.

Figure 2 shows a controlled experiment in which a grenade released silver iodide smoke in cumulus clouds previously surpressed by an inversion. The silver iodide acted to produce ice crystals, and the freezing released enough heat to explode a tower out of the top.

The same thing will happen when the materials from a steel mill get caught up in a cloud. They will freeze it. Or if you fly over it with a jet aircraft and ice crystals form up above and fall down through, they will produce the same results. The development of cumulus clouds and their ultimate achievement of shower status or thunder-

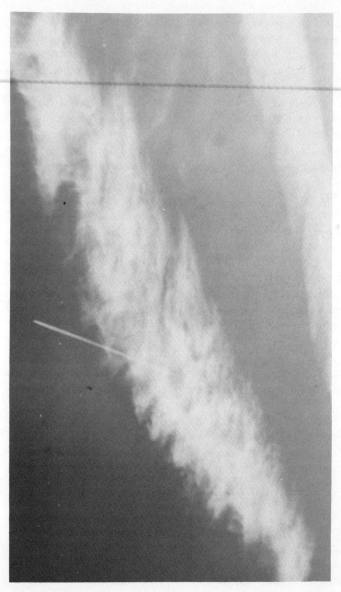

Fig. 1. Clouds from jets formed by exhalation of water vapor into very cold air.

Fig. 2. Result of cloud seeding. Tower shoots out of the top of a cumulus cloud.

storm status is determined in part by ice crystal availability and in part by man's role in when and where ice forms.

The production of clouds does several things. Of course, the solar energy coming in is reflected back out into space, but also infrared radiation coming up from the surface is absorbed and reradiated or reflected back to earth. The cloud layer acts like a grid in a triode tube; it regulates the heat balance of the earth. Now, if you put 300 SST's above 50° north latitude operating in the northern hemisphere, that will produce a complete overcast of cirrus clouds all the way from 50° to the North Pole in the wintertime. This will have a profound effect on the flux of energy both in and out of the atmosphere. The atmospheric engine is driven by the thermal gradients that exist from one latitude to another. We must begin to consider what the over-all effect of this might be on global circulation patterns, which only have to shift by very minor amounts to get very large variations in the weather we observe at the surface at any given point.

The other thing that man does and has done from the earliest time is to modify the earth's surface by plowing up the grass, by cutting down the trees, by his use of the land where large contiguous areas of several square miles or more are of uniform character, so that they either absorb or reflect the solar energy in a similar way. Temperature anomalies are produced on the ground, which affect the temperature and density of the air. These in turn induce vertical motion of air, which cause vertical momentum transport. The momentum transport then deflects the flow of the atmosphere over these areas and the lifting or sinking that occurs has a profound effect on the formation of clouds. Downwind of some midwestern cities now we begin to see that there are precipitation anomalies induced by the city acting as either a heat source, a water vapor source, and as a source of pollution, or as a source of a difference in the frictional character of the surface of the earth from one place to another.

To observe that this occurs in nature, see figure 3. The thunderstorms and showers are building up over land areas but not over water. The cooler air is flowing from over the water to over the warmer land and being lifted up. Every little lake, if it is more than two or three miles across, even though it represents a temperature anomaly of only a few degrees (five degrees at the most) can be identified by the absence of clouds above it. This illustrates the profound effect a temperature anomoly can have on

Fig. 3. Absence of clouds over rivers and lakes in Florida shows influence of small negative temperature anomalies.

cumulus development and subsequent showers and thunderstorms.

It is entirely conceivable that within the next century, when we get the kind of society that people seem to be determined to get, there will be rules about who is allowed to come out and sun on Wednesday from 3:00 to 4:00, e.g., those whose names begin with H through J. Land use will be determined by the patterns of weather to be induced downwind. There will be certain areas where thundershowers are planned at certain times, other areas where they are not.

II

Air pollution usually contains visible and invisible particles. The visible particles can be removed by electrostatic precipitators, but the invisible particles remain and have long residence times in the atmosphere. They penetrate deep into your lungs, and act in meteorological processes. Even if not removed at their origin, the big particles fall out like rocks; and they may annoy the housewife in getting on the windowsill or the bed, but they do not make as much difference as far as the atmosphere is concerned. In the atmosphere the things that are important are the very small particulates of less than a micron, or often of less than a tenth of a micron. These have a profound effect on the character of clouds.

Out over the ocean in the tropics there are about a hundred cloud drops in a cubic centimeter, but in Ohio there are anywhere from three to five hundred. There is the same amount of water in a cubic centimeter, but more drops. The reason is that the air is polluted. It is polluted with materials that facilitate the formation of water drops, hygroscopic materials that lower the energy necessary to form a drop. The drops form in greater numbers, and so a cloud has a different character. The clouds with the many little drops have great difficulty

Fig. 4. Steel mill releasing small particles and water vapor to form artificial clouds and fog in the early morning.

in producing rain because a raindrop requires a collison between about a million cloud drops, and the only way a million cloud drops can get together is if a few of them are fairly large and run into the other ones. The net result is that many little cumulus clouds that would precipitate in the tropics do not precipitate here. It takes a bigger cloud and a longer time for precipitation to develop in this area.

Figure 4 illustrates the process. It shows a cold, hazy morning in winter and a steel mill putting out few visible particles. It is the invisible particles together with the water vapor that is put into the air that produce an artificial cloud. I followed this particular cloud in a light airplane from Pittsburgh to Columbus, Ohio. The separate streams merged into a swath about forty miles wide that extended all the way to Columbus. People there found it a cloudy, foggy day, which the Weather Bureau had not forecast. In fact, of course, the clouds and the fog were artificial. People ran into bridge abutments and each other, and blamed it on the Lord.

A similar situation is shown in figure 5, except in this case the fog is coming out of a valley that has two paper mills in it, sixty miles apart, putting out sodium sulphite, sodium sulfate, and other pollutants. On cold mornings, of course, the valley fills up with cold air. There is a layer of warm air above. The air that comes out of the stacks is hot, but very quickly it cools off upon mixing with the cold air. It becomes about the same temperature as the air in the valley, and naturally the cold air in the valley cannot rise through the warmer air that lies above. So the valley fills with the foggy, smoggy air, and serves as a conduit to the cut in the mountain at Bellefonte, thirty miles from either of the two paper mills, where it spills through to the adjoining valley, as shown in figure 5.

The same cut is shown in figure 6 eight years later.

Fig. 5. Man-made fog spills from a Pennsylvania valley in 1962, Bellefonte, Pennsylvania.

Fig. 6. The same Pennsylvania valley in 1970. The interchange between two major highways especially designed to remain in the fog.

Fig. 7. A large power plant injecting energy into the atmosphere by evaporating water. On cold stable mornings fog can form.

An interstate highway has been built down the length of the foggy valley, and another interstate highway passes through the cut. There is an intersection of the two interstate highways in the foggy valley. During the first five weeks that the highway shown in figure 6 was open, five people were killed at the intersection, certainly not a tribute to man's foresight in designing the highway or his effect on the atmosphere in this particular area.

Another source of pollution is the large power plant. Figure 7 shows one of the earlier big plants. This particular plant generates about 1,800 megawatts. Most of the power plants being designed now in my part of the country are twice this big. Some of them go up to 4,500 megawatts. In order to get rid of the waste heat released by condensing the steam on the low pressure side of the turbines, one must dissipate energy into the atmosphere at the rate of about 10^{14} ergs per second, which is about the same energy dissipation rate as in a thunderstorm. We are putting tremendous amounts of energy into the atmosphere at one location; we do not put the energy into the river any more because the fish would cook (those that are left). The size of these plants is difficult to comprehend. The stacks shown in figure 7 are 1,000 feet tall. Out of those stacks come more than thirty tons of sulphur dioxide every hour. A little black smoke appears in figure 7, but normally you do not see any black smoke. The electrostatic precipitators remove almost all of the visible fly ash, but sulfur dioxide still comes out. Eventually, all the vegetation in the area will be affected by the sulfur dioxide coming out of those stacks.

Fumigation conditions and inversion conditions will inevitably occur in this location. Stagnation of the air over a period of several days will lead to some major disasters. The United States is in for some major pollution episodes in which people drop over in the streets. We have continued to escalate the rate of pollution while nature still operates on the same level to remove pollution.

The shorter towers shown in figure 7 are 400 feet high, and they evaporate 25 million gallons of water a day into the atmosphere. It is just harmless water vapor, and that does not cause any problem. Except, of course, it does cause some fog on cold mornings, as shown in figure 7, and it can cause artificial clouds. These are 8,000 feet tall, and they extend about a hundred miles downwind. Now, the newer nuclear plants that are twice this big in megawattage will be putting out about three times this much water, so you can imagine what it's going to look like. Nobody thought about this, incidentally, before it actually happened; until two years ago nobody had even examined this problem. In the summertime when there are showers and thunderstorms forming in the area normally, the additional water vapor will mean that they will be triggered preferentially in the same area. This will be the first place where the cumulus clouds will form, and there will be a preferred avenue downwind where the bigger cumulus clouds will form and the most showers and thunderstorms will develop.

III

As we increase the global pollution level, the entire atmosphere may accumulate so many small particulates that the clouds are stabilized. Figure 8 illustrates the problem on Saint Croix in the Virgin Islands. It shows cumulus clouds in various stages of development. The one on the right has dissipated, but rain is falling down. A shaft of rain is falling into dry air and evaporating. Had that rain formed five minutes earlier in the life cycle of the cloud—these clouds last about 20 to 25 minutes—it would have fallen through cloudy air; and instead of evaporating, it would have grown. It would have reached the ground as a quite heavy shower.

The east end of Saint Croix is a desert, and the west end of the island is a tropical rain forest. The line between the two is determined by the time required for precipitation to form in a cumulus cloud such as shown in figure 8. As the atmosphere gradually becomes more polluted, the time required for precipitation to form is increased. The more it is increased, the higher is the risk of having the clouds go all the way off the west end of the island before they rain, the rain fall in the ocean, and the entire island become a desert. Cloud-seeding might be a remedy, but the actual extent to which natural precipitation has been retarded is not yet established.

The same kind of precipitation shift occurs around Buffalo, New York, due to the steel mills in that area. In the winter the cold air comes across Lake Erie, forms clouds on the lee shore, and deposits a foot to three feet of snow on the lake shore. The reason that happens is because as the air speeds across the lake, it suddenly encounters the lake shore where there is more friction, the surface air slows down, the air coming behind it has to go over it, and there is a local lifting action. This lifting produces a narrow band of clouds that are, for the most part, super-cooled and contain very few ice crystals, so that the few ice crystals that are in there form big, fat snowflakes that fall very rapidly and come down in great numbers on the lake shore.

Now, the snowfall can actually be moved by reducing the size of the ice crystals. We have done this experimentally by releasing chemicals upwind of the snow clouds to raise the temperature at which ice forms and produce a lot more ice crystals to compete in the clouds. Smaller and lighter flakes are formed that have a flatter trajectory and are carried twenty to thirty miles downwind before they reach the ground. Three kinds of people were threatening injunctions to stop these experiments: the people who had the ski resorts on the lake shore did not want anybody

Fig. 8. Cumulus clouds in St. Croix, V.I. show the vault of precipitation developing too late. It falls through dry air and evaporates.

moving the snow; the people who had the ski resorts with snow-making equipment inland did not want their competitors to get snow free; and the people who made the snow-making equipment did not want anybody getting snow on order from nature because they would not be able to sell their equipment. Weather control has its problems. Of course, the steel mills in the area are doing the same thing by injecting seeding agents into the clouds in an uncontrolled way, but no one is concerned about this.

Cloud control may lead to lightning control. We know, of course, that lightning is formed when there are big charge centers in the clouds. The charge centers are the result of charge generation, mostly from the process of the freezing of water drops and the melting of ice crystals. And since we do have some controls now over the phase transitions in clouds and over the freezing of water drops, there is some hope that we will be able to regulate the amount of lightning coming to the ground. This is only a hope, and it cannot be demonstrated as of this time. (See figure 9.)

Cloud effects of pollution today are inadvertent. Tomorrow they may be deliberate. A city, by adding pollutants, may cause clouds in certain areas to develop at the expense of those in the surrounding areas because the clouds affected may prematurely have the ice phase introduced into them. This may then release the latent heat of fusion, promoting the growth of bigger clouds. Some of these swaths of rain that we are beginning to observe downwind of the cities are due to the effects of pollution and the city itself on cloud development.

Eventually, I suppose, we will get around to doing this deliberately. We will design our watersheds, and we will design our recreation areas to take advantage of man-made precipitation patterns. Certainly it behooves us to expand our understanding in this realm. To do this requires a

Fig. 9. There is some hope that control of cloud processes will eventually lead to control of lightning.

lot of sophisticated radar gear to measure cloud properties from the ground and to direct aircraft. It requires aircraft to penetrate the clouds and take measurements. There are about eighteen different parameters to be measured to define the state of a cloud. We must be able to dispense materials into the clouds and provide deliberately certain types of pollutants that will affect the cloud in a certain way. We must have access to very large and fast computers that can take the cloud data and the numerical models used to simulate the cloud process and predict what the cloud will do naturally. The next step is to put in the new parameters and see what the cloud would do artificially. Finally, we observe whether the result coincides with what we hypothesized would happen.

The above phenomena can be observed on a global scale over the earth as man increases his pollution-generating activities. Photographs taken from satellites show unnatural lines and bands emanating from the east coast of the United States. These are formed by man-made sources of pollution and their impact on the character of clouds. There are streaks and bands even out in the middle of the ocean. These are due to ships; the pollution injected into a relatively clean atmosphere by ships has affected fog and cloud formations. The streaks from the east coast can be traced back to industrial centers where the centers have either put in nuclei that dissipated the clouds or nuclei that made the clouds more persistent.

IV

So now the question arises, Are we going to go on dumping things into the atmosphere with unknown effects and produce unknown impact on our children and on the people of the world in general? Will future pictures of the earth show changed cloud patterns on an even larger scale? Will we begin to see shifts in the long-wave patterns that distribute precipitation over the hemisphere? Will we indeed bring about disaster? I am not saying we will or can, but as a matter of fact it seems to me to be a very highly possible thing from what we know about the atmosphere. We know that we do get major changes in the global circulation apparently in response to very minor shifts in the heat balance of the earth. And we certainly know that some of the things we are doing are going to produce changes in the heat balance of the necessary magnitude. A change may come by way of the production of artificial cirrus clouds, the alteration of the amount of atmospheric ozone in the stratosphere, the amount of carbon dioxide in the troposphere, or alterations in the thermodynamic and physical processes in clouds.

The fact is that many of these things are poorly understood, but we certainly know that they have an impact of about the same magnitude as those things nature does that do bring about major shifts in atmospheric circulation. We can speculate even further and say that we know from geological evidence, of course, that there have been major, almost cataclysmic, changes in global circulation and in atmospheric behavior in eons past to give glaciers and interglacial, postglacial periods; and we also would be inclined to believe and would feel intuitively that whatever brought those things about was not of any greater magnitude than some of the things that we see being brought about today by man's activities.

We should note in conclusion the extreme sensitivity of the world's economy and political structures to very minor changes in the atmosphere, to very minor changes in rainfall. A simple 10 percent reduction in rainfall in the United States and Canada would have profound effects on food production. In 1969 the rate of growth of the gross national product in the Soviet Union was the lowest in the last thirty years. Soviet growth was only 2.7 percent, down from an average of 6 percent, largely due to shrinkage in agricultural output as a result of adverse precipitation patterns. The fact is that the economy and the political structure of the world are very sensitive to minor changes in atmospheric circulation. A people or group of individuals who would, without regard for what they do, pollute the atmosphere and change the behavior of the atmosphere without knowing what the consequences will be, it seems to me, is a very foolish one.

part two

COMMUNITY

Robert Bierstedt

chapter seven

THE QUALITY OF SOCIETY

The young among us, reverting unaccountably to ancient superstition, tell us that we are living in the Age of Aquarius. It would be more appropriate, and surely more sophisticated, to say that we are living in the Age of Ecology. Suddenly we are all conscious of the environment, what we have done to damage it, and what we have to do to prevent its further deterioration. When we talk about the environment, we are inclined to regard it first of all as a physical environment, and to think about such things as the erosion of the soil, the pollution of rivers and lakes and now of the oceans themselves, and the poisoning of the atmosphere. With respect to the last of these, the atmosphere, we can see that Hamlet was indeed prophetic when he said, "This most excellent canopy, the air, this brave o'erhanging firmament . . . appeareth nothing to me but a foul and pestilent congregation of vapors." We have now given Hamlet even more reasons to complain. Space itself has lost its immunity to the infestations of man. As of a recent reckoning there were well over one thousand rocketed objects in one orbit or another, and the space in the vicinity of the earth was beginning to resemble a flying junkyard.

The physical environment, however, is not the only environment to which the exigencies of the day require us to pay attention. Another environment is the cultural environment. This, of course, consists of the products of man, some of them intangible, that surround us and that affect and, indeed, determine the course of our lives. This environment includes knowledge, myth, and legend; folkways, mores, and laws; and all of the physical objects that art and craft and engineering have been able to offer. Whether this environment too is "polluted" in this twentieth century of the Christian era is a subject for social criticism and ultimately for the philosophy of history.

There is still a third environment, and this is the social environment. It is made up of people themselves. It is made up of so many people at the present time that—as I shall contend—the quality of society is impaired.

When Grandma Moses, the American primitive painter, was interviewed on her one-hundredth birthday, she was asked what, in her opinion, was the principal difference between the world on that day and the world she remembered of her childhood. She replied that now there are too many people. Too many people! What meaning can we attach to this far from primitive judgment, and how do people, in shear quantitative terms, affect the quality of a society? These are questions to which the following observations are addressed.

Let us begin with the great demographer Thomas Robert Malthus, whose famous and unforgettable essay *On Population* was written in response to the easy optimism of Godwin and Condorcet, both of whom were protagonists of the doctrine of progress. In this essay, as we all know, Malthus invited the attention of his contemporaries to the ineluctable fact that the world's population has some essential relationship to the world's supply of food. Whether the former is always increasing in a geometrical progression and the latter always in an arithmetical one, as Malthus thought, need not concern us here. The actual picture is not so clear and the Malthusian thesis requires many qualifications. We can also ignore Coleridge's criticism of Malthus, namely, that the proportion of sense to nonsense in the *Essay* was also related as an arithmetic to a geometric progression.

We should pause a moment, however, to examine the awesome properties of a geometric series. Consider the brainteaser of the amoeba and the milk bottle. Suppose we place one amoeba in the bottle, assume that it reproduces itself every two minutes, and that the bottle is then completely filled with amoebae in thirty minutes. The question is, How long will it take to fill the bottle if we begin with two amoebas rather than one. If you answer, too quickly, fifteen minutes because fifteen is half of thirty, you will, of course, be wrong. Remember that we are dealing with a brainteaser. The correct answer is twenty-eight minutes. If we start with two amoebas rather than one we are in exactly the same position at the beginning that we were in at the end of two minutes in the first instance and have thus cut two minutes off the time required to fill the bottle.

What happens at the beginning, however, is not nearly so important as what happens at the end. If, beginning with one amoeba, it takes thirty minutes to fill one bottle, it is perfectly apparent that it takes not sixty minutes, or one hour, to fill two bottles but only two more minutes— thirty-two minutes in all. To make matters worse, we are assuming throughout that the rate of reproduction is constant. If the rate itself increases, we must contend with an even larger swarm of amoebas and need to hurry to find more milk bottles with which to contain them.

Now we do not need to agree with Malthus that human population growth in fact resembles a geometric progression. For many, many centuries—at least a hundred—it did not do so. Birth rates only slightly exceeded death rates, and so the rise in numbers was steady, but slow and unspectacular. But we do need to stop and think when the increase begins to approach, in some degree however small, the properties of a geometric series. Something of this sort began to happen in the middle of the seventeenth century. A line that rose almost imperceptibly for 100,000 years dramatically changed its direction and gave us the problem we face today. And today Thomas Robert Malthus is here again, insisting that we pay attention.

Let me cite a few frightening facts. It is estimated that some 77 billion people have enjoyed a longer or shorter sojourn on this planet since the misty beginning of the human race. Ninety-nine percent of this vast expanse of time produced only 6 percent of the 77 billion. The remaining 1 percent produced the remaining 94 percent. Of all of the people who have ever lived—in a time span of 600,000 years—4 percent are alive today. All of the centuries of human existence were required to produce a world population of one billion people by the year 1830 A.D. Only one hundred years, from 1830 to 1930, were required to produce a second billion. Only thirty-one additional years, from 1930 to 1961 were required to reach a figure of three billion. At the current rate of increase only fifteen years will suffice to increase the figure from three to four billion, and only ten years after that to increase it to five. At current rates of increase the population of the world could reach the incredible figure of six billion by the end of the present century. All the years of human history to the year 1900 produced a population of 1.5 billion people. The twentieth century alone, in a minute span of 100 years, will have produced at its end another 4.5 billion, or three times as many. When one century contributes three times as many people as all of the preceding centuries combined, we are confronting something more than idle arithmetic.

The time required to double a population differs, of course, in different countries. In the so-called underdeveloped countries, which at least one demographer calls the "never-to-be-developed" countries, it ranges from 19 or 20 to 35 years. In this group we would find such countries as Kenya (24), Nigeria (38), Turkey (24), the Philippines (20), Brazil (22), Costa Rica (20), and El Salvador (19). The industrialized countries, on the contrary, exhibit a range in doubling time from 50 to 200 years. In 1968, for example, the doubling times of Denmark, Norway, and Poland stood at 88 years and that of the United States, Russia, and Japan at 63 years. But consider what it means for a country to double its population in 20 to 25 years. In one generation, and with few technological resources, it must also double its food supply. Since this is clearly impossible, the result is poverty and starvation, and the human misery that accompanies these evils. The doubling time for the entire population of the world is now 36 years. What this means is that the present population of 3.5 billion people will be 7 billion in the sixth year of the twenty-first century. We rapidly approach a demographic Armageddon.

The disparities between the more fortunate and the less fortunate nations, of course, are great indeed. One-third of the world's population now consumes two-thirds of the world's food supply, leaving only one-third of that supply for the other two-thirds of the population. For that matter, the United States, with 6 percent of the world's population, consumes 40 percent of the world's non-renewable resources. For that reason, and somewhat paradoxically, the birth of one new American child endangers the dwindling food supply much more seriously than the birth of many more children in the underdeveloped countries.

Consider again that two-thirds of the people in the world go to bed hungry every night and that every morning there are 180,000 newborn infants clamoring for breakfast. Every week enough people are born to add to the world's population another Baltimore, Houston, Cleveland, St. Louis, Milwaukee, or Washington, D.C.; every two weeks another Philadelphia; every month another Chicago, and every two months another New York. Every year Asia adds to its population a number larger than the entire contingent of immigrants who came to the United States from Europe in the one hundred years of the nineteenth century. To conclude this sad recital of demographic facts, in the time it takes the average American family to have dinner, 418 people starve to death. David Riesman's "lonely crowd" in short, is hardly lonely any more; and as John Updike expressed it in one of his short stories, "The race is no longer a tiny clan of simian aristocrats lording it over an ocean of grass; mankind is a plague racing like fire across the exhausted continents."

So far as we in this country are concerned, we are inclined most of the time to think that population is not our problem. It is a problem that affects the Chinese, the Indians, the Brazilians, and other peoples far away. The problem of population however is one of our afflictions too, and it is one for which we have no privileged solution. It may be an anachronism, but we have to acknowledge that in this most prosperous nation on earth we have a serious problem of poverty. We may or may not reach a total population of 300 million by the end of the century, but by that time three out of every four of us will be living in congested metropolitan areas. In the United States today 15 million of our citizens, a number equal to the entire metropolitan area of New York City, are suffering from starvation. Even in our scientific and sophisticated age there are deprived Americans, and there are wards in the city of Chicago where the birthrate is as high or higher than that of any place in the underdeveloped countries. All of us know that some of our families have been on welfare for three generations. What I am trying to say is that although our problem is less serious than that in many parts of the world, we nevertheless have a problem and that it is not likely to go away.

It is only fair to say that the domestic picture at least does not appear to be quite so bleak as it was only a few years ago. The director of the Census Bureau, George H. Brown, in a speech delivered in New York City on 7 October 1970, said that the "population bomb" is being "defused," that the American woman is now having fewer children, and that the total population as of a given future date will be significantly less than that indicated in earlier estimates. The fertility rate of women of childbearing age declined from 3.35 children in the 1950s to 2.78 in the early 1960s, and to a current figure of 2.45. This is not too far from the 2.11 that would be required for a zero growth rate—the slight excess over 2.0 attributable, of course, to the mortality of those who do not live long enough to reproduce themselves. Even if the decline continues, however, a stationary population could not be achieved until around the year 2045. The population picture, however, so far as the United States is concerned, looks a little brighter now than it did a decade ago. The baby boom of the early fifties has subsided (although its effects will continue to be noticed in recurring cycles of diminishing amplitude as these babies and their successors arrive at reproductive ages), and it is less probable now that the population of the United States will reach 300 million by the year 2000. This note of optimism, however, must be tempered by the sober reflection that it does not apply to pullulating populations in other parts of the world. As the *New York Times* reminds us (editorial, 17 October 1970), "Fundamentally the population problem is a global one and good news about slowing birth-rates in this country alone cannot and should not end anxiety about the much darker picture in the world as a whole."

I have invited your attention to these unpleasant quantitative facts because they have qualitative significance, and it is now the latter on which I want to dwell. In turning from quantity to quality, however, I trust you will not think me less than sensitive to the misery of starvation, the *ranchos* and *favellas* of Latin America, the ghettos of Chicago and New York, and the teeming streets of the cities of India. I want to invite your attention, however, to the fact that many of the activities that we might be inclined to call middle-class are also in jeopardy because of too many people, and to this degree the quality of society is impaired. As John Stuart Mill wrote in his *Principles of Political Economy*, "A population may be too crowded, though all be amply supplied with food and raiment. It is not good for man to be kept perforce at all times in the presence of his species."

Examples can be drawn, of course, from many areas of endeavor—education, religion, business, the administration of justice, and so on. Let me choose a few examples from the area of recreation. The quality of a society is measured in part at least by the facilities it affords for recreation, those hours in which the day's work is done and those weeks in which one appropriately enjoys a holiday. What can crowds do to diminish and sometimes destroy these amenities?

The *New York Times* of 8 October 1970 had as the lead story in its travel section an article entitled "Will Success Spoil Amishland?" Amishland, of course, is Pennsylvania Dutch country, Lancaster County in southeastern Pennsylvania. Some eight thousand Amish live there, members of a strict Mennonite sect whose European origin dates back to the year 1698. They are strict fundamentalists, reject infant baptism, Sunday schools, and even, many of them, churches, preferring to worship instead in one another's houses. They speak a dialect of German, wear the plainest of black clothes fastened by hooks rather than buttons, indulge in no household decorations, reject all mechanical and electrical devices, including the telephone, and drive along the roads of the county in horse-drawn buggies. They have, unfortunately, become one of the leading tourist attractions in the United States for people who live on the Eastern Seaboard.

The author of the article to which I have referred, Ann Geracimos, not Amish herself, remembers her childhood in Lancaster and describes it in lyrical language as follows:

> I grew up here in the nineteen-forties and nineteen-fifties surrounded by a privileged isolation. Near my home, I could sit on a picket fence late at night under a clear sky, bright with stars, and listen to the bells of two dozen burly sheep nibbling grass. I used to think I could detect definite rhythms in the bell tones.

Sad to say, this idyllic countryside has disappeared in a press of people, no fewer than three million (!) of whom came as tourists in 1969, and who spent there an estimated $90 million dollars. What they found was not the simple homespun Amish they were looking for but traffic on U.S. Route 30 and State Route 340 so dense that at times it hardly moved and a clutter of neon signs advertising everything from "Sno-Cones" to pizza—yes, pizza. The roads are full of fake museums and stores selling the products of Amish craftsmanship, a commercial fraud because the Amish themselves never make anything for sale in stores. Finally, the famous farmer's market in Lancaster is now so crowded with tourists that the townspeople frequently find it difficult to do their shopping. One housewife says rather testily that she stomps on tourists' toes with her cane, and a local judge suggests that a balcony for sightseers will have to be built around the market, "just like the New York Stock Exchange."

Look now at another part of the world, Expo '70, the world's fair in Osaka, Japan, and reflect upon the following news dispatch transmitted by Reuters on 6 September 1970:

Expo '70 declared an emergency and closed its gates today as crowds reached massive proportions for the second successive day.

Some 4,000 people were stranded on the site overnight as transportation facilities reached saturation because of a record attendance of 835,832 yesterday.

Although officials stopped selling tickets at 3 P.M. and closed the gates two hours later, today's attendance was 777,098.

Expo officials believed a last-minute rush to see the six-month fair before it closes next weekened was responsible for the high attendance.

Officials had warned elderly people to stay away today and ordered restrictions on railway ticket sales to curb the crowds. Trains from the Expo site were extended to the early hours of this morning to cope with Saturday's crowds, but the trains were unable to accommodate about 4,000, who were forced to spend the night at the site.

The crowds surpassed the previous one-day record of 703,664, recorded at the Brussels Fair in 1958. . . .

An exposition designed to show the wonders of the future began itself, in short, to exhibit some of the future's inconveniences and discomforts as well. Visitors to the United States pavilion, for example, had to wait in line for two hours on week-days and from three and one-half to four hours on Sundays.

Let us return to the United States and consider what is happening to California, now the most populous state in the Union. Only twenty-five years ago the Santa Clara Valley, at the southern end of San Francisco Bay, was a lovely oasis of vineyards, orchards, and vegetable gardens. Today it is an urban anthill. Row after row of houses—"developments," so-called—succeed one another in architectural monotony. The gardens have disappeared and so have the gardeners; and so also have the plum and the pear orchards, once so lush—all in the short period of twenty years. What else can be expected when a population grows from 95,000 to 436,000 in two decades?

If we move our sights somewhat farther east we come

to Yosemite National Park. Here, this year, the traffic became so unmanageable that a part of the park had to be closed off to campers and automobiles. If we move all the way east to New York, we find the mountains of the Adirondacks subject to a new kind of erosion—erosion caused by the feet of too many hikers. Camping grounds in the Catskills begin to look, in the words of one observer, like a cross between a used car lot and Tobacco Road. The author of an article on this subject stumbled wearily into a camp's restroom area at 8 A.M. one morning last summer only to find herself standing in a line crowded with equally uncombed women. Is this how we now commune with nature and enjoy the great outdoors?

Consider next our streets and sidewalks and the everyday use we make of them. Once upon a time—how quaint the expression sounds—one of the pleasures of life in New York City was to stroll down the Avenue—Fifth Avenue, of course—and to enjoy the elegant shops and the chic and beautiful women passing by. Today the shops are still elegant (although economic pressures are forcing some of them out of business and others to move to Madison Avenue), but it is hard to stroll there. The sidewalks are too crowded. We all know about traffic congestion in mid-town Manhattan. But pedestrian congestion is something new under the sun—or at least recognition of it is new. On several occasions automobiles have been banned entirely from the avenue, as they are now on Sundays from Central Park, but in both places one is still awed by the mass of humanity. The crowds one used to see only at Coney Island on a Sunday afternoon in summer have become the rule rather than the exception in other locations as well. If rooms and buildings and other enclosed spaces can induce claustrophobia, one might find here another affliction called "demophobia"—namely, the anxiety engendered when one finds himself in the presence of too many people.

One of the pleasures of living in Rome, as in New York, used to be the nearness of the sea. With the beaches of Ostia only fifteen miles away a resident of the city, as recently as ten years ago, could easily drive there during his three-hour luncheon break, have a swim, drive back, and be in his office again in time for the afternoon stint at his desk. Unfortunately, this is no longer possible. The highway is clogged with traffic. If he tries to go by train, he will suffer a similar defeat. The city's streets at the noon hour are almost impassable, and unless our citizen lives or works close by, he will find the railroad terminal an unattainable destination.

And what do these contemporary Romans find even if they reach the sea? They find a scene of incredible pollution. The mothers who used to call to their children to get out of the water and come in for lunch now forbid them from entering the water at all. The entire Mediterranean has recently been described as Europe's cesspool, "an undrained tank, noxiously brimming with human waste matter, oil, and garbage." Once more the quality of life is diminished, and one begins to entertain a fond nostalgia for a century earlier than our own.

As a final example, consider Cape Cod and the offshore islands. On the cape itself on a given day at the height of the summer season accommodations must be found for 260,000 overnight visitors, and the Cape Cod Planning and Development Commission, once eagerly seeking tourists, now talks about limiting the number of motels that may be built. On Nantucket Island, thirty miles out to sea, the commissioners have to decide whether the beaches may now be used for sleeping in view of the shortage of accommodations elsewhere. And on Martha's Vineyard Island, a forty-five-minute ferry ride off the coast of Massachusetts, gigantic tourist busses now contaminate the once rural roads that lead to the fishing villages. Martha's Vineyard, incidentally, has a land area of ninety-three square miles, compared with the twenty-two square miles of Manhattan Island. Even now the editorial writer on the *Vineyard Gazette* wonders whether the former island is in danger of reaching a density comparable to the latter. One can still swim at Squibnocket, the town beach of Chilmark, but only if one can find a place to park; and at Menemsha, a tiny fishing village, the basin is now so polluted that it is a serious hazard to the health of the inhabitants.

I should like to add a brief note on another subject, the need for privacy and for personal space, a need that our society is increasingly unable to satisfy. Every one of us appreciates the privacy that space affords. When we enter a movie theater, for example, we are pleased if we find it uncrowded and take a seat, if we can, in an empty row with the hope that no one will occupy the seats on either side of us. Aisle seats are preferred seats because on one side there is no adjoining seat. Similarly, we have all watched the pattern passengers adopt when they begin to fill the cabin of an airliner prior to flight. They look not only for an empty seat but for an empty row and, once ensconced, hope that the flight list is small enough that no one will come along to occupy the seat next to them. An inch or two extra of elbow room may not seem to be a matter of cosmic importance, but the airlines of the United States are nevertheless currently engaged in what has been called "the battle of the inches." On 14 September 1970 United Airlines removed one seat from each row in its economy class DC-8 jets on the New York-Los Angeles run, thus reducing the number from six to five and increasing the width of the seats by 2.3 inches. The result was more than satisfactory. In a total market that was down about 24 percent United Airlines chalked up a passenger increase of 15 percent. The company also increased the distance between rows of seats from 35 to 38 inches with similarly favorable results. Needless to say, as we have all seen from recent advertisements, other airlines had to enter the competition too, some with fold-down center seats, with the result that those of us who fly economy class are going to have more elbow and leg room on our flights. The amount of space, in quantitative terms, that individuals need for the various activities in which they indulge has only recently become a subject of serious sociological research. That such research should now seem necessary is itself a testimony to the nature of a crowded society.

The examples I have offered surely suffice to indicate that beside the "foul and pestilent congregation of vapors" to which Hamlet referred there is a new kind of pollution, a pollution that Shakespeare knew not of—the pollution of people, the pollution of too many bodies too close to us. Our own American society, among others, is now a crowded society, one that has lost something of its quality, and one that has so far failed to understand that "bigger" is not always a synonym of "better." Our society is now flawed, whether or not the predictions of the demographers are accurate. There are too many people, and there will continue to be too many people in the foreseeable future. The momentum of population growth is such that, as suggested earlier, even if the size of the average family in the United States were immediately reduced to 2.1 children, seventy years would still be required to achieve a stationary population, and by that time the total population would be 40 percent higher than it is now.

Are there any remedies? Unfortunately, sociologists are better at finding problems than they are at finding solutions. It seems clear to me, however, that only a planned reduction in the population can provide the answer. The next question is how such a reduction can be accomplished, short of such extreme measures as infanticide and geronticide. Here again there are no easy answers. Malthus recognized both positive and preventive checks to population growth. In the former category he listed epidemics, wars, plagues, famines, and climatic exposure; in the latter—those that only man can employ—celibacy, late marriage, sexual abstinence, or, as Malthus put it, "moral restraint"; and the last of these, as he acknowledged, "does not at present prevail much among the male parts of society."

In actual fact, the number of preventive checks is rather limited. Some of them are repulsive, some are ineffective, some are impractical, and others are speculative. There is no known solution to the problem. Let me nevertheless briefly survey some of the possibilities.

The first way perhaps would be to rearrange the mores of society so that homosexuality would become an acceptable and indeed a desirable mode of existence. It has the obvious advantage that it is a system of sexual expression that has no reproductive consequences. Fortunately or unfortunately, depending upon the point of view, it is a system that would not work. The vast majority of us, men and women alike, prefer the opposite sex, and would regard the homosexual suggestion as an uncomfortable alternative. Furthermore, how can we rearrange the mores? The mores, as William Graham Sumner taught us long ago, are crescive, not enacted. They arise by slow accretions and not by conscious determinations. There is no solution here.

Contraception is another obvious preventive check. But it is no panacea. Needless to say, contraceptive information should be disseminated in every part of the world, and the use of contraceptive devices encouraged in spite of religious taboos. We ought to recall, in this connection, that many practices once prohibited by ecclesiastical interdiction are now acceptable in every society. In the nineteenth century in Europe, for example, it was considered blasphemous to introduce fertilizers into the soil in order to increase the yield of crops. The practice was considered an offense against nature and nature's God. In this respect one might argue that the wearing of spectacles to remedy a weakened vision is similarly an interference with nature and with a divine plan and ordination. Taboos sometimes, if not always, do succumb to rationality.

One reason, however, why contraception is no panacea is that it reduces, at best, only the unwanted births and not the wanted ones. As a matter of interesting fact, the birthrate in the United States began to fall five years before the general availability of the Pill and now, when the Pill is generally known and available, the birth rate is showing a slight increase again. This may be due, of course, to recent alarms about its safety.

Relaxation of the taboos, legal and otherwise, on abortion, is similarly difficult to evaluate. It could be that women who, prior to this relaxation, had resort to illegal abortions now resort to legal ones and that the net result is changed only slightly. Here we are almost wholly in the realm of speculation. But we cannot hope, whatever our moral attitudes, that abortion is the solution to our problem. It may help; it may not. Only time and statistical studies will tell.

With regard to our central question, therefore, none of these proposed solutions is a certain help. One might enlist instead a force that is still mysterious to sociology, namely, the force of fashion. Somehow we need to reduce the wanted births as well as the unwanted ones. Somehow we need to introduce the notion, into our own society, at least, that it is unfashionable for parents to have more than a single child, and indeed exceedingly fashionable for couples to have no children. Photographs of candidates for political office showing three, five, seven, and even more numerous offspring should be greeted with disapproval. The world can no longer accommodate these numbers.

This answer too, however, suffers from the fact, mentioned earlier, that it is difficult if not impossible to change the folkways by fiat. On the other hand, folkways arise in the first place to satisfy societal needs, and once a need is recognized—and recognized as urgent—there is every reason to enlist fashion in support of its satisfaction.

In lieu of everything else, it may be necessary to seek a political solution; that is, to resort to the authority of government to limit the number of children permitted to a family. This could be accomplished in various ways, and a number of formulas have been suggested. One obvious way would be to eliminate the dependency deductions for all children over one or even increase the income tax either at a steady rate or at a rate that increases with each additional child. Childless couples might be given a special tax advantage. Or, even more stringently, the government might sell licenses to have children, again increasing the price directly with the number of children. It might even be wise for the government to pay an annual bonus to every woman of reproductive age for every month that she is not pregnant.

There are two major objections to these proposals. The first is that they would give to the rich an alternative unavailable to the poor. The second is that civil libertarians would regard them as unconscionable incursions upon the freedom of the individual and especially upon the freedom to use one's own body as one wishes. The answer to this second objection, however, is that an increasingly crowded society will require increasing restrictions upon freedom, including even the right to move from one place to another. One civil liberty, in short, can easily be detrimental to another. If it is argued, however, that the state has no right to determine how many children its citizens may have, it could similarly be argued that it has no right to determine how many wives or husbands they may have. To this invasion of freedom, of course, we have all accommodated ourselves. To conclude the matter, no state so far, however authoritarian, has found it necessary to employ the extreme device of compulsory sterilization. But that too, as people heedlessly reproduce themselves, may become a genuine possibility.

Finally, if these preventive checks cannot be made to work, there is a positive check that is paradoxical and perhaps—I say it with a shudder—ineluctable. There is indeed, as I have written elsewhere, a solution.

> The trouble with it is that it is too effective a solution—it would finish mankind as well. The dreaded engines of nuclear warfare are more potent by an infinite factor than any known to history and there is no question that they can reverse the demographic trends that have been in operation since the beginning of the sixteenth century. It is possible indeed that they can decimate the race for centuries to come and make room on all the continents for new numbers of human beings—beings genetically different, perhaps, from ourselves in ways unpleasant to contemplate. Thus a new species would inhabit the earth, begin again to reproduce itself, and, in some sidereal time, have a population problem of its own.

Arthur A. Atkisson

chapter eight

HABITABILITY, THE METROPOLIS, AND
ENVIRONMENTAL POLICIES

The concept of a public environmental management policy is of only recent vintage within the United States. The environment traditionally has been viewed as a common resource, as something that is always there, always available for use, and of constant and unchanging quality. When comparatively sudden and unwanted changes in environmental quality have occurred, these ordinarily have been viewed as temporary aberrations that are readily correctable and that usually ought to be tolerated.

Consistent with these views, the protection of environmental quality has been viewed primarily as a private, rather than a public, matter. If one individual's pursuit of self-interest led to environmental degradation damaging to his neighbor, then the common law provided a remedy. The damaged party had simply to carry his problem to a court where, in theory, the equities of the situation would be judged and an appropriate remedy prescribed.

Unfortunately, the circumstances of life within an industrial and urbanized society have rendered the theory all but useless to modern requirements. For example, one New York court has held that, under the common law,

> each member of society must submit to annoyances consequent upon the ordinary and common use of property, provided such use is reasonable both as respects the owner of the property, and those immediately affected by the use, in view of time, place and other circumstances.[1]

On the basis of this view another court concluded that air pollution is "indispensable to progress" and, in 1931, classified the pollution from fifty coke ovens in Buffalo, New York, as only a "petty annoyance."[2] Twenty years later, the City of Buffalo took legal action against the same pollution source and, like the plant's neighbor, met with little success.[3]

Attributes of Contemporary Environmental Policies

Perhaps prompted by such experiences, many legislative bodies now have recognized the need for *public* control of environmental quality and have evidenced increased willingness to use their police power to deal more effectively with environment-disturbing activities. Contemporary policies rest on the view that exclusive reliance on private litigation is inappropriate to modern environmental management requirements and recognize that some environmental changes are neither temporary nor readily correctable, that some changes ought not to be tolerated, and that public controls over environment-changing activities ought to be preventive rather than simply corrective.

This shift in policy emphasis is of immense importance.

1. *Cogswell v. N.Y., New Haven and Hartford R.R.,* 103 N.Y. 10, 13–14 (1886).

2. *Bove v. Donner-Hanna Coke Corporation,* 142 Misc. 329, 254 N.Y.S. 403 (1931), aff'd mim., 236 APP.

3. *People v. Savage,* 1 Misc., 2d 337, 148 N.Y.S. 2d 191, aff'd mim. 309 N.Y. 941, 32 NE 2d 313 (1955).

To one exposed only to the folklore of American government, the ship of state may appear as a noble vessel plying its way relentlessly through troubled seas to some appointed destination. To other observers, however, it more frequently seems to be an almost rudderless vessel whose crew has not yet been briefed on their ultimate destination and are therefore occupied almost entirely in fending the vessel away from the rocks and shoals that mark its uncharted course.

Instead of moving steadily and serenely toward a density that has been defined and charted, it moves erratically along a path whose twists and turns have been dictated by the need to avoid some point of possible disaster. On the bridge its officers know only that the ship must sail and, being ignorant of their ultimate destination, judge the adequacy of their navigation by the mere fact that the ship has survived.

In terms of environmental policy the latter image seems much more accurate than the former. As boundless as the "police power" of government may be, its past exercise with respect to environmental concerns has been dictated principally by the need to guide the republic out of recurring crises. If the horse is stolen, then barn-locking policies spring like magic from the head of our governmental Zeus; if populations are laid low by water-borne bacteria, then policies for abatement of water-pollution discharges are framed; if earthquakes level the structures of a city, then policies for policing the structural quality of buildings are born.

Perhaps this approach was adequate for a simpler and more slowly moving society, but its inadequacies for a post-atomic age are so apparent as to warrant little comment.

Our propensity to wait upon the actual occurrence of unwanted environmental states before we take social action to deal with them inevitably leads to unwanted and undesirable human consequences. The problem-causing environmental change must occur before we control the change-producing activities, and the problem-afflicted population must endure its lot until control strategies have produced the desired environmental result. Unfortunately, the lag times associated with this system have been so large that some adverse human responses to environmental conditions have become the permanent lot of whole generations.

Consider the case of the automobile. Nearly ninety years have passed since Carl Benz demonstrated the first commercially successful gasoline-powered automobile; fifty years have passed since the automobile revolution got under way in the United States; twenty-six years have passed since the first photochemical smog blanket descended on Los Angeles; twenty years have passed since science established that the pollution emissions from gasoline-powered vehicles were the cause of this problem; twelve years have passed since the California legislature was moved to curb smog-causing emissions from motor vehicles; and four years have passed since the federal government assumed responsibility for controlling smog-causing pollution emissions from motor vehicles. Most informed observers now predict that an additional ten to fifteen years of comprehensive federal activity will be required before the air pollution problems occasioned by our expanding vehicle population will be solved. Meanwhile, of course, an infant born during the first Los Angeles smog attack will become a grandparent before experiencing a smog-free environment in his home town. Moreover, a technologic "innovation" will have become more than one century old before one of its adverse social consequences will have been abated!

Influenced by such lessons, the need for public environmental management policies and programs now seems to have been accepted, and there appears to be general agreement that these should be preventive rather than merely corrective in their orientation. The need to anticipate adverse future states and to mobilize remedial action in the here and now seems now to have been recognized. Debate over the appropriate properties of environmental management policies and programs now focus on such matters as the appropriate ends of such policies; the extent to which such ends should be developed through rational processes of choice and through use of empirically derived data; and on such matters as the means to be employed to achieve environmental quality objectives.

At least in respect to air quality management, rational processes for the development and implementation of environmental quality objectives have been fashioned by the Air Quality Act of 1967 and its successor the Clean Air Act of 1970. Under these acts environmental quality objectives are developed through a two-step process involving, first, the issuance of air quality criteria and, then, the promulgation of air quality standards. The former are viewed as scientific conclusions concerning the relationship between ambient burdens of pollution and a range of environmental and other effects. They are defined as descriptive or predictive statements that "describe the effects that can be expected to occur whenever and wherever the ambient air level of a pollutant reaches or exceeds a specific figure for a specific time period."[4]

In the purest meaning of the term, air quality criteria are products of scientific inquiry, not the results of a political process in which personal values, barter, personal or group advantage, and compromise are the guiding considerations. They are expressions of existing knowledge, and may be only feeble approximations of the truth in circumstances where knowledge is incomplete.

4. Arthur A. Atkisson and Richard Gaines (eds.), *Development of Air Quality Standards* (Riverside, Calif.: Merrill Publishing Co., 1970).

In contrast, air quality standards are unabashedly presumed to be the products of policy, political, and economic considerations. They are prescriptive in that "they prescribe pollutant levels that cannot legally be exceeded during a specified time period in a specific geographic area."[5] Through use of data concerning the costs of optional pollution reduction methods, air quality standards presumably are to be set on the basis of some reasonable relationship between the costs of achieving and maintaining a standard and the benefits to be derived from such a quality level.

The final planning step in the process required by the Clean Air Act of 1970 involves the development, by the states, of implementation plans that specify air quality standards to be achieved in specific regions, the present and probable future community factors influencing the achievement of such standards, the mix of strategies and methods to be employed by public agencies in securing and maintaining levels of air quality consistent with such standards, and the time schedules to be observed in the programs.[6]

The three-step decisional process required by this legislation suggests the range of considerations appropriate to any environmental management program: the relationship between environmental variables and specific consequences; the environmental quality objectives appropriate to a specific area or population group; and the mix of methods to be employed in achieving those objectives.[7]

In these terms, I suggest that three factors are of

5. Ibid.

6. Environmental Protection Agency, "Requirements for Preparation, Adoption and Submittal of Implementation Plans," *Federal Register*, Vol. 36, No. 158 (14 August 1971), pp. 15486–15506.

7. For a more complete discussion of decision models appropriate for environmental management programs, see discussion by Seymour Schwartz in Atkisson and Gaines (eds.), *Development of Air Quality Standards.*

ascendant importance to the current development of environmental management policies and programs: the changing environmental quality aspirations of the U.S. population; the fact of our metropolitan existence; and the need for environmental quality criteria and management strategies appropriate to the probable future circumstances of life within the United States.

Environmental Quality Objectives

However beneficial the "invisible hand" of the economic marketplace may be in regulating the production, distribution, and consumption of private goods and services, it seems clear that the "hand" also is "blind" to a number of socially valued considerations. Powerful economic disincentives to pollution control and environmental protection have led to environmental degradation as an almost inevitable concomitant of economic and industrial progress.

That environmental quality compatible with the wants of a substantial fraction of our population cannot be obtained through the workings of the economic marketplace now is evident. Unlike a can of tomatoes or a hula hoop, community environmental amenities cannot be purchased in the private economic marketplace. Try as one will, the lone consumer in our society cannot purchase a guaranteed personal supply of clean air, an unimpeded view of a distant scenic vista, an unlittered coastline, an "unimproved" and unsullied wild river, or an aesthetically pleasing community environment.

On the whole, environmental quality is a public, rather than a private, good and therefore is purchasable primarily in the political marketplace rather than in the private economic marketplace. Processes appropriate to the establishment of environmental quality objectives therefore must respond to democratic imperatives rather than to criteria appropriate to some hyperrational cost-benefit model. In these terms the perceived environmental wants and needs of population groups are more important to the establishment of such objectives than mere empirically derived statements concerning the relationship between environment-changing activities, environmental variables, and the effects of such variables on humans and their biosphere.

It seems clear, therefore, that the environmental quality aspirations of important population segments are variables of more importance to the "environmental objectives" equation than any arbitrarily defined point purported to measure the objective severity of an environmental impact on life quality.

Factors intruding on the quality of human environments have been much discussed in recent years. Usually, however, these factors are defined only in terms of specific chemical-physical parameters, such as noise; pollution burdens in air, water, and soil receptors; ecologic responses to pollution burdens, such as rainfall, atmospheric turbidity, and temperature changes.

Similarly, human responses to environmental quality changes also have been much examined but usually in terms of physiologic responses to specific stresses or to specific environments exhibiting a mix of attributes. Ordinarily, such responses are monitored in terms of human morbidity, mortality, or other clearly evidenced adverse symptoms, such as mental illness or absence from work.

Both types of information are of obvious importance and have loomed large in recent efforts to develop criteria and standards for the management of environmental quality. Neither, however, sheds much light on the primary variable of interest to those charged with responsibility for promulgating environmental quality objectives: the environmental quality aspirations of the constituent public.

Homo scientificus incurs great risks whenever he contemplates so basic a question as the quality of his own existence. Driven by the imperatives of rationality, he seems compelled to consider only those phenomena that can be measured and, therefore, to give consideration only to those matters for which measures have been devised. Within the bounds of this system what is ordinarily deemed to be "important" is, not surprisingly, that which can be measured, and that which is deemed to be "unimportant" is typically that which is immeasurable or for which no measures have yet been devised.

Sadly, the circumstances of human life and of scientific inquiry have made it easier to measure that which is "bad" than to define—much less measure—that which is "good." Premature death, morbidity, incapacity, deviance from a norm, economic gains and losses—all these things can be measured and therefore have been the object of much inquiry into the nature and effects of man-environment relationships. On the other hand, science has contributed little to our understanding of the "good life," and to our capacity to measure such life quality outcomes as "happiness" and "self-fulfillment." We know a great deal about subnormal human performances and the characteristics of the environments in which such performances are produced, but we know very little about the biophysiologic and psychosocial states that man may be genetically capable of achieving, and still less about the environmental circumstances that impede such human evolution.

Thus, formidable constraints now limit the capacity of science to guide man toward the design and construction of environments more congenial to his evolutionary destiny.

Yet, by whatever yardstick we measure the "habitable" environment, it seems clear that the scale must be appropriate to more than the mere measurement of the capacity of an environment to assure the biologic survival of the human species. If the rules of semantics lead us to define an environment as habitable if it is "fit for human life," then democratic imperatives lead us to understand the measures and motivations that guide public judgments concerning the "fitness" of their surroundings and the "humanness" of their lives

In these terms, recent history is suggestive. The now condemned environmental changes of recent decades have been inextricably associated with such benefit-producing phenomena as industrialization, improved productivity, advanced and more widely available medical services, greater economic affluence, and mass education. In the United States the combined impact of these factors on the nature of human existence has led to a prolongation of life and to substantially lower death rates among all age groups in our population. In the first sixty years of this century, life expectancy at birth increased by nearly 40 percent[8] and death rates in some age groups declined by as much as 84 percent.[9] As a whole, the U.S. society is now better clothed, better housed, and better fed than any other which has preceded it. We have produced several generations of human beings to whom illiteracy, famine, and plague are simply words, not the prevailing circumstances of human existence.

However, as threats to the survival capacity of major elements of our population have been controlled, it seems clear that the environmental and life-quality aspirations of these groups has increased.

As A. H. Maslow has observed, man's motives seem to be organized into a hierarchical system beginning with those related to survival, security, and safety and ending

8. Louis I. Dublin et al., *Length of Life* (New York: Ronald Press, 1949); U.S. Bureau of the Census, *Statistical Abstract of the United States,* 1968. Washington, D.C., 1968, p. 53.

9. U.S. Bureau of the Census, *Statistical Abstract of the United States,* 1963, Table 67; U.S. Department of Health, Education and Welfare, National Center for Health Statistics, *Mortality Trends in the United States,* 1954–63, Series 20, Number 2 (June, 1966), Table 4.

with those related to self-esteem and self-fulfillment.[10] As a lower-level need is satisfied, its motivational power decreases, and man instead is motivated to satisfy some higher-level need.

In these terms it seems likely that the establishment of environmental quality objectives consistent with the perceived needs of the several groups and strata within our society will not be unlike shooting at a moving target. As soon as one need is satisfied, another will replace it. If a "safe" environment is provided, then the fact of that accomplishment will lead to public demands for an environment of comfort, convenience, and beauty.

In short, public environmental wants will shift from those related to the "life-maintaining" qualities of human habitats to those related to the "habitability" of such environments.

That human responses to environmental conditions are a function of a complex mixture of physical and social factors is suggested by evidence dating back at least as far as the now-famous Hawthorne experiments. In those studies both "favorable" and "unfavorable" changes in work environments resulted in higher worker productivity, presumably as a function of the workers' perception of the social quality of the work environment and of management's interest in their welfare.[11]

In a recent symposium on the habitability of human environments, participants personally experienced much the same kind of response to environmental conditions.[12] Approximately eighty environmental scientists and design

10. A. H. Maslow, *Motivation and Personality* (New York: Harper, 1954).

11. F. J. Roethlisberger, *Management and Morale* (Cambridge: Harvard University Press, 1950).

12. Edward Wortz et al. (eds.), *Proceedings: First National Symposium on Habitability.* (Volumes I–IV) (Houston: University of Texas School of Public Health, 1970 [mimeo]).

engineers were convened under the auspices of the National Aeronautics and Space Administration, the University of Texas School of Public Health, and the Garrett Airesearch Corporation.

Instead of meeting in a conventional conference environment, the group was transported to an urban renewal area in the coastal community of Venice, California, where artists in a local colony had designed a number of experimental environments.

As judged by middle-class values, Venice would be viewed as uninhabitable. Located at the mouth of Ballonna Creek, the community was constructed in the early 1920s by an ambitious real estate promoter who sought to re-create some of the amenities of the community's namesake. However, his plan was never fully realized, and the canals fell into disuse. Pools of stagnant, swampy water environed the area; canals became filled with debris and sewage; buildings deteriorated; and annual public expenditures for mosquito abatement within the area finally exceeded the annual yields from property tax levies. Following construction of a new public small-boat harbor adjacent to the community, public pressures for physical redevelopment and "improvement" of the area mounted, and an urban renewal program now is under way within the community.

On the morning of the first day of the symposium, participants were bused into Venice and deposited in an alley. One's first impression of the area was of a profoundly blighted place; condemnation signs were much in evidence on buildings; drunks were observed to be still sleeping on sidewalks and in parking lots; the alley was lined with empty bottles, litter, and much debris. Astounded, symposium participants were directed through a hole that evidently had recently been chopped in the wall of a brick building adjacent to the alley.

We emerged into a chairless all-white room, lined with columns and lighted by a decorated skylight. The experience was much like reentering the womb. The room was a congenial shelter from the ugliness and alienness of the Venice environment. Throughout that first morning many of us believed that this was the essential message being transmitted to us by the room's designer: that urban man must be provided with congenial "shells" to protect him from the misery of his community environment. The sounds of some of that misery could be heard within the meeting room: the deafening roar of a hovering police helicopter, the shouts of passersby, the clamor of a patroling police motorcycle, the strident voices of local inhabitants.

At noon, the room's designer pulled down several columns along the Market Street side of the meeting place, and symposium participants were asked to hunker down at curbside to eat a catered meal. Horrified, many retreated to nearby bars for martinis and sandwiches in more conventional surroundings.

The second day the experiment was repeated. Now, however, we found that the Market Street wall of the meeting place had been totally removed and replaced by cheesecloth through which we could view the flickering shadows of passing pedestrians and the almost inarticulate outlines of the Market Street environment. For the first time many of us became aware of the hippy colony across the street. Within the room modest changes also had been made. Pillows and great blocks of pressed cardboard had been provided, and we were able to fashion our own individual sitting or resting places from which we could participate in the day's discussions. At noon a great hole was slashed in the cheesecloth and we again were asked to eat a catered lunch at curbside. Most complied and ate their lunches while engaged in conversation with each other and with the now-curious residents of Market Street.

On the third day the transformation was complete. The meeting room had been completely opened to Market Street. Moreover, the first part of the morning was devoted, not to scientific discussions, but to a program arranged by the local artists. In the center of the room was a shoeless young lady whose long hair hung to her waist and whose dress draped her to the ankles. A nationally known harpist, she explained she wished to communicate with us in the language she knew best—her music. From the back of the room I could see Market Street through the strings of her harp. As she played, Venice became a part of the meeting room. Mothers hushed their children as they passed us and stopped to listen to the haunting strains of her composition; the roving motorcycle officer halted his rounds and joined the Market Street population at curbside to enjoy the music.

When the performance ended the people of Market Street flooded into our meeting room and engaged us in conversation. At noon, coatless and tieless scientists and engineers hunkered down at streetside with bearded, shoeless Venicians, sharing their lunches and engaging in conversations that none wished to end. The sun seemed brighter, the sky bluer, the street warm and friendly, and our meeting place, ideal. That evening an enthusiastic and enchanted group of adopted "Venicians" returned to their hotel.

Reflecting on our experience at a later seminar, the group for the first time severely questioned the validity of our previously heralded search for "hard" data concerning the physical environmental variables that influence the habitability of human environments. We pondered four central questions: (1) To what extent do the quality and character of the social interactions within an environment influence the habitability of that environment? (2) To what extent does one's capacity to alter his environment influence his reaction to that environment? (3) To what extent do one's prior conditioning and values influence his adaptability to a new environment? (4) To what extent does one's perception of the mission or function of an environment influence his reaction to that environment?

Although the physical reality of Venice and of Market Street had not changed during our three-day symposium there, the participant's reactions to, and perceptions of, the quality of that environment had undergone profound—and apparently enduring—change. Before our experience each of us knew what a conference environment "ought" to look like; we could perceive the difference between ugliness and beauty, and we expected a "sitting-place" to be delivered to us—rather than to be fashioned by us—at any official meeting. Now we had changed. The artists had slowly and carefully stripped us of our prior conditioning; we had been introduced a step at a time to the environment of Market Street; in the midst of our astonishment and "suffering" we had developed new patterns of interaction between ourselves and with the Market Street population; we now wondered why anyone would wish to "renew" such a place.

Moreover, a simple and basic set of questions had occurred to us: Can one define, much less design, a habitable environment without defining the mission to be performed by that environment? Are function and environment a single system? If so, on what basis should one design a city? What is the function or mission of a metropolis? On the basis of what functional criteria is a scientist to appraise the "fitness" and habitability of a human environment?

That mere survival is not the only factor motivating man in his search for congenial habitats and in his measurement of "habitable" environments is suggested by recent patterns of human migration and settlement within the United States. As observed earlier by Edward

L. Ullman [13] and Jean Gottman, [14] these migration patterns suggest that the population is responding to the "lure of amenities" and is flowing "toward areas that are richly endowed with either cultural or physical amenities." [15]

Migration and Habitability

The variables that are important in environmental wants, as seen by the American public, can be observed in patterns of migration. They fall into two groups: (1) those variables that have to do with material income; and (2) those that are produced by environmental amenities. In some cases they work together; in other cases they work in different directions. Migration patterns show different results depending on ethnic and other group characteristics.

Viewed as a whole, the U.S. population seems not only to be tilting westward but to be flowing out of the interior landlocked states of the nation to the peripheral coastal areas. Moreover, within the context of this centrifugal movement of migrant streams is a further pattern suggesting a shift in population away from areas with cold winter climates and other environmental disabilities, such as overcrowding and physical blight.

In terms of eight large population regions of the nation, population movements over the past several decades have been comparable to those shown in table 1. See also figure 1. Clearly evidenced by these data is a general population movement away from the inland areas to the coastal periphery of the nation, and away from the densely populated and cold-winter areas of the Great Lakes and

13. Edward L. Ullman, "Amenities as a Factor in Regional Growth," *Geographical Review*, Vol. 44 (January 1954).

14. Jean Gottmann, "The Rising Demand for Urban Amenities," in Warner, *Planning for a Nation of Cities* (Cambridge: MIT Press, 1966).

15. Ibid., p. 168.

TABLE 1

SELECTED DATA FOR EIGHT POPULATION REGIONS OF THE MAINLAND UNITED STATES, 1960

Population Region	No. of Whole States	No. of Urban Places	1950 Population (1000's)	1960 Population (1000's)	Increase (1000's)	Expected Increase (1000's)	Excess Population Growth (1000's)	No. of Urban Places per 1,000 Square Miles	Population Added per Square Mile
(1)	(2)	(3)	(4)	(5)	(6)	(7)	(8)	(9)	(10)
1. Interior States	14	919	25,309	26,723	1,414	4,226	(−2,812)	0.94	1.45
2. Sunbelt-Rocky Mt.	5	173	3,799	5,497	1,697	634	1,062	0.33	3.19
3. Pacific Northwest	2	146	3,924	4,651	726	655	71	0.85	4.24
4. California	1	388	10,586	15,717	5,131	1,767	3,363	2.48	32.78
5. Gulf Coast	4	636	16,459	19,753	3,294	2,748	545	1.51	7.80
6. East Florida	1	137	1,654	3,042	1,388	276	1,111	3.57	36.14
7. South Atlantic	3	322	9,536	10,773	1,237	1,592	(−355)	2.36	9.05
8. Great Lakes-Atlantic	19	2,744	79,429	92,304	12,874	13,264	(−390)	5.11	23.97
Totals	49	5,465	150,700	178,464	27,764	25,166	2,597	1.84	6.97

Source: Columns (2), (3), (4), and (5): U.S. Bureau of the Census, *Statistical Abstract of the United States, 1968*, 89th ed. (Washington, D.C., 1968), table No. 13, p. 14. Urban place data were derived from table A-2, U.S. Bureau of the Census, *County and City Data Book*, (Washington, D.C. 1967). In those cases where metropolitan centers or regions crossed state lines, the entirety of the center or region's population was credited to the state in which resided the majority of the center or region's population. Portions of Florida have been assigned to the Gulf Coast and East Florida regions, respectively.

Column (6): Computed from columns (4) and (5).
Column (7): Computed from column (4) × 16.7% (national *natural* population increase, 1950–60).
Column (8): Computed from columns (6) and (7).
Columns (9) and (10): Computed from data in table 2, *County and City Data Book*, in combination with data in columns (3) and (6).

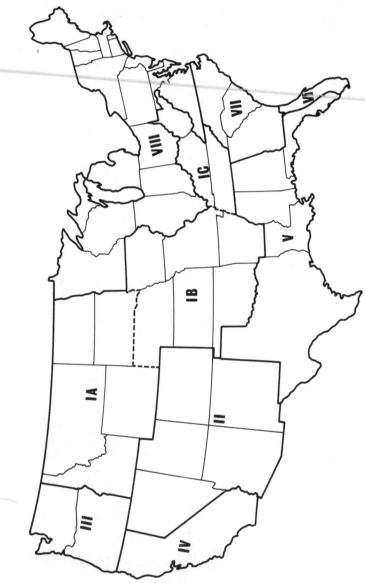

Fig. 1. Population regions of the United States

the northeastern Atlantic Seaboard to the more congenial winter climates of the Pacific Coast, the Sunbelt, the Gulf Coast, and the South Atlantic.

Within this broad pattern of population movement is an interesting, and perhaps significant, difference in the migration patterns exhibited by the white and nonwhite segments of the population (see tables 2 and 3). The

TABLE 2

WHITE AND NONWHITE EX-MIGRANT AREAS
IN THE UNITED STATES, 1950–60

WHITE			NONWHITE		
State	Net Ex-migrants		State	Net Ex-migrants	
	Number (1000's)	Percent		Number (1000's)	Percent
(1)	(2)	(3)	(4)	(5)	(6)
1. Pennsylvania	553	13.7	1. Mississippi	323	18.7
2. W. Virginia	406	10.1	2. Alabama	224	13.0
3. Kentucky	374	9.3	3. S. Carolina	218	12.6
4. Arkansas	283	7.0	4. N. Carolina	207	12.0
5. Iowa	236	5.8	5. Georgia	204	11.8
6. Tennessee	216	5.4	6. Arkansas	150	8.7
7. District of			7. Louisiana	92	5.3
Columbia	213	5.3	8. Virginia	70	4.1
8. Oklahoma	192	4.8	9. Tennessee	57	3.3
9. Missouri	158	3.9	10. Hawaii	52	3.0
10. Alabama	144	3.6	11. W. Virginia	40	2.3
11. N. Carolina	121	3.0	12. Texas	27	1.6
12. Nebraska	121	3.0	13. Oklahoma	26	1.5
13. Massachusetts	119	2.9	14. Kentucky	15	0.9
14. Mississippi	110	2.7	15. Arizona	10	0.6
15. N. Dakota	103	2.6	16. Six other		
16. Minnesota	101	2.5	states	12	0.7
17. S. Dakota	90	2.2	Total	1,727	100.0
18. Wisconsin	82	2.0			
19. New York	72	1.8			
20. Maine	68	1.7			
21. Illinois	64	1.6			
22. Eight other					
states	211	5.2			
Total	4,037	100.0			

Source: U.S. Dept. of Commerce, Bureau of the Census, *Statistical Abstract of the United States*, 1968, table 38.

TABLE 3

WHITE AND NONWHITE IN-MIGRANT RECEPTOR AREAS
IN THE UNITED STATES, 1950–60

WHITE RECEPTOR AREAS			NONWHITE RECEPTOR AREAS		
State	White In-migrants		State	Nonwhite In-migrants	
	Number (1000's)	Percent		Number (1000's)	Percent
(1)	(2)	(3)	(4)	(5)	(6)
1. California	2,791	40.8	1. California	354	20.8
2. Florida	1,516	22.2	2. New York	282	16.5
3. New Jersey	465	6.8	3. Illinois	189	11.1
4. Arizona	340	5.0	4. Ohio	133	7.8
5. Maryland	284	4.2	5. Michigan	127	7.5
6. Ohio	276	4.0	6. New Jersey	112	6.6
7. Connecticut	195	2.9	7. Florida	101	5.9
8. Colorado	149	2.2	8. Pennsylvania	77	4.5
9. Texas	141	2.1	9. District of		
10. Virginia	84	1.2	Columbia	54	3.2
11. Nevada	80	1.2	10. Indiana	45	2.6
12. Washington	70	1.0	11. Connecticut	39	2.3
13. Ten other			12. Maryland	36	2.1
states	443	5.4	13. Wisconsin	29	1.7
			14. Missouri	28	1.6
Total	6,834	100.0	15. Massachusetts	25	1.5
			16. Washington	18	1.1
			17. Colorado	15	0.9
			18. Twelve other		
			states	41	2.3
			Total	1,705	100.0

Source: U.S. Department of Commerce, Bureau of the Census, *Statistical Abstract of the United States*, 1968, table 38.

presumably more affluent white migrant seems drawn to the high amenity states of the Pacific Coast, Florida, Arizona, and Colorado, whereas the still-struggling nonwhite is flooding into the very areas abandoned by the amenity-driven white. For example, New York, Illinois, Massachusetts, Pennsylvania, and the District of Columbia account for 25.3 percent of all interstate white ex-migrants but are receptor areas for 36.8 percent of all nonwhite interstate migrants. Only the states of California, Florida, New Jersey, and Ohio individually attract 4 percent or more of both the white and nonwhite interstate migrants. Since both New Jersey and Ohio are in a region that has now begun to donate substantial numbers of persons to the interregional migrant stream, their population gains may be little more than "local" phenomena and might be viewed as an intraregional population shift responding to the same circumstances that have led to the region's recent white ex-migrant loss.

Within the bounds of interregional population movements are still other patterns of migration and settlement providing clues to the environmental and life quality aspirations of the U.S. population. These include apparent movements away from areas of both low and high population densities as well as movements toward metropolitan areas exhibiting particular attributes.

The general and continuing population flight away from low-density rural areas has been well documented and much discussed. Urbanization, which is measured as the rising fraction of an area's population found to be in residence in urban settlements, has been occurring in the United States since the first census in 1790. Involving the migration of population from rural to urban territory, urbanization has since resulted in continuing escalations in the urban fraction of the U.S. population. By 1870 urban settlements were recording larger total decennial population increases than all rural territory, and, in 1920, the urban fraction of the population finally exceeded the rural.[16] In the last two decades an absolute decline in the population of rural territory has been recorded, and the urban fraction of the U.S. population has jumped to a current level of 73.5 percent.[17]

16. U.S. Bureau of the Census, *Historical Statistics of the United States, Colonial Times to 1957* (Washington, D.C.: U.S. Govt. Printing Office, 1960).

17. Philip M. Hauser, "The Census of 1970," *Scientific American* 225 (July 1971): 17–25.

Not only has there been a steady stream of migration from rural to urban territory, but so also has there been a persistent movement away from the isolated urban settlement to the sprawling metropolis. Involving a system of urban settlements oriented around a nodal urban place ordinarily containing 50,000 population or more, the metropolis is rapidly becoming the primary habitat for *Homo North Americanus*.

Currently, the nonmetropolitan mainland counties of the United States are donating approximately 800,000 ex-migrants per year to 527 counties organized into 86 separately definable metropolitan centers and regions (see table 4). Counties containing slightly more than 75 percent of the mainland territory of the United States are donating population to the remaining 25 percent, and counties representing nearly 60 percent of the mainland U.S. land areas are being depopulated.

Whether pushed out of rural America by the pressure of low income or pulled into urban and metropolitan settlements by the promise of a better quality of life, it is clear that the U.S. population is voting with their feet in favor of an urban style of life. In spite of a distinct anti-urban bias in American literature and philosophy, the U.S. population has been rejecting the low-density environment of rural America in favor of the more populous and densely populated urban and metropolitan settlement. In spite of much-publicized data suggesting that human longevity is adversely affected by life within urban communities, the great bulk of the U.S. population apparently has deemed the urban environment more "habitable" than the rural.

However, within the U.S. system of urban and metropolitan communities there also has been a substantial migration of population away from the more densely populated central cities to low-density suburbs, and away from densely populated or blighted metropolitan communities to more congenial metropolitan areas.

As shown in table 5, cities of 100,000 population or more seem to attract and repel migrants as a function of their population densities: the higher the population density, the greater the rate of ex-migration; the lower the density, the greater the rate of in-migration. As in the case of interstate migration, however, the large central cities showing high rates of white ex-migration are also those that show high rates of nonwhite in-migration. Thus, the 29 large cities showing a decline in total population between 1950 and 1960 also revealed substantial increases in their nonwhite population.

In terms of metropolitan centers and regions, in-migration seems to be a function of several factors, including total population size, climate, population density, and regional location. Generally, the larger the population of an area, the greater its lure to potential in-migrants and therefore the greater its rate of population increase. However, this factor seems to be of primary importance in the 250,000 to 1,000,000 size range. After achieving a population level of 1,000,000, the principal factor influencing the growth of a metropolitan area is the excess of births over deaths within the area. Similarly, metropolitan communities in cold winter regions and in the interior block of states fare less well in attracting in-migrants than those in other regions. Metropolitan communities in coastal areas such as California, Florida, and the Gulf Coast, as well as those in regions richly endowed with natural amenities, such as the Pacific Northwest and the Sunbelt-Rocky Mountain regions, generally experience the highest rates of in-migration. Even within individual states these factors seem to be operative. Thus, the Gulf Coast states inland metropolitan communities exhibit lower growth rates than those in coastal or near-coastal counties. Also, areas with notoriously blighted environments and high age-adjusted mortality rates (such as the mill-town

TABLE 4

POPULATION CHANGES IN METROPOLITAN AND NONMETROPOLITAN COUNTIES BY POPULATION REGION, 1950–60

Population Region	METROPOLITAN COUNTIES				NONMETROPOLITAN COUNTIES			
	No.	Change, 1950–60 (1,000's)	Expected Change 1950 × 16.7%* (1,000's)	Excess (1,000's)	No.	Change, 1950–60 (1,000's)	Expected Change 1950 × 16.7%* (1,000's)	Excess (1,000's)
(1)	(2)	(3)	(4)	(5)	(6)	(7)	(8)	(9)
1. Interior System	69	2,442	1,362	1,079	1,014	(−1,028)	2,836	(−3,892)
2. Sunbelt-Rocky Mt.	18	1,391	360	1,031	138	305	274	31
3. Pacific N.W.	20	624	458	166	56	101	196	(−94)
4. California	28	4,997	1,662	3,335	30	133	109	28
5. Gulf Coast	70	3,102	1,241	1,860	409	192	1,506	(−1,314)
6. East Florida	15	1,397	240	1,156	38	(−8)	35	(−44)
7. South Atlantic	36	1,049	579	469	266	188	1,012	(−824)
8. Great Lakes-Atlantic	271	11,960	10,500	1,460	626	914	...	...
Total	527	26,965	16,402	10,556	2,577	798	8,756	(−7,957)

Source: Derived from U.S. Bureau of the Census, *County and City Data Book* (Washington, 1967), table 2.
*The natural rate of population increase for the United States was 16.7 percent from 1950 to 1960.

TABLE 5

RELATIONSHIP BETWEEN POPULATION DENSITY AND 1950–60 POPULATION CHANGE
IN 125 U.S. CITIES OF 100,000 POPULATION OR MORE IN 1960

Density per square mile, 1950	No. in category	Population		Change		1950 Density	1960 Density	Population Range 1950
		1950	1960	Total	Percent			
1. 16,000+	10	16,287,203	15,819,280	(−467,923)	(−2.87)	20,258	19,676	114,167–7,891,957
2. 14,000–15,999	2	1,436,928	1,282,785	(−151,143)	(−10.51)	14,088	12,576	580,132–856,796
3. 12,000–13,999	7	5,556,297	5,178,163	(−388,134)	(−6.97)	12,796	11,904	124,555–1,849,568
4. 10,000–11,999	2	291,202	273,446	(−17,756)	(−6.09)	10,785	10,127	113,805–117,397
5. 8,000–9,999	8	1,780,468	1,738,280	(−42,188)	(−2.36)	9,225	9,007	112,817–521,718
6. 6,000–7,999	16	4,524,587	4,816,211	291,624	6.44	6,664	7,093	101,531–637,392
7. 4,000–5,999	22	6,476,342	7,503,285	1,026,943	15.85	4,862	5,633	102,213–1,970,358
8. 2,000–3,999	24	5,069,928	6,323,197	1,253,179	24.71	2,949	3,678	104,477–570,445
9. 2,000	9	2,204,020	3,807,947	1,603,927	72.7	1,333	2,302	104,511–596,163
10. Cities less than 100,000 in 1950 but more than 100,000 in 1960	25	1,935,852	3,284,531	1,348,679	69.66	2,584	4,385	14,556–98,884
Total	125	45,572,827	50,027,035	4,454,208	9.77	5,294	5,812	14,556–7,891,957

Source: Calculated from data presented in U.S. Bureau of the Census, *Statistical Abstract of the United States,* 1968, table 20.

and mining areas of Appalachia and Pennsylvania) score low in-migration rates, and many actually show absolute losses in total population. Although masked by regional factors, gross examination of the in-migration experience of metropolitan communities suggest that the higher the population density of a metropolitan center or region, the lower its rate of population increase; the greater the package of natural amenities and public services offered by a metropolitan community, the greater its rate of in-migration.

Although only suggestive at this point, these data provide important clues to the environmental choices of the migrant fraction of the U.S. population. As part of a larger study of factors entering into the habitability of community environments, the data are being exposed to multivariate analysis in a current study within the University of Texas School of Public Health.

Metropolitanization

Whatever the properties of a "habitable" environment may be, and no matter what the nature of the terminal objectives of public environmental management policies and programs, it seems clear that these policies and programs should be constructed in consonance with the fact of our metropolitan future.

Currently, more than 97 percent of the U.S. mainland population increase is occurring in 86 metropolitan centers or regions containing less than 14 percent of our land area and 524 of the mainland's 3,104 counties. The 30 centers and regions individually boasting 500,000 or more population account for more than 87 percent of our mainland population increase but represent slightly less than 10 percent of our mainland land area.

Four sprawling metropolitan regions are of particular significance. BOS-WASH extends from north of Boston to south of Washington, D.C., sprawls over all, or parts of, eleven states, occupies the whole of 98 counties, and now boasts a population of nearly 40,000,000 persons. CHI-PITT, extending from northwest of Chicago around the rim of the Great Lakes and southward to Pittsburgh, now contains 85 counties, parts of six states, and houses a population in excess of 25,000,000 persons. SAN-SAN reaches from north of San Francisco southward along California's coastline to San Diego at the Mexican Border. Now adding more population per square mile per decade than any other metropolitan region, its 1960 population was slightly less than 14,000,000 and it was growing at the rate of 52 percent per decade. The fourth and most rapidly growing region is along the Atlantic coastline of Florida, extending almost from the Georgia border southward to Miami.

As shown in table 6, these five regions alone account for nearly 63 percent of the U.S. mainland population increase, and ten free-standing metropolitan centers with populations of one million or more account for an additional 16 percent of the U.S. population increase.[18]

Agglomerating substantial numbers of people, industries, and power-generating and consuming sources on limited fractions of our total land area, these places are of significance to environmental management policies for two central reasons: first, because of the extent to which they represent massive alterations in the natural environment and points of stress upon the natural ecosystem; second, because they represent a type of environment of consequence to the health of the human population and to the quality of human existence.

The consequences of the metropolitan milieu on the quality of human existence have been much discussed,

18. U.S. Bureau of the Census, *County and City Data Book,* 1967 (Washington, D.C.: U.S. Govt. Printing Office, 1967), Table 2.

TABLE 6

POPULATION AND OTHER CHARACTERISTICS OF FIVE METROPOLITAN
REGIONS OF THE UNITED STATES, 1950–60

Metropolitan Region	Number of Counties	Population (millions)		Population Change (millions)		Land Area, Thous. of Sq. Miles	Population Density per Sq. Mile, 1960	Percentage of Mainland U.S. Population Increase, 1950–60	Percentage of National Net Migrant Flow, 1950–60
		1950	1960	Total	Percentage				
(1)	(2)	(3)	(4)	(5)	(6)	(7)	(8)	(9)	(10)
1. Boston-Washington	98	31.4	36.5	5.1	16.4	44.7	817	18.6	n.a.
2. Great Lakes	85	19.8	24.1	4.3	21.5	54.6	442	15.4	9.07
3. California Coast	23	9.2	13.9	4.8	52.0	33.9	411	17.2	30.69
4. East Florida	15	1.4	2.8	1.4	96.9	15.2	186	5.0	10.96
5. Gulf Coast	42	3.9	5.7	1.8	46.6	31.7	180	6.5	11.00
Total	263	65.7	83.1	17.4	26.4	180.1	462	62.7	n.a.

Source: Tabulated from U.S. Bureau of the Census, County and City Data Book (Washington, 1967), table 2.

and usually in unfavorable terms. Ian McHarg has referred to the environment of the modern U.S. metropolis as "the least humane ever fashioned by man."[19]

In 1898 Josiah Strong viewed the development of large cities in the United States as a corrupting influence on the morality and health of the nation, alleging that improper sanitation in cities resulted in 150,000 unnecessary deaths in 1890.[20] More than thirty years later, Maurice R. Davie and Niles Carpenter published major works alleging adverse impacts of city life on health, personality, family stability, mortality, and mental health.[21] In 1938 Lewis Mumford charged that

> most of our cities, not least those big ones built mainly during the last fifty years, are biologically speaking life-inimical or life-destructive environments. . . . At almost every stage in life the rural area with poor medical facilities and a crude system of sanitation is nevertheless decisively superior as an environment of life to the urban area, though the latter be equipped with all the latest services in medicine and sanitation.[22]

In 1964 an expert panel of the World Health Organization cautioned:

> The tremendous increase in urban population clearly justifies the warning that after the question of keeping world peace, metropolitan planning is probably the most serious single problem faced by man in the second half of the 20th century.[23]

19. Leonard Duhl (ed.), *The Urban Condition.* (New York: Basic Books, 1963), p. 49.

20. Josiah Strong, *The Twentieth Century City* (New York: Baker & Taylor, 1898).

21. Maurice R. Davie, *Problems of City Life* (New York: John Wiley, 1932).

22. Lewis Mumford, *The Culture of Cities* (New York: Harcourt, Brace & Co., 1938), pp. 422–23.

23. William B. Dickinson, Jr. (ed.), *Editorial Research Reports on the Urban Environment* (Washington, D.C.: Congressional Quarterly, Inc., Jan., 1969), p. 27.

In spite of the already-mentioned improvements that have been recorded in the mortality experience of the U.S. population since the turn of the current century, some evidence suggests that metropolitanization may now be altering this trend. We may now have turned a corner, and the very forces of urbanization and economic progress that led initially to improved levels of health and life expectancy may now be producing circumstances that occasion the opposite effect (see table 7). A number of investigators have shown significantly higher age-adjusted death rates in urban than in rural places as a result of such causes as arteriosclerotic heart disease, cancer (all sites), hypertension, diabetes mellitus, cirrhosis of the liver, peptic ulcer, suicide, homicide, bronchitis, and emphysema.

For white males, death rates in all age groups under age 55 are lower in the noncentral city portion of metropolitan counties than in nonmetropolitan areas. For white females the portion of the population under the age of 45 exhibits the same difference in death rates (see table 8). Similarly, both infant and maternal mortality rates per 100,000 live births are lower in metropolitan than nonmetropolitan counties for both white and nonwhite populations.

Thus, any adverse impact of metropolitan environments on human death rates is to be found primarily in the adult population and, even then, primarily in the adult population segment over age 35 or 45. The data therefore suggest—but do not conclusively demonstrate—that any excess deaths related to life in metropolitan communities are a result of long-term exposure to these environments. A similar suggestion of adverse effects of the urban environment appears in table 9. As there shown, the larger the urban place, the higher the death rate.

In other respects the distinction between the urban and nonurban parts of metropolitan areas is significant. For

TABLE 7

CHANGE IN DEATH RATES PER 100,000 FOR AGE GROUPS
FOR SELECTED DISEASES, 1954–63

Disease	Age Groups								
	1–4	5–14	15–24	25–34	35–44	45–54	55–64	65–74
1. Arteriosclerotic heart disease, including coronary disease	−0.1	N.C.*	−0.3	+0.5	5.4	11.4	42.5	188.0
2. Malignant neoplasms of respiratory system	−0.1	N.C.	−0.1	+0.2	2.7	9.2	24.0	48.2
3. Pneumonia (except pneumonia of newborn)	−1.7	−0.1	N.C.	+0.8	1.4	3.3	10.8	37.8
4. Diabetes mellitus	−0.2	−0.2	−0.3	+0.5	1.0	1.5	3.9	10.4
5. Cirrhosis of liver	N.C.	N.C.	N.C.	1.1	2.3	8.4	7.3	2.0
6. Suicide	—	0.2	1.8	3.1	3.5	1.8	−0.3	−0.7
7. Other bronchopulmonic diseases	−0.1	−0.1	N.C.	+0.1	N.C.	1.4	6.3	18.3

Source: *Mortality Trends in the United States, 1954–63.* U.S. Department of Health, Education and Welfare, National Center for Health Statistics, Series 20, Number 2.
*N.C. = no change.

TABLE 8

DEATH RATES PER 10,000 WHITE PERSONS, BY AGE AND SEX, FOR METROPOLITAN AND NONMETROPOLITAN COUNTIES, UNITED STATES, 1959-61

Age Group (Years)	MALES				FEMALES			
	Metropolitan Counties			Nonmetropolitan Counties	Metropolitan Counties			Nonmetropolitan Counties
	Total	With Central City	Without Central City		Total	With Central City	Without Central City	
Under 15	2.5	2.6	2.3	2.7	1.9	1.9	1.7	2.0
15–24	1.2	1.2	1.2	1.7	0.5	0.5	0.5	0.6
25–34	1.4	1.5	1.3	1.9	0.8	0.9	0.7	0.9
35–44	3.2	3.3	2.7	3.5	1.9	2.0	1.7	1.8
45–54	9.4	9.7	8.2	8.7	4.8	4.9	4.4	4.2
55–64	23.0	23.5	20.6	20.3	11.1	11.2	10.7	9.7
65–74	50.1	50.6	47.5	44.0	28.6	28.7	28.3	25.7
75–84	104.6	105.1	102.6	98.3	77.8	77.9	77.7	73.8
85 and over	214.3	215.1	213.3	217.6	192.9	194.1	187.4	192.4

Source: Tabulations from the National Center for Health Statistics, U.S. Dept. of Health, Education, and Welfare.

example, based on crude deaths in 1960, it appears that the least hazardous living places in the United States are located in that fraction of metropolitan territory classified as "rural" by the U.S. Bureau of the Census (see table 10). For both white and nonwhite persons, the "rural" sections of metropolitan counties exhibit the lowest crude death rates. Metropolitan counties in the two highest death rate deciles exhibit death rates ranging from 1,188 to 1,429 per 100,000, and those in the two lowest deciles range from 850 to 1,026. If the counties in the latter group include primarily the low-density semirural communities

TABLE 9

URBAN-RURAL DEATH RATES IN THE
UNITED STATES, 1960
(PER THOUSAND)

Location	Death Rate
Urban, in metropolitan counties	
Places of 1,000,000 or more	11.5
500,000–999,999	11.2
250,000–499,999	10.6
100,000–249,999	10.4
50,000– 99,999	9.8
Rural, in nonmetropolitan counties	9.4

Source: U.S. Department of Health, Education, and Welfare, *Vital Statistics of the United States, 1960,* Vol. II, Mortality, Part A (1963), table 1-0.

TABLE 10

CRUDE DEATH RATES BY COLOR AND
PLACE OF RESIDENCE IN UNITED STATES, 1960

Place of Residence	DEATH RATES		
	Total	White	Nonwhite
Metropolitan counties	9.3	9.3	9.6
Urban places	10.1	10.2	9.8
Rural places	6.8	6.7	8.2
Nonmetropolitan counties			
Urban places	11.0	10.7	12.8
Rural places	9.4	9.3	10.1
Total U.S.	9.5	9.5	10.1

Source: National Center for Health Statistics, U.S. Dept. of Health, Education, and Welfare

of the more affluent metropolitan residents, the difference is not surprising.

Not only within metropolitan areas, but also between metropolitan areas, there are substantial variations. Table 11 shows age-adjusted mortality experience of metropolitan and nonmetropolitan areas. The former are represented by Bureau of the Census Standard Metropolitan Statistical Area classifications. Guided by age-adjusted death rates for white males, the author has found a number of high-death-rate metropolitan areas. Characteristically, these are areas in which in-migration is depressed. For example, the metropolitan triangle including Philadelphia, Harrisburg, Scranton, and Wilkes-Barre, Pennsylvania, and Trenton, New Jersey is now experiencing little or no in-migration and, except for nonwhite males, has age-adjusted death rates ranging from 20 to 378 per 100,000 population more than for all nonmetropolitan

TABLE 11

Total Age-adjusted Death Rates per 100,000
for All Causes in Selected Places
in the United States, 1960

Place of Residence	WHITE		NONWHITE	
	Male	Female	Male	Female
1. Nonmetropolitan	1,113	709	2,984	1,092
2. Total U.S.	1,138	722	1,435	1,064
3. 201 Standard Metropolitan Statistical Areas (SMSA)	1,151	729	1,409	1,050
4. Highest death rate, SMSA	1,429[a]	936[b]	2,098[c]	1,400[d]
5. Lowest death rate, SMSA	850[e]	499[f]	855[g]	465[h]

Source: Lines 1 and 2 are from U.S. Department of Health, Education, and Welfare, *Vital Statistics of the United States, 1960*, Vol. 2, *Mortality*, Part A (Washington, 1963), table 1-E and "standard million population table," p. xvi. The calculations assume the same age and sex distribution in nonmetropolitan as in metropolitan areas. Lines 3, 4, and 5 are from Edward A. Duffy and Robert E. Carroll, *United States Metropolitan Mortality, 1959–1961*, U.S. Department of Health, Education, and Welfare (Cincinnati, 1967), table 5.

[a] Wilkes-Barre–Hazelton, Pa.
[b] Scranton, Pa.
[c] Portland, Maine
[d] Wilkes-Barre–Hazelton, Pa.
[e] Tuscaloosa, Ala.
[f] Midland, Texas
[g] Ann Arbor, Mich.
[h] Madison, Wis.

counties of the United States.

Thus, suggestive—if not definitive—evidence leads one to conclude that some types of metropolitan environments exert adverse effects on human longevity and a negative influence on potential in-migration.

Summary

The task of identifying the mix of variables that negatively or affirmatively influence life quality within metropolitan environments is one that is a long way from being completed. Yet, such data are sorely needed if defensible criteria are to be made available to guide the formidable task of city building and renewal that lies yet before us.

Not only are criteria needed that express the relationship between the variables immediately contributory to a range of human consequences—such as unusually high or low human performances—but so also are criteria needed that express the relationship between controllable community factors—such as traffic densities—and such human performance–influencing variables as ambient levels of air pollutants derived from motor vehicle traffic. Moreover, much more data are needed concerning the value that various population segments assign to varying environmental configurations.

Nearly two hundred years ago Edmund Burke commented that "the public interest requires that we do today what men of intelligence and good will would wish, five or ten years hence, had been done." Understanding that the metropolis is the most probable future habitat for the overwhelming proportion of the U.S. population, that its design and construction is the result of a web of identifiable institutional decisions, the public interest now requires that we forge new criteria and environmental standards to guide us in the decisional activities that will shape our developing metropolitan habitats.

This incursion into still-uncompleted research, into findings of the most tentative character, and into a variety of perspectives, impressions, and viewpoints has been intended to suggest the range of variables and the kinds of studies that may contribute to the resolution of these needs.

Adolf Ciborowski

chapter nine

ENVIRONMENTAL PLANNING IN
URBAN RECONSTRUCTION

I have chosen the topic of environmental planning in the reconstruction of cities not only because of my personal experience in this area, but also because the tasks of planning for rebuilding and implementation represent together probably the most exciting and, simultaneously, the most difficult challenge in the field of city planning.*

The existing population of a destroyed city, which, in dramatic circumstances lost the roof over its head, and most probably, also lost the means of livelihood, is looking for immediate relief. To meet the urgent demands of this population, to help life return to the shattered city, to introduce immediate and mostly temporary, technical services, facilities, and accommodations is an enormous challenge in itself. But all this immediate action in rebuilding should not create as a consequence physical obstacles to further stages of reconstruction, when the best use should be made of the opportunity presented by catastrophic destruction to improve and modernize the city's shape, functions, and land uses.

*This article represents the author's personal views and not those of the United Nations or any other organization.

The planner who prepares the scheme for reconstruction is working under permanent stress and the pressure of the survivors' daily needs. He must make immediate decisions, although his efforts to create long-range concepts of improvements in rebuilding and development must be based on time-consuming studies and planning tasks. Only the well-developed instinct of an experienced planner can help solve this basic conflict.

Furthermore, the remaining population of a destroyed city has its own social and cultural identity. It has its traditions, customs, and, rooted in both of these, its expectations and preferences. In the majority of cases these expectations are limited by accumulated experience, are modest and sometimes naïve in what concerns the improvements of the city. Therefore, the planner who is forward-looking and is thinking in modern terms will very soon find himself in conflict with the inhabitants. He must convince them that the new city that will be built on the ruins of the old will be of a different shape and will form new living conditions, because the main aim of the rebuilder is to improve environmental conditions. In most cases the planner must find a sound compromise between his vision and actual social attitudes and expectations.

He must find two additional compromises: one between his vision and the actual socioeconomic conditions, the available economic means and the most crucial social needs; another between his dream to build a fully modern city with a modern architectural environment, and the necessity to protect and retain cultural and traditional values, to reconstruct the landmarks of the cultural heritage of the city and its inhabitants. This last is an extremely important social and even political task, because it is decisive for communal or national identity and, therefore, for the spiritual well-being of a society.

I shall later direct my remarks to the reconstruction of my mother city, Warsaw, Poland, which suffered destruction at the hand of man, and Skopje, Yugoslavia, which suffered destruction from a natural cause, an earthquake. I will contrast the results and the problems created by these two different kinds of destruction. Unfortunately, humanity is too much concerned with the task of destruction and too little concerned with creative work. This is an additional reason why I want to direct my remarks to reconstruction.

A General Framework

Human settlements are composed of two basic groups of components, the natural and the man-made. To simplify somewhat, the natural components are, of course, air, water, soil, and light. The man-made components are functional uses and developments that serve the purposes of human life and activities, housing, industry, traffic and transportation networks, services, recreation, and others. There is constant interplay between both kinds of components. This interplay directly influences the conditions in which human beings have to live, work, and find entertainment; also it influences all the conditions of health and culture that we expect the environment to offer the human being. The interplay is carried on also on another level, namely, among the industrial, the residential, and the transportation areas in a town. Finally, there is still another level of interplay. This is among three basic components of human relationships: social relations, economic relations, and physical relations.

The whole system of interactions between the components of a human settlement and the activities of its inhabitants is rather complex. Therefore, the process of planning for environmental development of a settlement is of a broadly intersectoral and interdisciplinary character, especially when the planner tends to correlate the social, economic, and physical aims and aspects of development and to indicate the critical path to harmonious and balanced environmental development.

The interdependence between the socioeconomic aims of development, their translation into the physical shape of a city or a town, resulting environmental qualities, and the achieved level of social satisfaction are set forth in figure 1.

This diagram is, of course, brutally simplified, and it does not pretend to present a complex system of city-planning. It also takes into account only some of the bricks from which the whole social, economic, and physical structure of a city is built. Nevertheless, despite all its limitations, the diagram illustrates the process of thinking (or planning) when formulating a model of a city, and also it could illustrate the CITY *in statu nascendi.*

I would like to explain this diagram briefly.

The upper box represents the formulation of social and economic aims of a city's development. They will be expressed in terms of number of inhabitants, of demographic and social structure, of economic role and model of a city, and further in terms of living standards (housing conditions, level of social and technical services, and so on), and, finally, in terms of means for construction and for maintenance.

The above socioeconomic model must be translated into the physical shape of a city. For that purpose we have to have various sets of tools. They are indicated on the diagram by two boxes below the upper one.

One set of tools is of a physical character. This is, in the first place, the building industry—building materials, technologies, building enterprises. Further, it is equipment necessary for the functioning of various components of the city (transportation of goods, people and energy, manufacturing, servicing, and so on).

The second set is composed of administrative, legislative, and fiscal tools. It is well known that the quality of the

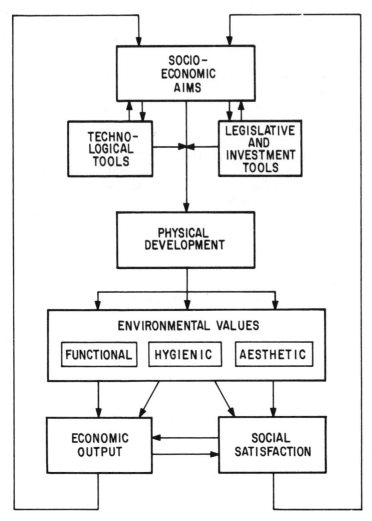

Fig. 1. The planning process

end product depends on the skill of the producer and on the effectiveness of productive tools. There is nothing closer to truth in the case of city-building. Obsolete land tenure laws, outdated administrative machinery, or an inefficient building industry will damage, through the implementation process, the best concept of socioeconomic development.

But let us hope that the tools are appropriate and that by using them in skillful ways we can build the physical shape of the city, represented as the box bringing together the products of physical development.

Next in the diagram, the oblong box represents the environment of such a city. It has its physical frame, its technical characteristics, and its social life. Natural components of this environment are affected and adjusted to the new role they play in a city. In our diagram we are interested in some of the qualities of this new environment, since they result from the process of city-building and from performing human activities within the urban framework.

The diagram points to three important environmental qualities:

1. functional (spatial distribution and interrelation of various urban functions, as industry, housing, recreation, efficiency of network services);

2. hygienic (impact of environmental conditions on human health: density of development, quality of water and air, access of light, microclimatic conditions);

3. aesthetic (environmental specifics that have direct impact on human spiritual well-being, such as scenic beauty, architectural form, or, on the contrary, aesthetic pollution and dirt).

The two lowest boxes of the diagram represent the

economic output of a city and the social satisfaction of its citizens. Both are interdependent, but both depend basically on the above-described environmental qualities. Both of these boxes, which represent the ultimate goal of city development are linked, on the diagram, by a feedback path with the upper box of the city program. It indicates that the process of planning and development is a continuous one and that the results of one stage of operations should be taken into account when rectifying the aims formulated for the next stage of development.

Two Examples

After this somewhat theoretical intermezzo, I would like to describe briefly two cases of destruction and re-building of cities. These are: Skopje, Yugoslavia, which was destroyed by an earthquake, and Warsaw, Poland, which was destroyed by the deliberate acts of man at war.

There are important differences between a town that was destroyed by man and a town that was destroyed by nature. All of my investigations and my personal, sometimes tragic, experiences show that human beings are much less human in the process of the destruction of a human settlement than is nature. The number of human beings killed by a natural disaster is, with very few exceptions, much lower compared with the physical destruction of a town than it is in the case of man-made destruction by war. Here are a few figures. Warsaw was 85 percent destroyed physically; 65 percent of the population was killed. Skopje was 65 percent destroyed by earthquake, but only 0.6 percent of the population was killed. The same proportions, more or less, are repeated through history: in the cases of other European towns destroyed by war and at Hiroshima, as well as for towns destroyed by earthquakes, such as Chimbote, Peru, where the destruction of the town was approximately 70 percent but less than 1 percent of the population was killed. Of course, there are exceptions such as the recent tidal wave in East Pakistan.

The difference between the level of physical destruction and the damage that is done to the population creates, of course, quite different challenges when planning for reconstruction.

Moreover, a human being who is destroying a town is selective in a different way than is nature. The human being attacking or bombing a town selects those elements that are most important, most valuable. In Warsaw the whole center of the town was destroyed, as it was in Rotterdam, Hamburg, Dresden, and in other towns attacked during war. In the cases of Skopje and Chimbote, and many other towns destroyed by earthquakes, including the famous one in Tokyo, the best buildings, the most modern elements of the town resisted. The worst, the poorest, the shantytowns, the slums were totally destroyed.

Development of a Plan. In planning reconstruction, what are the specific considerations? The first is that we know the town before its destruction—its failures, its characteristics, and what should be improved when planning the new one. I must admit that in many past cases of reconstruction this opportunity was lost. Some political, fiscal, legal, or administrative limitations are often of such a character that they do not allow this opportunity to be used for improvement, and the town is rebuilt in exactly the same way it was before the catastrophe.

The next problem is that when planning for the reconstruction of a town we know the client, we know for whom we are working. There is the existing population that has its traditions, its customs, its expectations, its values. From one side this offers additional stimulus to the work of the planner, but from another side it offers simultaneously some very specific kinds of limitations. When we are planning a completely new town, as in the case of Brasilia or of Chandigarh, we are planning for unknown members of society. We are thus able to shape this society somewhat through our concepts and through our ideas of how the town must be built and how the people will live there. In the case of Warsaw, or Skopje, or Chimbote, the position was quite different. The people knew, or they believed that they knew, what they wanted and needed. Most of their expectations were built on their traditions and on their experiences up to that time, which meant that the majority of the population in the town to be reconstructed were traditional and reluctant to accept too far-reaching and modern solutions. And this is one of the limitations that confronts a planner.

There are other, even more serious, limitations. The planner working in a town for reconstruction is under the enormous pressure of immediate urgent needs. In Skopje 170,000 people were living in tents on the streets and in the parks and demanding that they have by tomorrow, or at the latest the day after tomorrow, a roof over their heads and places for them to work; the same also, of course, in Warsaw. There is not only pressure from the population but, in all cases of reconstruction, there is a very strong economic limitation.

In my introduction I pointed out the need for sound compromise. But what do we wish to achieve? What are the key issues of the improvement program?

The very first answer is that we have to revise the land uses when planning for reconstruction, and in the revision of land uses the very first consideration is to decrease the density of land use, to decrease the number of people living in the central area, to introduce more greenery. Further, it is important to improve the functional scheme of the town by appropriate division in land uses among the industrial, commercial, residential, and other zones.

We seek also to improve the microclimate. In planning for reconstruction, we investigate existing microclimatic conditions and introduce measures that will improve them. In Skopje we had to make an investigation, using wind tunnels, of the different models of development of the central area before we knew how the local microclimate would be influenced by the shape of the buildings and their density, size, and height. There would be, depending on the three-dimensional shapes of development, more or less wind, more or fewer foggy days, more or less smoke; as a result there would be more or less specific, local endemic diseases. Of course, there are also other tools in microclimatic control, as for example, the introduction of reservoirs of water. Such reservoirs have rendered a very important influence on the changes and improvement of microclimatic conditions. Further, there are aesthetic problems and aesthetic values. Landscape and cultural values have to be retained—and not only retained, but the cultural heritage and the historical buildings must be incorporated into the new life and must be given new functions.

My last general remark is that success in planning and implementation depends very much on social participation by the inhabitants, on how much they are involved, how much they understand the aims and goals of the planner. It depends on the extent to which members of the local community feel a responsibility for what happens in the town. After we had been working a year in Skopje as an international team, we organized a public exhibition, a rather professional exhibition of diagrams, maps, and drawings, that were not easily understandable to the average citizen. But we were surprised: the exhibition was visited by roughly 40 percent of the total population of the city. A few weeks later there was a national day for the republic of Macedonia, where Skopje is the capital. The children in all primary and secondary schools in the town wrote about the most important issue in the history of their town. About 80 percent of the children wrote about the master plan for the reconstruction of Skopje. This was probably the highest award I ever received for professional work.

Skopje. The development and reconstruction of Skopje envisaged not only the full restitution of the pre-disaster economic and technical potential of the city, but also its further growth and development. The population will increase from approximately 200,000 in the days of the catastrophe to 350,000 by 1980. Proportional growth is envisaged in the number of working places and in all kinds of services and facilities.

Figure 2 shows the scheme of development and reconstruction of Skopje.

Seismic conditions of Skopje Valley demanded the avoidance of any great concentration of human settlements and of any urban development at all within some zones along the Vardar river. Therefore, low-density development was recommended for the majority of residential zones. Open areas were established along the river in the form of public parks and sport facilities. This greenbelt, which occupies the most dangerous areas, crosses through the entire town and becomes a kind of ventilation corridor for the city. Many other, narrower, green corridors cutting through the town were also introduced. The green areas aid the microclimate, provide ventilation, and also provide access routes for rescue activities if there is another catastrophe.

Another consideration was related to the location of industrial plants. The configuration of land and the microclimatic conditions indicated as the best choice the areas located downstream, on the eastern side of the town. These areas are located downwind in the prevailing wind direction. However, if all industrial activities were concentrated at one end, there would be commuting problems through the central area each day. For this reason, we located

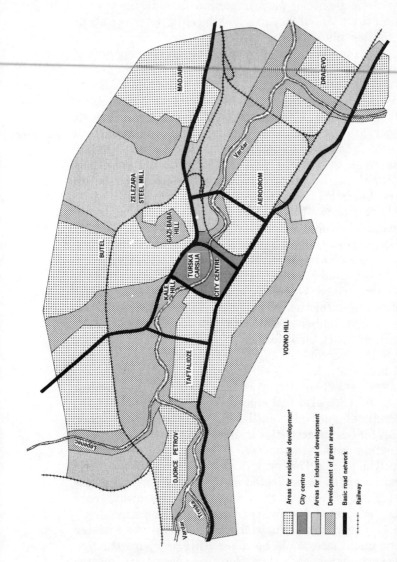

Areas for residential development*
City centre
Areas for industrial development
Development of green areas
Basic road network
Railway

Fig. 2. Reconstruction of Skopje (From United Nations Development Programme, Skopje Resurgent [United Nations, 1970])

some nonpolluting industries, with strict bylaws on the kinds of activities in which they could engage, on the residential side of the town.

Warsaw. Before the war, Warsaw had a population of approximately 1,300,000; of this population, roughly 850,-000 lost their lives during the war. The destruction was concentrated in the central areas and amounted to 85 percent of the city's over-all development. This was an example of the selective action of human beings destroying a human settlement. As a result of the reconstruction,

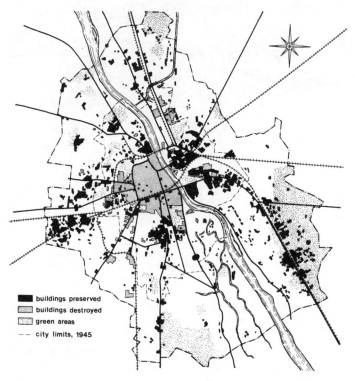

Fig. 3. Warsaw, 1945 (Adapted from Adolf Ciborowski, *Warsaw, A City Destroyed and Rebuilt* [Warsaw: Interpress Publishers, 1969])

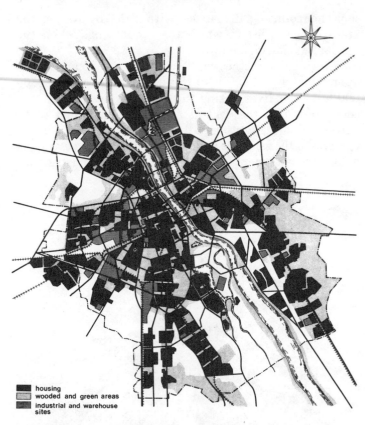

housing
wooded and green areas
industrial and warehouse
sites

Fig. 4. Warsaw, 1969 (Adapted from Adolf Ciborowski, *Warsaw, A City Destroyed and Rebuilt* [Warsaw: Interpress Publishers, 1969])

the area expanded about five times. Figures 3 and 4 show Warsaw before and after reconstruction.

In 1970 Warsaw reached the prewar level of population, but the industrial output in newly built industrial zones is more than six times higher then before the war, and the average density in housing dropped from 2.1 persons per room before destruction of the town to 1.25 persons per room in 1970. Over 300,000 new apartments were built in the process of reconstituting the city, with 90 percent of them connected to district central heating systems, which is one of the factors substantially decreasing air pollution. These figures indicate that the process of reconstruction was simultaneous with the processes of development and of improvement of living conditions.

The master plan for the reconstruction of the city not only expanded the territory of the town and diminished the density of development but it introduced careful functional zoning. For instance, industry was scattered throughout old Warsaw. It is now concentrated in six zones, and in each of them are combined specific kinds of industries in accordance with the microclimate and with functional conditions. In the south is the food industry, connected with the richest agricultural areas to the south of Warsaw. The electronics industry is near the center of the town. It is nonpolluting and does not create grave environmental problems. The chemical industry is located downwind from the city.

In the rush of planning, reconstruction, and development activities, it was, of course, difficult to avoid some mistakes. One example of a wrong environmental decision is the location of steel mills within the northern industrial zone. This location is somewhat too close to the city and closes possibilities for further residential development on the very attractive areas along the Vistula River.

Another new component of the city plan, which has substantial influence on environmental qualities, is a system of greenbelts. The whole town was designed in the shape of arms or belts of development. Between them the greenery, the open spaces reach to the center of the town and give a natural corridor for ventilation. All these corridors have further links through narrower greenbelts and parks. In some of its central areas Warsaw had a density of 1,500 inhabitants per hectare before the war.

Fig. 5. Old Town Market Square—Barss' Side, 1945

Fig. 6. Old Town Market Square—Barss' Side, 1969

The density in these areas was reduced about 3–4 times as a result of the new internal green areas and broad highways that were cut through the whole city. About 200,000 trees twenty-five to thirty years old were moved into Warsaw and replanted in the green areas. We now have in Warsaw about twenty-five to fifty square yards of open space per person. Not all of the green areas are parks; some are protective forest belts, and some are agricultural or gardening lands.

Besides the development of the town itself, attention was paid to the improvement of environmental and microclimatic conditions around the town. Protective forest belts were added, as well as artificial lakes, which have become important recreational areas.

Residences and working places are distributed in such a way as to reduce commuting traffic and transportation. We succeeded in getting an approximately 60 percent balance of residence and working place.

Finally, there is the issue of the cultural heritage, the historic monuments, the old part of Warsaw. The old town of Warsaw was destroyed in a systematic way, house by house, according to plans prepared in advance. All the documents of Polish culture were to be destroyed, using the occasion of the war.

We undertook all the efforts to restore and reconstruct the entire historical part of the town, so that the authentic shape and character emerged from the ruins. Figures 5 and 6 give examples from the historic part of town.

Conclusion

I have tried through these two examples to illustrate some of the important considerations in urban planning, particularly in reconstruction. Both examples show how the natural environment can be blended with cultural traditions and human values to produce maximum habitability and satisfaction. In reconstruction we look to the past for guidance. In expansion and in the planning of new settlements, we must search through the over-all national heritage for cultural values. When these are agreed upon, the principles of urban planning are the same for new settlements as for reconstruction of old: both the biological and the spiritual needs must be simultaneously taken into account when building an urban environment.

Paul F. Brandwein

chapter ten

EARLY EDUCATION AND THE CONSERVATION
OF SANATIVE ENVIRONMENTS

Pectinatella magnifica is a microscopic bryozoan; its habitat is the clear, cool, not overly unruly stream; its diet,
microscopic protozoans and algae and the detritus its cilia
bring to it; it occupies the usual food niche of microscopic
organisms in the presence of voracious young fish; somehow
its reproductive bodies manage to be distributed by the
unknowing largesse of birds who dip their feet into the
stream; thus far, in itself it has no market price—except
perhaps to gain some patient student a doctorate and to
furnish me with a study of the vagaries of a small country
stream. One might say, with Wordsworth, "and oh, the
world to me," but the harsher realities are that although
pectinatella is the result of some 3×10^9 years of evolution,
it is succumbing—in the stream I am studying—to various
new kinds of natural selection, and especially to one known
by the name of "pollution." The industrial product causing
the pollution has its market price; it is valued. *Pectinatella*
is not. That is to say, 3×10^9 years of evolution or not,
for the present *pectinatella* has no value. In *pectinatella*

we recognize the archetype of the sequoia, the elephant, the panda, the trumpeter swan, the passenger pigeon: we discern the archetype of events which stem from one form of exploitation pressure or another. I am tempted to call these exploitation pressures modern forms of natural selection, although one could say justly that it is man, not industrial products, that causes pollution; he uses pesticides; he exploits the land; he has the socioeconomic choices to make. He determines—or should determine—the quality of life he aspires to.

My choice of *pectinatella* may seem precious; who, after all, requires a bryozoan to make life complete? But the point is that *pectinatella* need not be destroyed, if reason and morality, or competence and compassion, prevail. What kind of education is relevant at this moment in history where comprehension of the fitness of the environment and the interdependence of environments, and of men, is essential to securing sanative environments and sane men? What kind of individual will bring competence and compassion to the examination of an environment affected by economic, social, political, cultural and ecological components? If we wish to secure healing environments in the future through public policy and practice, then we must secure healing environments for children now. There is an overwhelming literature that supports this view.

Education, definable as the conservation of man, has as its prime concern the fitness of man to the environment. Practically every school system has in its curriculum a series of activities under the heading of "conservation." These are generally conglomerates of readings, experiences, field trips and films. But if one examines what actually goes on, one finds in about 50 percent of the cases that the topic is glossed over or neglected, being viewed as not important or as having little intellectual rigor. In a city, what fields or ponds or streams are available for the necessary field trip? In the country, school experiences in conservation are too often thought to be redundant. In any event, more than any other curricular area, conservation is honored in the breach. Almost never does the study of conservation combine the biological and physical sciences, and the behavioral and social sciences, in one conceptual structure, an art-science, relevant to the kind of world now in the making.

Among other failings, education has not prepared young people for life in a changing environment, an environment in which science and technology have a rapidly increasing impact, a world in which, in Lewis Mumford's terms, "The moral sense needs mothering."

What kind of early experience is relevant to securing the sanative environments we seek? What kind of early experience produces the kind of men who comprise what Mead[1] calls "evolutionary clusters"—men who create and give life its quality, men who will create the philosophies, policies, and practices which will secure the future of the sanative environment?

Conservation may be defined as the recognition by man of his interdependence with his environment and with life everywhere, and the development of a culture which maintains that relationship through policies and practices necessary to secure the future of a sanative environment.

What experiences can we give the child, who is father to the man, which will give meaning to the environment? Einstein has defined science as experience in search of meaning. For me, all education, whether in science, the arts, economics or ecology, has always had the same aim: it is experience in search of meaning.

But which experiences? Which meanings? To make myself clear, I should like to deal with meanings first; these are the means to the end we seek: meanings are

1. Margaret Mead, *Continuities in Cultural Evolution* (New Haven, Conn.: Yale University Press, 1964).

anvils on which philosophies, policies and practices are forged. Education is a kind of ecosystem in which meanings, understandings and concepts are interrelated. We would propose that schools provide a *mental environment in which the teacher finds direction and scope, and the child finds psychological safety and freedom to experience as a part of the search for meaning.* Here the teacher would play a significant role, as a guide to full development of children, a guarantee to idiosyncratic development in a healing environment; he is not a mere guardian of the archives, not a Cerberus, nor Procrustes. To find and understand structure is to see the interrelatedness of things—whether parts of an ecosystem, or parts of a philosophy.

Substance: Structure and Meaning

Evolution (I modify Julian Huxley's thoughts in this matter) implies transmission and transformation of DNA. Various baskets of adaptation to the environment—that is to say, various experiments in creative evolution—occurred before matter was able to contemplate itself. That basket of contemplative adaptation we call *Homo sapiens cum faber* is, however, not the result of biological evolution only; cultural evolution has helped make man what he is. Cultural evolution implies transmission and transformation of knowledge, attitudes, values. A vast horde of evidence supports the claim that what happens to men and women in their school years presages what they become—or what is as important—do not become.[2]

2. For an excellent summation see Erik H. Erikson, *Childhood and Society* (New York: W. W. Norton, 1963) and Hans Gerth and C. Wright Mills, *Character and Social Structure* (New York: Harcourt, Brace & World, 1964). These are chosen as a kind of summary; the case for the general position we have stated is supported by much of the work in psychology, psychiatry, sociology, cultural anthropology, and general folklore. (See also the work of Sheldon and Eleanor Glueck.)

We speak of the "problems" posed by pollution, population, pesticides, pressures on resources. Why doesn't everyone recognize these as "problems"? They are not recognized
as problems because the clarification of a *problem*—in
counterpoint to a *question*—requires great skill, based on
searching knowledge. The ability to recognize and clarify
problems is precisely the ability to frame strategies for
solution: there is all the difference in the world between
asking a question and framing a problem.

Mental activity, I would affirm, is purposed and directed
not by problems but by objects and events.

*If the object or event is not recognized, a problem is
not clarified. Indeed, an object or event is recognized only
when the concept to which it has relevance is understood.
Otherwise, the problem is not clarified.*

To most of our population, the conservation of our
resources does not pose problems per se precisely because
the objects and events which signify ecological danger
are not clearly perceived. This is because the basic concepts
underlying the conservation of environments are not understood.

If the formulation of questions were all that was involved
in the process of inquiry, one would be at a loss to explain
why Leeuwenhoek did not ask, "What is the relation of
ATP to the energy consumption of my animalcules?" or
Adam Smith, "How is deficit spending related to the
business cycle?"

Understanding, that is, possession of a concept, is obviously antecedent to recognition of a problem. The activity
antecedent to clarification of problems is also antecedent
to insight into the kind of education with which we are
concerned, the kind of "evolutionary clusters" we seek
to develop, and the kind of knowledges, values, skills and
attitudes we engender in the young.

There was a time when it seemed sufficient to base
education on a recounting of facts. Facts were stable. Now

A. N. Sullivan tells us that in all probability nothing that was "true" in the last century is "true" today. Mere facts seem no longer to hold their authority.

Clearly the point is that the school can no longer be a place where the "facts are covered." Clearly that part of the early environment we call "school" must be a place where the student learns how to learn: that art should prepare him for a world whose technology does not presently exist. Is this possible? Yes.

There are continuities within discontinuities, uniformity within diversity, stability within continuous flux. Many *concepts* remain stable over several decades. These concepts become the *prelude* to recognition of new objects or events, leading perhaps to new concepts. Concept replaces concept, but the event occurs slowly: a concept is based on networks of inferences based on prior observation of objects and events.

Let us be specific. Suppose I were to ask you to think of a reptile. (Closing one's eyes helps.) One might see in the mind's eye a crocodile, a garden snake, or an iguana. One doesn't see a *reptile*. Similarly, one doesn't see a mammal, a fish, or a town meeting. These are conceptual structures, or *concepts*.

A concept is a network of inferences stemming from critical observation of objects and events leading to class identities; in turn, a comprehension of class identities enables us to identify as yet unobserved objects and events.

The possession of concepts helps us to associate or combine. The goose, frog, and rabbit are all vertebrates; the inclined plane, pulley, and lever are all simple machines. We expect a goose to have feathers and a warm body, and to lay eggs; these are associated in the concept, "bird." Concepts help us combine, associate and synthesize. The area of conservation is a congeries of concepts.

It was mentioned earlier that Einstein defined science as experience in search of meaning. May we not also define it as activity in search of concepts? *Concept-seeking, together with its end, concept-formation, thus becomes the central objective of the teacher.*

Similarly, if we accept science as consisting of a series of conceptual schemes which help us understand the physical world, then conceptual schemes are made up of concepts; concepts, of a series of related elements or facts; and facts, of the data which result from observation.

Curriculum planning is simplified when courses of study are developed around the major conceptual schemes of the area being studied. The very nature of learning consists of concept-seeking activities leading to concept-formation. The concepts formed need to be so important, so functional, that their understanding and application will help young people to live lives of maximum effectiveness.

One structure[3] basic to an intellectual grasp of the modern natural environment (ecological and technological) follows on pages 174–75. The levels of conceptual understanding are given in order to emphasize sequence; as soon as a child has come (through experience) to grasp one concept he proceeds to the next level; or if he is of high intellectual competence, he may encompass a group of these at one intellectual swallow.

This conceptual structure differs markedly from a curriculum based on a series of discrete compartments such as biology, chemistry, geology, ecology, etc., each subject to the whim of an administrator and to the vagaries of fashions in education. Note too how it differs from a curriculum based on a series of activities, e.g., "How to

3. This structure was first advanced in "Substance, Structure, and Style in the Teaching of Science" by Paul F. Brandwein, given at the General Motors Conference for High School Science and Mathematics Teachers, August 1964. Similar structures may be developed for the social sciences and the humanities. Mathematicians have begun to develop a structure for elementary mathematics. (See the work of the School Mathematics Study Group.)

Make an Aquarium," or from the so-called "processes of science," e.g., hypothesis making, problem framing, and the like. A hypothesis is not a process of science but a product, much as a laser is.

A conceptual structure is a home for original activity of all sorts; in fact, without some such structure, original problem-solving activity is merely problem doing. That is, the teacher knows the answer and the children's activity in inquiry is merely error reduction to come up to the teacher's standard. It is of utmost importance to the future of society that we develop each child's intellectual tools to their fullest and that we give fulfillment to all children, including those who did not choose their parents properly but will nevertheless comprise the majority. A sanative environment is not sustained by the minority.

Manner of Learning through Inquiry: The Nurture of Evolutionary Cadres

The Kipsigis are a people of Nyanja, a province in the southwestern corner of Kenya. Before they became colonials, their virtue, viewed ecologically, was that they lived within the environment, and were, as much as primitive technology permitted, part of it. When they became colonials, they began to plant corn as food, and then as a cash crop; today's Kipsigis cultivate tea, as well as corn and cattle. With the use of the land for cash rather than subsistence has come the inevitable growth of a class of artisans and service and professional people. One may predict that as more and more Kipsigis depend on wage labor, the population will expand and pressure will increase for the cultivation of the remaining land. The Kipsigis ecosystem is changing.[4]

4. Paul Bohannon and George Dalton, *Markets in Africa* (Garden City, N.Y.: Doubleday, 1965).

A Structure for the Elementary School Science Curriculum

	CONCEPTUAL SCHEME A	CONCEPTUAL SCHEME B	CONCEPTUAL SCHEME C
	Energy may be transformed; it is neither created nor destroyed. (Total sum of matter and energy is conserved: see *Conceptual Scheme B, Concept Level VI.*)	Matter may be transformed; in chemical change matter is neither created nor destroyed.	Living things interchange matter and energy with the environment (and with other living things).
CONCEPT LEVEL VI	Energy gotten out of a machine does not exceed the energy put into it.	In nuclear reactions, matter may be destroyed to release energy. (The total sum of matter and energy is conserved: see *Conceptual Scheme A, Concept Level VI.*)	Living things are adapted by structure and function to the environment.
CONCEPT LEVEL V	Once an object is in motion, it tends to remain in motion, unless energy is applied to produce an unbalanced force.	In a reaction, the totality of matter remains constant.	The capture of radiant energy by living things is basic to the maintenance and growth of all living things.
CONCEPT LEVEL IV	Molecular motion can be altered by the absorption or release of energy.	Matter consists of elements and compounds.	Living things capture matter from the environment and return it to the environment.
CONCEPT LEVEL III	Energy can be changed from one form to another.	Matter exists in small particles.	There are characteristic environments, each with its characteristic life.
CONCEPT LEVEL II (*Analogical*)	There are different forms of energy.	Matter can change its state.	All living things depend on the environment for the conditions of life.
CONCEPT LEVEL I (*Analogical*)	Energy must be used to set an object in motion (i.e., when work is done).	Matter exists in various states.	All living things are affected by their environment.

A Structure for the Elementary School Science Curriculum

CONCEPTUAL SCHEME D	CONCEPTUAL SCHEME E	CONCEPTUAL SCHEME F	
A living thing is the product of its heredity and environment.	Living things are in constant change.	The universe is in constant change.	
The characteristics of a living thing are laid down in a genetic code.	Changes in the genetic code produce changes in living things.	Nuclear reactions produce the radiant energy of stars.	CONCEPT LEVEL VI
The cell is the unit of structure and function; a living thing develops from a single cell.	Living things have changed over the ages.	Universal gravitation and inertial motion govern the relations of celestial bodies.	CONCEPT LEVEL V
A living thing reproduces itself and develops in a given environment.	The earth is in constant change.	The motion and path of celestial bodies is predictable.	CONCEPT LEVEL IV
Plants and animals reproduce their own kind.	Organisms are related through structure.	There are seasonal and annual changes within the solar system.	CONCEPT LEVEL III
Related living things reproduce in similar ways.	Forms of living things have become extinct.	There are regular movements of the earth and moon.	CONCEPT LEVEL II (Analogical)
Living things reproduce.	There are different forms of living things.	There are daily changes on earth.	CONCEPT LEVEL I (Analogical)

Why don't the Kipsigis maintain the values that come with living close to the land? Are the values learned in centuries of living in close harmony with the land to be easily set aside? Men almost always adopt new ways if they will enable them to control and modify the environment to the end of securing better food, longer life, and the amenities which eliminate drudgery.

What kind of education should the Kipsigis have? Indeed, what kind of education is useful for any people who would conserve the sanative nature of their environment while improving their food and shelter and reducing drudgery?

All children vary. Freedom to develop to one's fullest is the practical guarantee of biological and cultural variation. Which of these variations, which characteristics, shall we nurture and conserve?

Every child is of supreme moral worth; teaching is a mercy as well as a profession, and teachers—like physicians—must take all children who come to them. Equal opportunity does not mean identical opportunity but opportunities tailored to the individual child's capacities. Conservation implies wise use, and children are scarcely less important resources than land. Wise use means wise education, which in turn should at least mean full opportunity for fulfillment of personal capacities and destinies.

The characteristics of children who have become highly productive scientists and scholars have been studied in order to find clues to the special characteristics which have been central to their development. These are the gifted individuals who comprise the evolutionary cadres we have been considering.

Giftedness implies the ability to indulge in *fantasy*, without losing focus on reality, so that the free association arising in fantasy is eventually subject to sober analysis.

It implies the possession of what I have called "questing." *Questing* implies the inability to fully accept present explanations of reality, hence the need ever to seek fresh explanations.

Giftedness implies *persistence,* or the ability to work effectively in the face of failure, disapproval, or illness. Persistence implies the willingness to reject the ordinary goals of comfort.

It implies a certain amount of *physiologic vigor,* the stamina necessary to persist in the long drafts of work.

Given the qualities which I have sketched—the *intelligence* which permits critical analysis of alternatives and the ability to test by means of critically designed investigations, the *fantasy* with its highly creative free association constantly compared with reality, the *questing, persistence,* and *physiologic vigor*—we may have a candidate for the evolutionary cadres, provided:

> *The individual is given the early sanative environment which permits fulfillment of these characteristics, the environment in which he can become what he has the potential to be.*

What are the essentials of this early ideal environment? I should place the essentials (using Rogers' terms but taking license to extend their meaning) under two heads: psychological safety and psychological freedom.

Psychological safety requires that the interpersonal relationships within the family are healing, and that gentleness and warmth, firmness and quiet surround the child: the child is held to be of supreme moral worth and is loved for its own sake. In such an environment the child can develop self-respect and ego-strength.

The origins of delinquency—that is, disrespect for the environment—usually lie in a disruptive home environment. How can a child be expected to conserve the environment if he feels that he himself is not worth conserving?

Psychological safety demands a permissive environment in which failure is desired and expected, as a concomitant of growth. Ego-strength is best established in such an environment. Psychological safety cannot exist without psychological freedom, or the freedom to fail.

In a healing environment, *psychological freedom* secures

that "precious lawlessness" which ought to be the birthright of every child. Once, long ago, a child could truly be part of the natural environment. A step away from his doorstep wilderness began. To run free, to be part of an ecosystem, gave precious lawlessness. Psychological freedom, if not available to a child, must then become part of the corrective environment of the school.

To safeguard the psychological freedom antecedent to attitudes which would safeguard man's future ecosystem, the school might well commit itself to furnishing at least three models:

a. The intellectual environment (conceptual in nature) in which the alternatives the modern world presents might be considered

b. The psychological framework in which evolutionary cadres could survive, insuring the survival of all individuals, whatever their ancestry or destiny

c. The natural environment from which may come an understanding and appreciation of the environment whence man came

In the future, no school should be built without securing a good sample of natural environment—woods, field, and stream—which would be for the use of the children who in such a natural setting will see auguries of future environments. Films and pictures are fraudulent; they tell what has been, not what is; what has been missed, not what is being missed. If land cannot be acquired with every future school site, then there should be at least a modest wilderness, easily accessible, in which sense and sensibility may be encouraged to grow. There is no substitute for the woods, nor any education without it.

We must help the child to acquire the tools with which to ask *corrective questions* of society: he must learn to be obstinate in the face of custom and conformity.

The skill of inquiry is based on the understanding that personal desire or wish is not the key to understanding the universe. It is based on the understanding that explanations of the way the universe works—to be accepted by scientists—must be testable.

The teacher's framework of concepts enables him to *plan inquiries,* that is, to plot the child's experiences in search of meaning; but the arsenal of conceptual schemes thus learned must precede *free and true inquiry,* in which the child plans his own experiences and moves in his own unique manner in the search for meaning. The teacher's use of planned inquiries is merely a tool to make the acquisition of known concepts easier. In free and true inquiry, the fantasy, questing, persistence, intelligence—the total apparatus of the student—are energized and initiated by *his own processes;* in inquiry planned by the teacher, the initiating processes are those of the teacher.

Whatever educational environment utilizes and fulfills the idiosyncratic nature of the student by enhancing free and true inquiry may be furnishing the social corrective that will eventually produce the methods by which a sanative environment is brought about in the future. What is the nature of this free and true inquiry? Put another way, what is the scientist's "art of investigation"?[5] How does it bear on the teaching of our evolutionary cadres?

We do a disservice to both scientist and science teacher if we oversimplify the art of investigation by imputing to the scientist a "method" with prescribed steps leading inevitably to success. Further, we crown this folly by calling it the "scientific method." Bridgman sought to avoid this impropriety by calling it "a method of intelligence." Very

5. W. I. B. Beveridge, *The Art of Scientific Investigation* (New York: W. W. Norton, 1950).

few have adopted the term; nevertheless, to my mind, it is far more evocative than "scientific method." Elsewhere,[6] I noted that if the scientist did indeed have a method it was more in the nature of a melee, rather than a procession of one stately step after another, all crowned with discovery. Process and product feed on each other; there is feedback; there is unity between process and product, not dichotomy.

Nevertheless, an analysis of the scientist's art is useful if it reflects clearly the nobility of his task and its complexity, rather than describing a recipe. The classic procession of the rationalized "scientific method" runs somewhat as follows:

1. A problem is stated.
2. A hypothesis is developed.
3. Observations are made (an experiment may be part of controlled observation).
4. The observations are checked.
5. A conclusion is reached.

This series of steps, appropriately followed, leads inevitably to success.

For one thing, a scientist doesn't "begin" his work with a "problem." A scientist is highly informed. He reads avidly the work of his colleagues. He has a general *comprehension* of the conceptual schemes and concepts which explain the way the world is assumed to *work at this particular moment in time.*

Finally, he goes to the laboratory—or the field—or the

6. The Burton Lecture, "Elements in a Strategy for Teaching Science in the Elementary School," in Joseph Schwab and Paul F. Brandwein, *The Teaching of Science* (Cambridge, Mass.: Harvard University Press, 1962).

observatory—or the blackboard—or to a notebook filled with his mathematics—or to the armchair. The scientist's activity is a "mix," not pure unadulterated laboratory work.

Does a scientist, then, ever engage in mere problem solving? Surely, as part of an investigation, but the elaboration of the problem is part of the strategy of solving it; the statement of the problem is but one tactic. Problem solving may result in failure—intelligent failure; if it leads to insight into cause. Free and true inquiry defies description; it is idiosyncratic and creative; its satisfactions are aesthetic. Nevertheless, we may try to plot the general area of the scientist's art.

The scientist has a present comprehension of the way the world works. It is always assumed that his comprehension may be erroneous in some part. Because of the personality structure which led him into the area of scholarship and science, he is never satisfied with his comprehension. Experience as a scientist has led him to assume the only certainty is uncertainty; he has learned to live with change. He assumes that there are imperfections in any concept or theory; he is sensitive to discrepancy, to disconformities, to error.

From my own investigations into the way scientists work,[7] it seems that before the scientist enters his laboratory he has a decently clear idea of the *operations* which he will pursue to meet his confrontations. In some form or another, at the moment of true confrontation, the flashes of insight (*preconscious* in nature) point the way to a fruitful solution; a full-formed strategy and tactics (in broad outline) catch him, as it were, by surprise. In a word, his "problem" comes to him embedded in a matrix of probable solutions. Why not? All his life has been a

7. Paul F. Brandwein, *The Gifted Student as Future Scientist* (New York: Harcourt, Brace & World, 1955). See also Anne Roe, *The Making of a Scientist* (New York: Dodd, Mead, 1953).

preparation for this moment. Who was it who said speaking of so-called accidental discoveries, "Accidents come to him who is prepared."

The processes of science, to my observation, are preconscious; we have yet to identify processes of the mind which can be called "scientific." Simpson's[8] definition of science as an exploration of the material universe in order to seek orderly and testable explanations of phenomena suggests a more productive approach.

The scientific paper or report is one of science's major accomplishments. It assures the necessary critique through confirmation and collaboration. Anyone who abides by the rules of evidence of this highly refined method of intelligence may open his mind's work to others and receive the benefit of their advice. Scientists make wise use of each other; they conserve.

The Conservation of Evolutionary Cadres

Since *all* those who will make policy go through some form of school, it is self-evident that the early education of children determines whether man's future environments will be sanative. There is little, if any, evidence to the contrary. There is a vast amount of evidence that early childhood is the time of life when the seeds of leadership are sown. What the school does to children is of considerable moment insofar as evolutionary cadres are concerned.

Over these past years I have been observing 82 teachers who are considered excellent by their colleagues and by their community, and who have produced students who have gone on to contribute.[9] What is it that these teachers do?

8. George Gaylord Simpson, *This View of Life* (New York: Harcourt, Brace & World, 1964).

9. There are other criteria observable in the classroom. Their presentations are captivating, their personalities luminous; they are scholars who bring two loves together: children and their field of learning.

The teacher who conserves children, who unites their gifts with opportunity—what is his image? It is an unquenchable desire to construct and disseminate a meaningful world. It is a faith: the universe has its uniformities; it can be explained if explanations are sought honorably. Such teachers would say, with Einstein, "The universe is not fickle."[10] It is a creed: each child is of supreme moral worth; the fullest development and fulfillment of each child comprise the teacher's goal and duty. It includes morality: we must take all children who come to us; compassion is wedded to competence. It has a mode: teaching is not telling; a child must not be denied the right to discover. It is an attitude: individual differences are cherished.

Equal opportunity does not mean identity of exposure to identical experiences. To repeat, freedom to learn and grow is the practical recognition of biological and cultural variability. With these teachers the school environment is curative; it is luminous and illuminating.

Great teachers teach by freeing the youngster's energies. To teach the learner the art of learning is to teach him to find "hidden likenesses";[11] in short, to find relationships.

Creative teachers make opportunities for children to originate their own experiences in search of meaning; they give the children opportunities *to science* (a new and useful verb). Limited plans for experiences in search of meaning are made available to the student. If the problem can be solved in a planned period of time, it is within the domain of the calisthenics of discovery, or problem-*doing*. In problem-*solving* the solution may have to be deferred because the inquiry and data-gathering necessary for critical investigation take time. It is problem-*solving* that

10. Actually, "Der Gott is nicht boshaft."

11. Jacob Bronowski, *Science and Human Values* (New York: J. Messner, 1956).

evokes the free and true inquiry we have been discussing.

Where the teacher works only through lectures, work sheets, and assignments, and insists on recall of lecture and text, and when laboratory experience merely confirms what has already been shown in the text, then inquiry, and the motivation toward learning associated with it, is crushed. Teaching is then equated with telling; truly the road to impoverishment for young minds.

Where the student has the opportunity to do most of the work, then slowly but surely he assumes responsibility for learning, and the library becomes a tool along with the laboratory. The teacher becomes a guide and the classroom a place to clarify; the text and talk is a springboard for further work, not an end in itself.

In sum, we have put forward the thesis that a sanative, a healing environment developed for the young is our only guarantee that the young, when they become men and women, will place high value on a healing environment for their young. Conservation has both intellectual and emotional parameters. Indeed, judgment affecting conservation must include a strong intellectual component; love of outdoors, if diffused and not directed by the intellectual vector, may even be antagonistic to appropriate conservation measures.

In order that the environment make sense, we need to plot school experiences in search of meaning. A conceptual ordering permits us to see structure, and through structure, relatedness. An intellectual contemplation of structure is imperative for an appreciation of order (synonym: intellectual beauty). However, when *we* plot experiences for the young, even in the interests of the child's idiosyncratic development, we introduce *our own values* as ends.

When children are allowed to devise their own investigations in free and true inquiry, they will develop their own values: values that arise through healing experiences tend to be those that value healing.

When we establish a sanative environment for the young, we are extending the bounds of human sympathy. Conversely, extending the bounds of human sympathy through experience in the search for meaning builds not only a world of meaning but a world of beauty: a world fit for all life and for all life to come.

Edward Stainbrook

chapter eleven

MENTAL HEALTH AND THE
ENVIRONMENT: DO WE NEED NATURE?

This is the century of the self-conscious, self-studying, and self-directing man. We are nature having become aware of itself, and no revolution that one can name in the history of man is more critical, more fraught both with disaster and with promise than is the contemporary happening of the emerging consciousness of self-aware man alone in a centerless universe. Our expanding knowledge and understanding of our world and of ourselves gives us increasing freedom to decide the structure and meaning of our continued emergence as cultural and symbolic man. It also warns us that we are constrained by our evolved biological organization to collaborate understandingly with the natural and with the man-changed and the man-created environment as well as with our limits as an evolved body that is a unique but interdependent biological system in all the rest of the natural universe.

The cultural history of man has now led him from fate through tragedy to the emerging vision of humanistic responsibility for his own destiny. But human beings may have succeeded so well as thinkers and doers, as symbol-users and culture-makers, as fabricators and shapers, as inventors and constructors, as to unwittingly place themselves conceptually outside nature. Apart from too infrequent moments of deep self-reflection, modern man seems determined to seek his own elimination as natural man and to ignore, disguise, transform, and frequently to despoil unconcernedly the naturalness of the earthly space in which he lives. To a progressively accelerating extent, the widespread applications of science and technology are contributing directly to the denaturalization of man and the rest of nature.

Contemporary scientific thought and its technical implementation is, itself, conditioned by Western man's conception of his relation to nature. So much does culture—the symbolic, conceptual, logical, and evaluative transformation of a living experience in the particular life space people inhabit—determine their basic behavior in the world that Eastern and Western civilizations can be, as they long have been, contrastedly opposed as essentially differing life styles. In the West man behaves largely as if nature, especially the rest of biological and physical nature, is his opponent to be conquered, controlled, or malleably used and changed in his service. For Eastern man nature is perceived more as a possible ally to be identified with, understood, joined, sought for, and lived with in harmonious collaboration.

Even the concept of the progressive linearity of events and of the consequent dissociation of Western logical time from the eternally recurring seasonal circularity and the organic rhythmic cycling of natural time may be another evidence of modern technonomic culture's divergence from more isomorphic ways of perceiving and sensing natural order.

Provocatively, the many recent demonstrations both in

unicellular organisms as well as in complex animals and man of recurrent genetically programmed biological rhythms with twenty-four hour, seven-day, lunar and seasonal annual cycles point to an early evolved locking-in to biological processes of a correlation between once extant and coexisting sequences of bodily and environmental events. Modern environments with climatic and illumination controls, with work organizations and other social institutions structuring wakeful activity around the clock, with a distressingly high and insistent input of inadequetely integrated information demanding delayed and belated sleep-disturbing attempts at mastery, and with the rapid transportation of persons through space and time—all these transformations in and of the environment may now conflict with the innate tempo of the body and with the inherent biological scheduling and readiness for anticipated happenings in the world around. Fatigue and inefficiency and perhaps other and more subtle temporary or enduring impairments of adaptation and optimal biological responsiveness may be the price exacted for a mismatch between the preferential ongoingness of the body and the now out-of-phase demands of the surroundings.

But, although we must be aware of the trends of this society to dehumanize ourselves and to maintain a cold war against nature, we must urge a general consistent concern about the meaning and functions of the natural environment for reasons other than a romantic agony over the loss of natural man and of natural nature.

No one needs to argue the advantages of adapting and transforming the natural environs to satisfy better both the basic biological needs and the psychologically experienced and culturally derived motivations of man. Moreover, although the unforeseen or belatedly detected consequences of the adaptations to the natural surround are now what threaten us, the basic meaning of the word, survival, is to live on after a resolution of a life-threatening crisis. We cannot, even if we would, stop the progressively augmenting alterations of both man and his investing nature being made possible by the knowledge and skills of our technetronic society and culture. And many of us, freed from the worry of subsistence success, will respond to the consequent existential anguish by wondering what then shall man be for? If, however, we try to save our lives by losing them in the scientific and technologic inventions of change, we run the danger of being lost in process and of being completely programmed only by our own momentum.

Some of us, therefore, will have to forthrightly raise questions about what it is in the human situation we wish to conserve and potentiate, and what new values for man need to be created and accepted as directives for action in our time. Our basic task in assessing what man should do with nature is perhaps not so much a problem to be solved as a value to be established—not so much a discovery as a decision.

But we are confronted by what exists, and certain interrelations between urban man, particularly, and his natural ambience are the concern of every individual and of every social institution and agency.

Health concerns rank very high in the man-environment dilemma. A few years ago the President's Commission on Chronic Illness defined medicine as merely a branch of a more inclusive science of human ecology. This is a recognition that a population is constantly exchanging substances, energies, and information with its environment and is cross-organized with it. Usually medicine prefers to detect and describe disease and impairment as purely biological happenings. However, an adequate conceptual model of a living person accepts the fact that every self is a uniquely, genetically programmed body that has become humanized and socialized, that is to say, experience-changed and experience-organized. We do not have a body, as we wrongly so frequently assert, we are a body. William James had already posed the statement at the turn of the last century. "And our bodies themselves," he asked, "are they ours or are they us?" Our bodies are obviously and indissociably us, and we are in constant reciprocal transaction with the world around us.

Indeed, for some of our body organs, what is considered to be inside the body are, like the lungs, really an invaginated exterior with the internalized surface of the organ in direct contact with the contents of the natural environment. And just as the complex whole body learns to be human and social, so does each organ system. Depending upon the functions of each system, different organs participate more or less predominantly in different human and social transactions. Organs, therefore, can be differentially involved, more frequently, more intensely, or more openly and vulnerably, depending upon the character of the situation.

The adaptability of each organ system is related to a number of determinants, genetic, maturational, developmental, and situational, so that the survival capacity of a person may be limited and even completely diminished by the least favorable factor affecting only one organ system. Some conditions remote in time or space or subtly indirect in their relationship to an ultimate impairment may nevertheless be significant in the development of incapacity.

When impairment is monitored only at the biological level, usually after an ostensible structural or functional defect has developed, this information considered, in the case of cancer of the lungs, as feedback information from a noxious atmosphere is always years too late for effective prevention. Hence, many of the really helpful feedback sensors scanning either the internal environment of oneself or the external environment must be ideas in the mind, hypotheses, that is, conceptual anticipation. It is the function of the mind, the educated brain, to pick up information before the uninformed tissues of the body know and signal what is happening to them.

The contemporary toxicogenic environment is composed not only of the well-discussed air and water pollution but is also formed by objects and effects of a more psychological and sociological character. Most of the urban environment is full of noise and of people and of vehicles driven by people. The urban environment is, therefore, filled with relevant and irrelevant information that must be scanned and filtered out or suitably processed by all of the occupants of the city. As someone has suggested, silence in the city must be defined as unintended or personally irrelevant noise.

From birth onward human beings react with anguish and irritable distress to any excessive stimulation; hence, noise can insistently evoke a psychophysiological response from the hearer that under suitable subjective circumstances results in increased arousal both of brain physiology and an activation of the functions of other body organs, particularly of the heart and blood vessels. In a situation of sustained informational overload, and perhaps complicated by the subjective state of the person, the increased subjective irritability with which one reacts to the noisy surround may intensify, sustain, and increase the frequency of psychophysiological responses. Over a period of time this may make a contribution to the actual appearance of a disease. Chronically stressed persons who are busy with "noises inside" tend to react excessively to the noises outside. For some phychologically susceptible persons, therefore, the noisy external environment can be distress-inducing. Even in more purely physiological terms, prolonged high-decibel sound can produce inner ear changes that may, in the extreme, lead to the complete destruction of the sensitive hearing tissue. A metabolic degenerative change ensues as the finally irreversible reaction to the noise.

There is another indirect way in which the noisy environment contributes to the human stress. The recent study of sleep and dreaming in man has suggested that dreaming may be considered as a delayed processing of inadequately mastered information experienced during the day. As you know, Freud suggested that the dream protected sleep and that, therefore, we dream in order to sleep. Contemporary theory would suggest that we sleep in order to dream. Freed by sleep from the input of insistent external information, the dream experience may represent a time when we can integrate and rationalize the unsettled and unsettling issues directly or indirectly evoked in the waking state into our preferred ongoing conceptions of ourselves, of others, and of our idiosyncratic way of being in the world. When sleep is interrupted by the noisy night, dream time may be lessened and the dream work interfered with.

Obviously, the density of people in the urban environment has a great deal to do with informational overload and with the constant burden upon our attention, which must scan suitably and react to very frequent person encounters. One of the ways this task is handled in the city is by learning not to scan or not to respond to a great number of people. This leads to a learned indifference to others as protection against the density of the human encounter. It can also by generalization lead to a not-seeing and a not-responding to others even in a context where seeing and responding might be appropriate. City dwellers may develop by this perceptual defense of not seeing others a conceptualization of them as faceless and anonymous. So, too, one may become aware of one's own anonymity and facelessness by getting no response to oneself from the surrounding others. One cannot deface the other without at the same time defacing oneself.

The theologian Harvey Cox, who sometimes seems to take the position of apologist for the secular city, insists that we cannot approach the city with a village theology. Neither can we approach the problems of nature in the city with a rural conception of nature, nor can we expect in the urban environment rural neighborliness or a personally shaped reaction to every leisurely encountered passerby. And there are many positive psychological and social advantages to the anonymity and the personal freedom and the privacy in the city. But one of the basic human difficulties presented to the people in the city is that too many of them who are there are almost completely alienated from supporting primary face-to-face relationships. Consequently, because of their self-isolating and isolated containment, they frequently find themselves unable to find and establish a consistent and enduring environment of a very few people who can reflect back to them their continuity and existence as worthy selves. Moreover, many newcomers, particularly into the central cities, have migrated to the cities primarily because they have lost or moved away from significant supporting persons in their lives.

Perhaps one of the most urgent needs in the large central cities is some new kind of residential places for young people between the ages of 18 and 25 who spend a variable time in transition in central cities while they establish themselves in gratifying and economically supporting relationships in the new environment.

It is sometimes said that Los Angeles must be a very interesting place from the psychiatric point of view, as indeed it is. One of the reasons for that is that so many people have come west seeking the frontier and find only Los Angeles. So many coming into the city are unable to relate effectively to others and find no appropriate social space in which they can effectively reintegrate themselves into social living. Perhaps the basic consideration here is that it is quite possible and perhaps desirable to enjoy the anonymity, the impersonality, and the freedom and the privacy of the city. The anonymous environment, however, cannot be managed if one also feels completely anonymous. With the support of a few primary face-to-face relationships, however, the anonymity of the city may be transformed from despair into confident and gratifying living. Either implicitly or explicitly we are all asking, "Do you know that I am here?", "Do you value me?", "Am I doing all right?", "What can I confidently expect?"

The congestion of people and their social organization are, therefore, very relevant to the goals of the natural and social design of the city. We are fond of extrapolating, perhaps too uncritically, studies of the behavior of congested animal populations to the description of congested persons in the city, forgetting that man is a very resourceful symbol-user and has tremendous capacity for organizing himself socially or for failing to do so. Hence, we have to modify our thinking about the consequences of congestion in the city by considerations of the adequacy or inadequacy of the social organization of the congestion. It is not congestion alone, for example, that creates the hostility, the lack of love, the lack of esteemful supportive mutuality, and the psychological degradation that may exist in the ghetto residence of five or six persons in the same room, or ten to twelve persons in the same small apartment. Large families of ten to twelve were common occurrences in our own society not too long ago, and even larger families and numbers of people in the same small dwelling occur with minimal social pathology in many other cultures. An important pathogenic factor in ghetto congestion is the failure of the social organization of the people crowded into rooms and apartments. Lack of kinship ties and other socially enforced obligations and responsibilities may keep them a crowd rather than a group. Added to this is their inability to escape from this closed and entrapped situation in which they exist with their unrelatedness to each other, with their lack of reciprocal gratification and their high anxiety and hostility.

It is worthy of reflection here that one of the great benefits of designing cities for space and openness and for providing walkways by which people may traverse distances is that the possibility is created for persons to get out of the closed space of residential entrapment. Pathways are made out into the social space around, and if in that social space around there are also sufficient and accessible social resources in that openness, then you have invited persons to come out of their closed, entrapped pathology into the more resourceful, more self-esteemful and self-confirming environments of the world around them.

Closely associated with the space and social design of the city is the current recognition that in these times the city can be built anywhere. Moreover, urbanity is a culture, a whole way of life, that can obtain wherever the city may be located. In the next thirty years we will have to build the equivalent of 150 new cities in this country. These cities need no longer be anchored to the pathways of commerce or to the natural energy centers. There is now no technical reason why a city cannot be built anywhere. Hence, the question must be seriously debated as to how much we shall reconstruct existing urban centers and how much we shall build completely new cities in areas where openness and space need only be used and not obtained by renewal and reuse.

One might apply some of the experience we have had with psychiatric hospitals to our thinking about the inter-relationships between the physical and social environment of the city and the behavior of the people who live there. Much of what contributed to the impairment of people who lived for a considerable time in a chronic psychiatric hospital was the environment of the hospital itself. We were impairing people in the very act of trying to help them. We desocialized persons and diminished their self-esteem simply by the way in which we structured their life experience within the hospital's social and physical space.

The implications of this for the urban environment are obviously great. They have to do with the self-fulfilling prophecies invested in an external environment of ugliness, dilapidation, dirtiness, overbuilt space, and the lack of natural surroundings. These characteristics of the surroundings constantly reflect back the low worth, the isolation, and the segregated rejection implicitly communicated to the people who live there. In this sense, the surroundings increase and confirm the negative self-appraisal that is learned also from other ways of being in the contemporary society.

The characteristics of one's self-appraisal have some relationship to how destructive one may be both toward oneself and toward others. Individuals vary, of course, in how dependent they are for their own self-esteem and self-appraisal upon the reflections from the physical and cultural surroundings. However, it is usually those people who are most dependent upon external appraisal and most vulnerable to it who live in the greatest number in the most unaffirming and demeaning part of the city, both in terms of the physical and the natural surround as well as the social relationships.

Understandably, we give much attention to the behavior of others that makes us anxious or that threatens us. Violent and criminal behavior are concerns of high priority for city dwellers. Violence may be understood generally as a primitive regressive expression of destructive hostility that occurs more easily in psychologically disposed individuals when more constructive alternative action in the service of agression as a search for personal mastery is not available. It would seem to be true in human behavior that the more violent your behavior is, the less effective is your aggression, and the more constructively effective the aggression, the less violence. The task of the urban society and of the body politic generally is how to provide the social resources for the effective, constructive expression of dissent. Simple suppression leaves no alternative for the aggressive search for personal effectiveness except violence.

The most rational methods for shaping and directing the behavior of people in the city has to be executed through the various social organizations and institutions of the society in which people of all ages and characteristics come to do their human business with each other. The inhibitory anxiety about destructive behavior and the learning of a compact of concern about others and about the basic values of society have to occur and be maintained in the socialization process of education and, subsequently, in the social processes of human interaction all of one's life.

You cannot really socialize a child in a crowd, that is to say, in a crowded classroom. You cannot maintain the social reinforcement of concern for self and others that inhibits violence, predation, and self-centered greedy achievement and acquisition if no relationships even obtain between the body politic and those who have stayed out, never gotten into, or have dropped out in anger and despair. At long last all of us need a sense of confident mastery of ourselves in our situations. We need a constant reinforcement for feeling good about our concern about others. We need a sense of a predictable future. We need a society that binds undue anxiety but at the same time allows its people to worry resourcefully. We need a society that keeps man compassionately related to man.

The changing relationships of contemporary man and nature, particularly in the city, may also be determined by some of our basic attitudes toward our own bodies as part of nature. In a definite sense, not only has historical philosophy and religion alienated man from his body but current scientific thinking, even in the behavioral sciences, tends to support the same alienation. The analogy of the body with a machine, first in the Cartesian sense of a doing machine, and then in the contemporary sense of a thinking machine, makes a healthy, joyful narcissism about the body a difficult psychological experience. Not since the Greeks have we experienced a healthy narcissistic acceptance of our own bodies. Christianity taught that the body was bad, evil, and morally as well as physically dirty; and then before we could recover from that insult, the industrial and electronic society suggested that it was inefficient, ineffective, and much less omniscient and omnipotent than the contemporary machine.

The more implicit goal of what may overtly seem to be a resurgence of the hedonistic enjoyment of the body may indeed be a nascent attempt to repossess what for so long under cultural direction had to be dispossessed. The reacceptance of oneself as a body also implies the acceptance of that body as part of nature. Hence, one can see increasing evidence, particularly among the youth culture, of the return both to the enjoyment of the body and to living in and close to nature.

I would like to stress this theme of the reacceptance of the natural in the self because I think there are two basic themes relating to nature and man that are of tremendous importance to the contemporary society. The most familiar trend is our increasing acceptance of our relationships to nature and our knowledge of ourselves as being in the ecosystems of nature. The other great revolution, which has been partially innovated by increasing knowledge in the behavioral sciences, particularly in behavioral biology, is the reacceptance by man of himself as an organization of nature. We are not only love's body, as Norman Brown would have it, we are nature embodied.

The more we become aware of ourselves as nature's bodies, the more we can inform ourselves about ourselves as bodies and culturally and socially direct and translate this information and knowledge, then the more adequate we can be in our adaptation. Up to the present one might say that man has spent most of his time trying to teach the body how not to be natural. Increasingly, the task is to allow the body to learn to be natural resourcefully, adaptively, and effectively. That will then be a repossession of internal nature just as we are reaccepting and repossessing our relationship to external nature. Most of our concern about nature now relates to ecological concerns and man's relation to external nature. This is the revolution of the recognition and acceptance of man in nature. The other revolution is the awareness and acceptance of ourselves as nature.

It is true, of course, that the return to nature can be a cop-out. This might be what the psychiatrists would call a regressive use of nature, trying to restore earlier situations where one could be dependent without guilt or passive without self-castigation, and where one could experience for a time rather effortless pleasure and unconflicted satiation. Regression, however, can be used as an avoidance of development and responsibility or it can be used in the service of self-enrichment and growth. In our contemporary adolescent world some do seek the natural environment as a drop-out space, but others may use it as a place for creative restoration and for an extended intrapsychic transformation of the self as a preparation for resuming with more awareness and confidence a life career in a highly complicated and difficult world.

We must recall that some of our most basic metaphors and phrases that define our real feeling about nature are "Mother Nature" and "Mother Earth." Every time you lie on a sun-drenched beach and enjoy simply the tranquillity and ease of the moment, you are regressively enjoying a very basic human gratification. There are those persons who wonder whether children born in the ghetto and, therefore, quite out of the natural environment have the same kind of regressive longing and need for nature. The longing to return to Mother Nature may be a symbolic yearning, but I believe it is present in all of us.

There is another more subtle human need for the natural environment that has to do with the experience of permanency and of change. In a psychological sense time tends to get mixed up with space, and immortality and infinity are projected against the background of the permanent, relatively unchanging earth. As a support for his own striving for immortality, man needs the sense and the security of the timeless duration of nature. As contemporary society accelerates and multiplies the demand for constant change, both for individual persons and for the collectivity, the need for a relatively permanent frame of reference that can allow change to occur without the sense of being lost in the process becomes increasingly important. Just to be in frequent perceptual contact with the reassuring enduring earth is a psychological security factor of considerable importance.

This society has drastically foreshortened its history, and anxiety and insecurity create defensively a very constricted future. Hence, any moment of contemporary crisis will tend to become overwhelming because the crisis cannot be placed against a long reassuring historical background and a confident predictable future. The maintenance of a time and space background that reduces the moment of crisis to a manageable circumstance with which one can cope is, I think, one of the very important human contributions that is provided by contact with the natural environment. The natural environment endures. It is permanent.

As space exploration continues, changes in our conceptualization of the meaning of the permanence and stability

of the earth will undoubtedly occur. Whatever the issues
of the future in relation to man's conceptualization of
nature, contemporary American society has much to gain
from a reacceptance of man as indissociably and intrinsi-
cally a part of nature.

As René Dubos has recently insisted, "Life in the modern
city has become a symbol of the fact that man can become
adapted to starless skies, treeless avenues, shapeless
buildings, tasteless bread, joyless celebration, spiritless
pleasure, to a life without reverence for the past, love
for the present, or hope for the future." Well, perhaps
it is not that unremittingly pessimistic.

By the end of this century, this society may well be
able to go beyond material and economic affluence for
most of its people. But after problems of existence come
existential problems. How despairingly paradoxical that
modern man should have to come to a defense of nature
in his life and in his city. It is only as man can confidently,
securely, and exultantly repossess his own nature and the
greater nature of what we know as the world that he
remains resourcefully in the directing vanguard of his
own destiny. That is where the slowly evolving changes
of nature have placed him. We can only go with nature
and with our feet pressed against the earth. Otherwise,
we may follow the Pied Piper of our materialism and
technology to the desperate edge of our increasingly plastic
and synthetic existence.

The times cry out for some new ordering and stabilizing
myths for man's existence. The more man becomes known
by science, studying him as object, the more it becomes
crucial for man, the subject, the knower, to have a center
of infinitely enduring stability in time, and of utter faith
in the orderliness of the changing process so as not to
lose himself in time and space. He must remain able to
hear an accident occurring in his substance without feeling
that his substance is nothing but occurring accidents. A

humanistic mythology spiritualizing the permanence, the stability, the orderliness, the immanence, and the constantly renewed promise of the continual differentiation, novelty, and creative emergence of man in nature and of nature in man would seem to best express the necessary new faith of modern man. Then, to refute the poet, Yeats, we can say, "The center holds, things fall together."

A Special Address

Senator Gaylord Nelson

chapter twelve

MAN AND HIS ENVIRONMENT

Man's relationship with his environment is the most crucial issue he has faced in the long perspective of history. All other issues—war, racism, poverty, crime—will become irrelevant if he fails to solve the pressing problems of the environmental crisis.

Man has caused more desecration to the landscape, dissipation of resources, and degradation of the environment in the past one hundred years than was committed in all his previous years on earth. Man is the only creature to intrude massively into the environment and create great imbalances in life systems. He is the only one who is destroying the livability of his own habitat and that of all other living creatures.

Those who question, as many do, whether anyone really cares what happens to the whooping crane, the peregrine falcon, the bald eagle, or any other of the many creatures who are on, or soon to be included on, the endangered species list, would do well to remember the warning of the poet John Donne, "Never send to know for whom the bell tolls; it tolls for thee." There are many species on earth with a survivability capacity superior to that of mankind.

How long can the United States and the world consume basic resources at the current accelerating pace before we run out? The fact is, of course, that sometime we will run out of those resources that feed and fuel the world's industrial machines. Harrison Brown, in what I think is one of the finest books ever written on this problem, *The Challenge of Man's Future,* addressed himself to the question of how soon we will run out of resources. Extrapolating from current rates of consumption, he concluded that sometime within the next one-hundred years we will have exhausted many if not most of the critical resources upon which a highly sophisticated technological society depends. What then? A return to an agricultural society, he suggests, unless we find new ways to deal with the problem.

A second fundamental question is whether this planet, a living organism in every sense of the word, can sustain life in any acceptable fashion with a population of seven and a half billion in another forty years, or fifteen billion, eighty years from now? I doubt it. And will there be any water left on earth sufficiently unpolluted to support marine life in another thirty-five to forty years, if we continue to degrade it at the current pace?

A third fundamental question involves the organization of society: What social, economic, cultural, and political changes must occur before mankind establishes workable relationships with the environment? These relationships may be established voluntarily, by some sensible, rational plan. If not, they will be established involuntarily, because they will be imposed upon us by the condition of our resources, and undoubtedly with a good deal of human misery in the process.

We have to understand that we live on a finite planet that has a limited capacity to support life, as does any

finite body. It has limited resources, such as a thin envelope
of air that is being rapidly degraded and a shallow mantle
of soil, minerals, and water that is steadily deteriorating.
We should consider planet Earth a space ship, which is
also a closed life system. There is nothing that can be
taken out of the planet and nothing that can be brought
into it. We must live with what is here.

There are three general aspects of the environmental
problem: the philosophical, the physical, and the political.
I use the term *philosophical* to refer to the attitude of
the human species toward the environment. It is unfortu-
nate that Western man, as contrasted with primitive
peoples, has always thought of himself as somehow over,
above, apart, and separate from nature.

All the aboriginal groups around the world differ in
that they have always felt that they were a tiny, relatively
insignificant part of nature. So long as we arrogantly feel
that we are superior to nature and that what happens
to other creatures or what happens to the world's resources
really does not mean very much, then it will not be possible
for us to solve our environmental problems.

Physical aspects relate to what we can do from a scientific
standpoint to maintain the quality of the environment
and to preserve the habitat for a vast number of living
creatures. Needless to say, we cannot function beyond the
limits of our physical knowledge, which at the moment
is seriously inadequate. We do not know as much as we
should about refining the pollutants out of the air and
out of the water, or about the implications of introducing
into the atmosphere massive doses of herbicides and
pesticides. The whole field of scientific understanding of
the environment is in its infancy, and we need to dramatically expand our research. Then we must work on problems
where we have some understanding and where we can
do something.

This leads to the political aspects.

These refer, of course, to citizen's action at every level of government from city hall to the White House, supporting tough environmental legislation, requiring pollution standards, and demanding that new technology pass strict environmental impact tests. If the environmental problem is going to be solved at all, it will be solved in the political arena. There must be massive public support, and this in turn depends on public understanding. It is fundamental that we have environmental education starting in grade school and continuing through high school and beyond. Without widespread understanding and massive political support the problems will not be met.

Assuming now that public understanding and support are adequate, what should be done immediately? I am going to suggest nine programs. All are federal programs and, of course, do not eliminate the need for state and local policies nor do they reduce individual responsibility or the responsibility of private industry, both of which are essential. They represent national problems about which something should be done. Others may wish to add or subtract from my list. But the point is that we can and should recognize the important problems. The federal government at this stage in history has to do some fundamental things that are obvious and necessary to begin the attack on the total problem. We need:

1. *Tougher air and water quality policies.* The existing legislation respecting the air and water has made a good start, but establishment of a national policy on air and water is necessary. That policy, which should be simple and straightforward, should decree that all municipalities and all industries in the country are required to immediately install that equipment to refine pollutants out of the air and water that meets the highest current practical state of the art. As we expand our research and improve our technological sophistication, the advancements in the art should automatically become the new national water

or air quality standards that everyone must meet. If we established that kind of policy and funded the program for the municipalities, we could remove 85 to 90 percent of the pollutants from the air and water in the next ten to fifteen years.

Frankly, there is no sensible alternative to such action. The current cost of pollution in this country is massively greater than the cost of actually cleaning it up. Everyone of us has been paying a staggering annual tax in the form of costs for pollution damages, and the dirtier the environment gets, the larger the bill becomes.

Water pollution does an estimated $12 billion in property damage each year, not counting the immeasurable loss of Lake Erie or of a productive estuarine area, or of the life and protein productivity in the ocean itself.

The same is true of air quality. The cost of air pollution in this country is $12.3 billion in economic damages annually. An effective level of control over stationary sources could be achieved at a national cost of about four billion dollars. Los Angeles is already controlling air pollution from smokestacks and other stationary sources, but faces ever growing air pollution from the automobile, which accounts for 80 percent of Los Angeles' air pollution and 40 to 60 percent of the air pollution for the country as a whole.

One of the tragedies in this field is that the automobile industry, the largest of the American industries, which has fought against auto safety and tire safety, has also been fighting air pollution control equipment. The four major U.S. auto companies were actually charged by the government with engaging for fifteen years in a conspiracy not to compete in the development of pollution control devices for the heavily polluting internal combustion engine.

The automakers finally negotiated an agreement with the government to refrain from such collusion in the future.

Meanwhile, suits filed on the same basis by numerous states are still pending. If the automakers had been working all that time—from 1953 to 1968—to develop pollution control, we would now have a clean internal combusion engine.

2. *Greater financial aid to municipalities.* Municipalities today are faced with chronic revenue shortages and a costly far-ranging variety of needs. As a practical matter, they simply are not able to handle the cost of high-level waste treatment programs. Under present legislation, municipalities and states in combination can get federal matching funds for 75 percent of their municipal sewage facilities, depending on state financial assistance and other conditions. Municipalities should get a flat 90 percent. This is the same percentage of federal aid we have appropriated for the interstate highway system. It would seem only logical that environmental needs are at least as important as the interstate program.

3. *A national land use policy.* Land is a critical natural resource but has always been so abundant in this country that every landowner feels he has a right to use land to which he holds title in any way he pleases. We cannot continue this way.

For example, anyone who extracts minerals by strip mining must be required to save the topsoil. It took nature thousands of years to produce each inch of topsoil, which can be destroyed by a single act of carelessness. We must save the overburden, restore the topsoil, seed it, plant it, contour it, and guarantee its integrity. If you fly over Pennsylvania, West Virginia, Virginia, Kentucky, Arkansas, and parts of Ohio and Illinois, you will see open sores on the land that will be there forever. The open strip mines in these states, if placed end to end one hundred feet wide, would stretch hundreds of thousands of miles. Acid leaching from strip and deep mines in the same states has also destroyed some ten to twelve thousand miles of once clean rivers and streams, filling them with sulfuric acid and silt.

A second example is the San Francisco Bay. In recent decades, the bay has shrunk in area from 700 square miles to 400 square miles. A sensible land use policy would prevent the Corps of Engineers from issuing permits to San Francisco or Berkeley or Oakland to fill in the Bay to expand the property tax base. The bay is a unique natural scenic area and the spawning grounds for a wide variety of marine creatures.

As a general policy, no one should be permitted to drain any land except by special petition from an appropriate conservation control board. The wetlands of the country, as another example, are the irreplacable habitats of several species of birds and other creatures. If the wetlands are destroyed, the wildlife on these lands will be destroyed as well, resulting in ecological imbalances that ultimately will affect man's welfare.

We must stabilize the shorelines of lakes and rivers. Owners of lakefront property should not have the right to cut trees on the shoreline or to drain effluent from their septic tanks into public waters. Thousands of lakes throughout the country have received death sentences from recreational development, which is a euphemism for eroded banks and overfertilization.

4. *A minerals policy.* We need a national policy on the extraction of minerals that would take into account the environmental risks. Nobody should be permitted to drill any new oil wells on the continental shelf until such time as the technology is available to extract it without the kind of environmental disasters we have seen in the Gulf of Mexico and off the coast of Santa Barbara.

5. *Rejuvenated mass transportation.* We cannot continue our irrational love affair with the automobile, depending on it alone for our transportation needs. The reason we are so committed to it is that it gives us independence.

But we are rapidly losing that independence in irritating traffic congestion. Fifty years ago you could cross New York City twice as fast as you can cross it now by automobile. One of the by-products of the great popularity of the automobile is a decline in mass transportation. People too young or too old to drive, or too poor to own a car, are left without transportation. Furthermore, we cannot continue to pave America. We have now paved an area the size of the state of Kentucky.

6. *Recycling of waste.* Cities all over the country are negotiating for new sanitary landfills ten, twenty, or fifty miles away. At the same time, we are destroying resources that are recyclable. Half the material destroyed is paper, a large fraction of which can be reused. Another major part is metal. Some one or two million automobiles a year are accumulating on the countryside, and another seven or eight million find their way to junk yards. Last year, we used 85 billion disposable cans and bottles, about 25 for each man, woman, and child on earth. It is preposterous to continue to mine and harvest virgin materials only to create new sanitary landfills and more disposal problems. The answer is a national policy for recycling waste.

7. *Control of pesticides and herbicides.* Our national policy on pesticides and herbicides should be similar to our policy for prescription drugs. In essence, the company that develops a drug must prove it is effective against the target organism; must demonstrate its effect on animals and then on humans; must demonstrate its side effects, its safety, its efficacy; and only then apply to the Food and Drug Administration for the right to put it on the market. The FDA decides whether it should be used at all, and if so, for what purpose and under what circumstances. The same kind of protocol needs to be followed before anyone is permitted to introduce herbicides and pesticides into the atmosphere, since obviously those chemicals are medicating all living creatures, including

humans. The process would require appropriate ecological studies of the environmental effects and a decision on the circumstances and condition in which a pesticide or herbicide could be used, if at all.

We have spewed hundreds of millions of pounds of DDT into the atmosphere for more than a quarter of a century. There is hardly a marine creature in the oceans or the lakes, hardly an animal on earth that is not carrying DDT in its fatty tissues, and the consequences of this irrational activity are totally unknown. Some specific effects are now appearing, such as the destruction of the peregrine falcon all the way from the east coast to the Rocky Mountains, and the eventual extinction of the bald eagle. It has been discovered that DDT affects the bird egg's capacity to hold a chick long enough to survive. We have no notion what effects the use of these pesticides and herbicides have had in other life systems around the world. We do know that we find DDT in the fatty tissue of the Adélie penguin in the Antarctic, thousands of miles from any place the chemical compound has been used.

8. *Preservation of wilderness areas.* We need to preserve all the wilderness that is left, not only for the purpose of knowing it is there and enjoying the fact that it is there—to say nothing about enjoying wilderness visits—but because of the critical scientific value of these areas. Wilderness areas are the only places left in the world where we can study the works of nature extending back millions of years.

9. *Protection of the oceans.* A national policy on the oceans would stop the dumping of solid wastes and the introduction of effluents from our great cities into the oceans. We are rapidly destroying the productivity of the oceans. Every marine biologist that I have talked with agrees that because of the current accelerated pace of the use of herbicides and pesticides, and the dumping of industrial and municipal wastes into the oceans, the protein

productivity of the seas will be destroyed for all practical purposes in the next twenty-five to fifty years. The destruction of oceans would mark the end of the largest single resource on earth. That, even Rachel Carson believed, would never be possible.

The reason it is possible to destroy the oceans in such a short time, is that almost all of the breeding and spawning life cycle is in the first half-dozen miles or so off the continental shelf and in the marine estuaries.

Those are the nine policies we should introduce immediately and support with financial commitments adequate for the job. No president has adequately addressed the environmental problem in a way that approaches being financially significant. For example, President Nixon attacked Congress in October 1970 for being inflationary in authorizing a billion dollars for eight different municipalities for sewage treatment facilities. He wanted $214 million. Then, in 1972, Congress authorized $18 billion to be spent over a three-year period for municipal sewage treatment. But the president has only allowed the release of $9 billion, two billion of that for 1973, three billion for 1974, and four billion for 1975. My judgment is that we will need to be appropriating 25 to 30 billion dollars a year more for the environment than we have been spending at the congressional level. This is over and above what states, municipalities, and private industry must spend. Unfortunately, it is about the same amount at the federal level that we wasted in Vietnam for several years, and the environment is much more important.

What we need is an aroused public, effective conservation groups, and environmental public-interest law firms starting law suits all over the country. This action must be coupled with environmental legislation at all levels of government. We are seeing today the beginning of a great movement that has significant promise, and the promise comes from the concern of the people. It is interesting to note that neither candidate in 1968 gave any significant attention to the environment. Then, in January 1970, the president said that the environment is the issue of the seventies, which next to peace, is the most important issue facing us. How did the environment get to be the issue of the seventies in such a short time? It got there because politicians are hearing the voices of the people from all across the country.

Young people and old people alike spontaneously expressed their concern on Earth Day, 1970. Across the nation there were eight to ten million students, 3,500 colleges, and 3,000 communities spontaneously participating. This genuine display of concern is the reason the environment is the issue of the seventies. For if it is not, and we return to the indifference that has characterized our past history, then man may well destroy himself. In the decade of the seventies we must choose between the destruction of our planet and the survival of mankind.

part three

POLICY

Orris C. Herfindahl

chapter thirteen

DEFINING THE PROBLEM OF ENVIRONMENTAL QUALITY

Let us consider the nature of the problem of environmental
quality from the point of view of an adviser on public
policy, an adviser who takes the values and philosophies
of the members of society as given. From this viewpoint
it is useful to think of quality of the environment as a
kind of sum of the quality of the constant flow of substances
and stimuli that comes to each of us unbidden from other
persons, businesses, nature, and man-made objects. The
estimate of quality is to be thought of as depending on
both present and future effects, of course. This very
comprehensive concept of environmental quality is useful
because it ties in nicely with applicable economic principles.
The current concerns over environmental quality are
concentrated on only a part of these substances and stimuli,
however, especially on the harmful or problem-causing
emissions and also on the various kinds of congestion,
which may be regarded as cases of pollution. There are
a variety of reasons for concern over these emissions—effects on health, aesthetic reactions, and effects on the
functioning of various natural systems that in turn are

important to us either for reasons of aesthetics or production.

Every business firm and household generates substances that have to be disposed of in some way or stimuli, such as noise, whose disposition is coincident with emission. There are, for example, the products of combustion, the spent or contaminated chemicals, the waste rock after useful minerals have been extracted, the excrement, the garbage, the fertilizers and pesticides washed off by the rain, and so on. If these are disposed of so that other persons or businesses are not affected, they are not a part of the problem of environmental quality. The problem comes when other persons or businesses are annoyed or harmed.

The quantity and composition of residuals and pollutants is not fixed, of course. Proximately they may be viewed as depending on:

1. the size and composition of real final output—what is produced and how much;
2. the technologies used in production and in the handling and disposal of residuals;
3. size of population and its spatial distribution.

The bearing of each of these factors on the size and composition of the residual load is clear enough. Production of more of the same things will mean more of the same residuals; a society of beefeaters, for example, will find that its residuals include manure, whereas the vegetarian society avoids this. The impact of technology is obvious; bicycles produce less air pollution than automobiles, for example. Clearly, residuals are likely to increase with population, and its spatial distribution will affect congestion.

It is hardly open to doubt that many people in a number of countries feel they have experienced a substantial decline in various aspects of environmental quality over the last few decades, a decline large enough to have more than offset those improvements that have taken place. Why has this deterioration occurred? The key fact here is that the capacity of the natural environment to receive and process many types of substances without adverse aesthetic or production effects is limited. So long as the flows of residuals were low enough for the rivers, the soil, the atmosphere, the bays, and the oceans to process and absorb them, we perceived no over-all changes, and the noticeable consequences were so highly localized in relation to areas untouched that we were not much concerned by them. Indeed, all through human history we have been acting pretty much as if the natural environment had the capacity to absorb and process anything we might toss into it. In considerable part this has been true until recently, notwithstanding that the history of particular cases of human despoliation of the natural environment is a very long one. Because the capacity to absorb appeared to be unlimited, there was no thought of a charge for using this service. In any case, nobody owned the atmosphere, the rivers (roughly speaking), and certainly not the oceans.

In recent years the flow of residuals of many types has increased to the point where they are beginning to impinge on the capacity of these great natural reservoirs to handle them. Where the residuals themselves are directly obnoxious, high local concentrations are increasing in number, this being dramatically illustrated by air pollution. Where the substances are processed by nature, changes in the functioning of natural systems are beginning to appear, changes that many informed people view with apprehension. Man's production and consumption activities and the accompanying present flow of problem-causing residuals are so large in relation to the absorptive capacity of the natural environment that man now is quite capable of lowering its quality a great deal, and possibly to a catastrophic point.

In the face of what has happened, it would be a serious

222   **Environmental Quality and Society**

error to regard the growing concern over environmental quality as a fad or to attribute it to an unexplained change in values. It would seem a little like saying that the hurrying and scurrying that would accompany a cholera epidemic reflects a newly acquired emphasis on health values or just a passing health fad. It would be more likely that the value or concern had been there all the time.

Variation Among Pollution Problems

Our understanding of the real effects of the many different pollutant flows and concentrations varies enormously. These variations in understanding in turn have an important bearing on the responses that society appropriately may make to these problems.

The differences in understanding of the effects of various pollutants reflect the interplay of several kinds of obstacles to fruitful research. A frequent complicating factor is multiplicity and complexity of causation.

To take an extreme case, suppose that a decrease in life expectancy at age sixty and over is observed. How much of this decline is attributable to the survival to these ages of physically defective persons who would have died earlier except for improved medical care? How much is attributable to changes in the complex pattern of the way of life, including the amount of liquor drunk, obesity suffered, tension experienced, and so on? I do not mean to suggest that this and similar problems of multiple causation cannot be studied. Many methods are available, but they often are inadequate, perhaps because of insufficient variation in the variables or lack of suitable data if the method is statistical or because methods or ingenuity are not up to coping with chains of complex interactions.

Pollution problems also vary greatly with respect to their amenability to experiment and the cost of experiment.

eriment with humans is not feasible, usually reasons, recourse must be had to animals, but ions to pollutants cannot be transformed to eactions in a simple way.

.rge part of the cost of experiment with animals .umans is approximately proportional to the length . time over which the subjects are observed. In order to cut cost, high dosages may be substituted for long continued low dosages, but here again the transformation of results from the one to the other situation is a matter of great difficulty.

The difficulties in interpreting animal experiments with high-dosage rates suggest recourse to statistical study of humans with differential exposure over long periods. This has its cost difficulties, too, but perhaps more important is the introduction of many uncontrolled variables into the system, and we are back to the problem of multiple causation discussed above.

Finally, the study of pollutant effects never is able to catch up with the changing nature of the problem. First of all, the quantity or load of pollutants on various natural systems, including the human body and psyche, is changing. As a result, there may be new undesirable effects where none was suspected before. Second, there is a constant procession of new chemicals reaching different parts of the population—without being asked for—via air, water, foods, and other articles used and consumed.

These obstacles to research are of little consequence for some problems, present much difficulty for others, and may be insuperable in a few cases. At the one extreme, a comparatively simple system may be identifiable and amenable to study by straightforward experimental techniques. The study of the toxic effect of some substances may be a case in point. Here the problem of control is simple because specific ill effects are connected with particular substances. The goal of control, as in more complex cases, is simply to balance the costs of additional restriction of use or discharge against the additional benefits. If the ill effects are severe enough, the appropriate discharge may be zero, as no doubt ought to be the case with mercury discharged to natural waters, there being ample evidence of the horrible effects of methyl mercury on man.

A second category of cases that is well understood in some instances is that in which the effects of discharges become summated or combined synergistically either by receiving organisms or by natural processes in the receiving body such as a stream or lake. For example, the natural processing of organic substances discharged into rivers or lakes creates a draft on the quantity of free oxygen present in these waters and of course leaves certain residual products that in turn affect water quality. Air pollution is a somewhat similar case, with the processing being in part mixing, dilution, and dispersion. In each case, the receiving body—that is, the water body or the air—emits substances or stimuli that produce aesthetic, psychological, and biological effects when they are received by persons. In cases of this kind, the appropriate type of regulation will be much more complex than in the simpler cases of the first type. The relevant physical systems are much larger, the number of sources of emission is much greater, and the technical possibilities for coping with the problem are more numerous and complex. In the case of water pollution appropriate action may even involve regional treatment facilities—certainly regional design, if not the facilities themselves.

In making collective decisions on how, and how far, to reduce pollutants in cases of the types discussed to this point, there are several traps to be avoided. First, there is no point in taking the view that we need to understand everything about a pollutant—all its ill effects and how they are produced—before there can be a decision to curtail. For one thing, understanding never is complete. For another, if it has been established that one ill effect would in and of itself warrant a 10 percent reduction in exposure, there is no need to wait to find out that there are twenty other ill effects before taking that initial step.

If limited knowledge can be sufficient for action, it follows that esthetic or psychological considerations may be adequate in and of themselves to warrant control. Ill effects on health or on someone's cost of production do not have to be demonstrated in every case. If it is all right to use productive resources to produce automobiles whose appearance pleases their buyers (by using chrome, fins, and so on), it is just as reasonable to use productive services to improve the appearance of a stream simply because some like to look at it.

Another form of the urge to know it all before taking step number one takes the form of paralysis on contemplating the total cost of "cleaning up." Apart from the ambiguity of this notion, tomorrow's action requires only that the benefits from tomorrow's "cleanup" be greater than the associated costs. Of course, it is desirable to be able to plan ahead further than the figurative tomorrow, but there is no need to foresee the next several decades or to cost out states of cleanup that are unlikely ever to come into being.

The most difficult decision problems are encountered when there is great uncertainty over the possibility of highly adverse effects flowing from one substance or a class of substances. The candidates here are surprisingly numerous, including increase in carbon dioxide because of fossil fuel combustion, and increase in atmospheric dust from human activity, pesticides, radiation, and population increase. In the case of a class of substances, the ill effect may result from a summation operation by human or other organisms. For example, the condition of the asthmatic may be worsened by a variety of substances. Similarly, pesticides as a group may combine to produce an effect or group of effects.

In cases of this type, one of the possible courses of action is to reduce the flow of the pollutant involved even though there may be great uncertainty over the magnitude of the ill effects or even though it has not been conclusively demonstrated that they come from some or even a number of substances in the quantities usually received.

Obviously a decision in such cases presents great difficulty to public bodies, since the argument for control involves weighing demonstrable costs against problematical gains. To explain that the problematic gain is very large—avoidance of catastrophic cost a few decades from now—seems not to be appealing. The view that our relations with the natural order will continue as in the past, a view usually based on personal experience and a limited knowledge of human and natural history, seems to have great appeal to many people. This confidence in stability is misplaced, however, for there is ample evidence that man can produce large changes in the great natural systems. Continuation of their past behavior is not assured.

Formally similar decision problems involving uncertainty are faced by individuals rather often. One example is provided by the case of a person invited to participate in a card game with stakes that are very high for his financial resources. What should he do? He could plunge ahead, refusing to even consider the possibility of disaster. Second, he could carefully compare his and his opponents' abilities and try to estimate his most probable financial outcome. This would indeed be appropriate if his financial resources were very large relative to the stakes so that he might participate in a number of such games. (In the case of society, the large financial resources would be analogous to its having a chance to play the "Pollute the Ocean Game" several times).

But his resources are not large, and he may be wiped out. Suddenly it occurs to him that he really does not have to participate? (The analogy in the case of society is that it does not have to pollute the ocean.) By not participating he loses the chance for great gain (corresponding to the product that has to be given up if the pollutant is controlled) but avoids the possibility of complete disaster.

The public is not the same as the individual, of course, and this makes its decision problem far more difficult. In the first place, it seems to me that the public ought to be a good deal more careful about avoiding physical catastrophe than most individuals are about avoiding the physical disasters associated with unhealthful living, driving automobiles, and the like. Nor do individuals seem to be very impressed by the possibility of cataclysmic effects that may come after their own lifetimes or possibly one generation beyond. This characteristic may have its uses, of course.

If anything, the public—that is, individuals viewed as a collective body—is even more myopic than the individual. A sizable catalogue of cases could be drawn up in which the well-demonstrated imminence of serious adverse effects or even their actual presence has been insufficient to move the representatives of the public. The history of air pollution provides many examples, as does also our failure to take many actions that would reduce deaths by automobile at very low cost in money or inconvenience.

The lessons to be drawn from all of this are ambiguous, of course. But one thing clear is the great desirability of rapidly improving our understanding of these potentially cataclysm-producing substances so that we can speak with some assurance about what lies ahead. For example, suppose it could be said that if we continue to spew out carbon dioxide at present and prospective rates, average temperature will go up two degrees by 19xx and at that time cities A, B, C, and so on, will be under water. That might not be enough to get action, but it would be a good deal more persuasive than having to say that temperature might rise, but then again it might not because of offsetting factors.

Within limits, we *can* buy a better understanding of these systems. Whether that understanding can be quite complete is not the relevant question. We could make very good use of even a little more precision.

An understanding of the physical-biological facets of environmental quality—where and how pollutants are produced, how they are transmitted, the effects they have on natural systems and on man and other organisms within these systems, the technical possibilities for altering quantities of pollutants or their destinations—all of this knowledge is indispensable if we are going to make any progress toward achieving levels of environmental quality that are technically achievable. No matter how profound this understanding, however, it touches only one of the two major aspects of the problem of improving environmental quality.

The economic, political, and administrative side of things is of equal importance. Consider the following problems, for example, which are very different from the physical or the biological: What should government do when some are willing to pay for improvement of quality and some are not? Will uniform standards for effluent discharge give better results than varying standards? Will effluent charges yield better results than standards? What governmental unit is appropriate for taking action?

A major obstacle to effective public action is that the boundaries of the physical systems involving pollutants are not the same as those of the political units with the power to take action. Those who produce and those who receive the pollutants may not even be members of the group with power to decide on and adopt remedial measures. On the other hand, a political unit that does embrace the relevant physical system may be so large that the task of regulating pollution is neglected or handled in ways that are not well adapted to local conditions.

In the case of water and air pollution, the creation of special pollution control districts corresponding to river basins and the less well defined airsheds with power to design control for the relevant pollution region has worked out well in some cases and deserves further trial. The great advantage of a system integrated in this manner is that it facilitates the attainment of cost-minimizing solutions.

The problem of bringing the political system to grips with pollution control is far from solved in this country, this situation largely reflecting the fact that pollutants do not respect jurisdictional lines. This problem is far more severe in those cases where pollutants touch the interests of other nations, as is or may be the case with DDT and other insecticides, crude oil spills from wells and ships, radiation, and air pollution of certain types, including carbon dioxide and atmospheric dust.

Cultural diversity and national sovereignty complicate every phase of international problems of environmental quality. For example, reasonably strong consensus must be attained on many matters before appropriate action can be taken in a particular case, but even the development of a common view of the physical-biological aspects of a particular pollution problem is accomplished more easily in one country than among several.

The really serious difficulties come with design and administration of remedial measures, however. Exactly what tools should be used to reduce the rate of pollution? How is the cost of collective action to be divided among the nations? In proportion to pollutant produced, in proportion to income, or how? One question that is sure to arise is whether those countries which have used up the absorptive capacity of the oceans or the atmosphere by their past dumping activities—mainly European countries and the United States—should compensate those which have consumed this capacity in lesser degree.

Implementation of any international control scheme is sure to pose serious difficulties. The fact of national sovereignty will impede the coercion of noncooperators in some cases. Even where governments are genuinely inclined to enforce agreed procedures, their good intentions may be frustrated by weaknesses in their political-administrative systems.

The difficulties appear to be so formidable that the outlook for successful control of a pollutant on a worldwide basis—if this should ever be necessary—is doubtful. Our experience to date with programs for regulating whaling, fishing, crude oil spills, and so on is not encouraging at all.

Population

Control of the level of population may become an environmental quality issue in one of two ways. First, the effects of certain pollutants can be lowered by curtailing their production, and one way to do this is by reducing population. Second, it may well turn out that certain types of congestion can be dealt with best by reducing population. Whether population could be reduced if the necessity arose is doubtful, however.

A wide variety of tools is already available, any one of which is capable of lowering population if used widely enough. These range from abstinence and contraception through sterilization, abortion, infanticide, and euthanasia. However, the mere availability of this wide array of tools—and no doubt more are on the way—in no way assures that any one or several of them *would* be used more widely even if society were willing. The all-important question is, How is the greater use of the tool to be induced and controlled?

Several measures for inducing increased use of some of these tools could be adopted and implemented with no great difficulty. These measures include, for example, official attempts to persuade individuals to limit the number of children they beget, modification of tax and other laws to penalize large families instead of subsidizing them as is done now, and provision of contraceptives free or below cost. There is no way to know in advance whether any of these or other measures would or could suffice to bring population increase to a halt in a particular curcumstance, for relevant experience is quite limited.

Population control does not require that nobody be permitted to have more than, say, 2.2 children in his family but merely that the average be no higher than this. Thus a tax advantage for smaller families might be sufficient if it were large enough. If we should ever adopt a well-formulated negative income tax, the tax advantage from a number of children at or less than the standard number could then be extended to all income levels.

Birth tickets are another device that would give a financial advantage to small families, but unlike the tax advantage it would automatically adjust the reward to the level needed to get the desired total number of births. Under a simple version of this plan, each female would be given 2.2 tickets at birth, or whatever number is required to attain the life-time birth rate per female born that is desired by society. Every time she has a child, she would have to surrender a ticket, either one received at birth or one purchased on the market. Tickets could be fractionated and could be bought or sold at any time.

The initial issue of tickets would be independent of income, but a decision to have more than, say, two children would be equivalent to deciding to purchase the privilege of having a child from those whose desires or circumstances lead them to have less than three children. The market for these tickets, which ought to function well-nigh perfectly, would automatically find that price which would adjust tickets purchased or retained for use or later sale to the number available. The result would be that a decision to "consume" more than two children would have to be paid for just as in the case of a decision to consume more of any good that uses up the services provided by scarce resources. Clearly a control system like this could function only if the lowest levels of real family income were high enough so that society could in good conscience inflict a penalty on women who have too many children even though their incomes are low in a relative sense. An additional requirement would be that women know how to avoid having children and have the means to do so.

Obviously only a minority in this country feels that strong efforts to reduce the birth rate should be initiated now. Whether population will grow to the point where a large majority shares this feeling is not at all clear. First, we do not know how successful we shall be in coping with the effects of congestion by methods other than reducing population. Second, we may become accustomed to congestion. Indeed, we appear to be curiously apathetic about traffic congestion right now. Third, it is by no means certain that population itself will continue to grow.

Population growth from one year to the next is exhaustively determined by the death rate at each age, the fertility rate at each age, the age distribution, and the size of the population. Since life expectancy at birth is quite great (now about 71 years), only a small fraction of the population is replaced each year (1/71, or 1.4 percent, if population were stable). This plus the fact that death rates are changing very slowly means that the age distribution can be changed only slowly even with changes in fertility rates large enough ultimately to produce large changes in the rate of population growth. Since fertility rates exhibit considerable short-run stability, the result is that short-run population forecasts are very accurate, but much experience shows that accuracy falls off rapidly as the forecast attempts to reach further into the future.

The bugaboo of long-range population forecasts is change in fertility rates. In view of the large changes that have taken place in many factors influencing fertility—for example, availability of, and attitudes toward, the use of contraceptives and abortion, not to mention other more subtle factors—it is possible that fertility rates soon may fall to a level that finally would stabilize population if death rates did not change. Of course, that ultimate stable level might be considerably above the level at the time of the fall in fertility rates simply because the age distribution is not in a reproducible equilibrium. For example, there are now a lot of females of child-bearing age or younger.

Two suggestions emerge from this discussion of population. First, it is important that we become aware of the large amount of inertia that can be present in population movements. When population is increasing, the wrong kind of age distribution may make it very hard to slow down this increase even if the forces slowing down the growth would ultimately be successful.

Second, initiation of control—if the need should arise—would be delayed without advance agreement on the measures to be used. Suppose that in the year 2000 we decide that population ought to be reduced but that we have not decided how to go about doing so. To form an idea of how long it might take to agree on how to proceed, ask yourself how long it would take to arrive at a common view of the effects of population control on minority groups. Or try asking a few women and men what they think of a scheme that would permit them to have as many children as they want at a price that would be adjusted so that families as a whole would decide to have no more than 2.2 children on the average. Although present reactions may be somewhat misleading because most people do not feel that the need for curtailment has yet arrived, it seems likely that it will be difficult to develop a consensus on *how* to go about reducing the rate of population growth. To start this task now so as to have a common view in hand would eliminate delay in instituting acceptable measures if the need should arise.

Choosing Methods for Improving Environmental Quality

In general terms, there is only a limited number of things that can be done if environmental quality is to be improved. The possible actions are the following:

1. Reduce discharges of harmful residuals by
   a. recovering them for reuse (recycling);
   b. changing residuals to a harmless form for discharge to water, soil, or air for dissemination, storage, and natural processing, if any, by treatment, modifying production processes, or using substitute inputs or processes;
   c. reducing the output of the products whose production entails the residual output, whether the products are consumer goods or intermediate goods used by other firms.
2. Reduce damage from harmful residuals by
   a. increasing the assimilative capacity of the environment (e.g., by stream aeration or low flow augmentation);
   b. discharging to a place where less damage results;
   c. moving the activities or organisms subject to damage.
3. Reorganization to reduce congestion effects.
4. Reduction of population.

Rational action to improve environmental quality or to prevent its deterioration probably would make use of a combination of the above measures, although many people appear to be familiar with only one or two of them and greatly underestimate the potentialities of the others. For example, few appreciate the great variation that is possible in production processes. In many industries there now is a tremendous variation in processes, which depends in large part on geographical differences in the relative prices of inputs. For example, water intake per dollar of value added in petroleum refining in the Delaware and Hudson water basins is about ten times higher than in the Arkansas, White, and Red regions as well as in the Great Basin region.

The lesson is clear. The mere fact that a particular process is in use—perhaps even in all plants in an industry—does not rule out the possibility that an alternative process that would reduce pollutant output is available at very slightly higher cost. It frequently is.

Similarly, we often seem to have little comprehension of the enormous flexibility that is possible in the consumer's budget. The basic wants of consumers can be satisfied in a wide variety of particular ways, as is suggested by the large variation in the details of the consumer budget in single countries that is observed over time or the variation between countries in the budgets of social classes that have many characteristics in common.

More complex forms of reorganization are possible. For example, it really is not necessary that people live ten to thirty or more miles from their place of work and that they all try to go to and from work at the same time of day. There *are* other ways to do things, perhaps at some additional cost, but cost may be lower in cases where there is some defect in economic and social organization. The defect may prevent progress to a situation that is both preferable and cheaper. In the case of urban transportation the defect has been recognized for a long time—it seems to be very difficult to organize so as to take into account the delay and inconvenience I impose on those already driving when I decide to drive to work.

The problem of finding the appropriate combination of methods from the array open to us is a difficult one, and if we are not aware of its subtlety, the result is likely to be the selection of methods much more costly than need be. Consider, for example, the setting of a uniform standard for effluent discharge that is to apply to all producers in all locations. Although this is certainly one way to reduce the discharge of a pollutant, it makes it impossible to cope with the pollution damage problem by changing the place of discharge or by moving those who are damaged, and these methods might be preferable.

The use of subsidies to encourage the installation of certain types of equipment to reduce pollutant discharge has similar defects. Since a subsidy cannot be granted simply for the amount of money that a businessman says he needs for the socially optimum method of handling a pollution problem, the result seems always to be a provision that the subsidy be granted for the installation of a certain type of plant or equipment. This means that one particular method of handling the pollutant problem is encouraged to the exclusion of other and perhaps better options. To subsidize the construction of municipal sewage treatment plants, for example, is literally to discourage the installation of treatment facilities inside industrial plants, change of processes, or relocation.

Designing systems of control that will lead to adoption of the socially optimum combination of methods for handling pollution problems is far from simple. The economist's study of economizing mechanisms leads him to advocate the use of charges imposed on the action or emission causing the damage insofar as this is possible. The usual economic incentives will then insure a search for the most efficient responses, which may turn out to be process change, relocation, recycling, or use of substitute products. Some production operations will find it easy to avoid the charge, and others will find it difficult and will continue to emit the pollutant. This *is* the desired result if the charge has been set at the right level—that is, so that the benefits from further reduction would be less than the additional social costs. If emission of a pollutant is to be reduced by a given amount, it is in the social interest to do so in the cheapest way possible.

Summary

The principal lesson of this tour of the environmental quality problem is that it is complex and many-sided. There is not one but many problems at the physical-biological level with wide variation in complexity, and the same is true of the economic-political-administrative side of things.

It was noted that the societal decision problem is especially difficult in cases like the carbon dioxide problem that involve very serious but uncertain effects. The indicated course of action was to try to reduce the uncertainty by enlarging research efforts.

One of the main problems in bringing the political system to grips with environmental quality is the lack of correspondence between the boundaries of the natural systems involving the pollutant and its effects and those of political units with the power to act. The political-administrative difficulties encountered domestically are greatly exacerbated in those cases where international control is or may be necessary.

Although it is not certain that population reduction will be regarded as essential in this country to improve environmental quality, an advance consensus on *how* to reduce it would permit timely initiation of control measures.

Finally, a variety of methods is available for use in most problems of environmental quality. The imposition of charges on pollutants is one of the best tools for seeking out the best combination of technical methods.

Richard A. Tybout

chapter fourteen

TWO MARKET BIASES

If we focus on the essential features of the market mechanism in contrast to its principal alternative, allocation by central directive, the advantages of the former are conspicuous in many well-known respects. The market provides an automatically operating mechanism for guidance of production and distribution of the material output of society through literally trillions to tens of trillions of transactions per year in the United States alone. It permits the buyer and the seller an infinite range of alternatives as to type of commodity, size, style, adaptation to particular usage, and many other characteristics. There are problems aplenty in getting and keeping markets working well. But the fact remains that the market mechanism has brought, and continues to bring, material goods to the consumer in unprecedented abundance and without the spectacular fallibilities of central direction.

And yet we feel that something is wrong. As our material welfare increases, our quality of life decreases. The connection is not coincidental, nor is it limited to the capitalistic society. The attributes of social decision-making that produce market biases in the United States are just as effective in producing market and production biases in the Soviet Union.[1] Each year we are left with less of our natural heritage to enjoy as more of it is converted to material goods and related land uses. What is worse, we have in its place increasing quantities of waste products, which remain to impair environmental quality in all too many ways.

We need to take account of the costs of material output in terms of environmental quality losses that accompany it. An ideal social decision-making mechanism would strike a balance between utility from conventional consumer goods and utility from the environment. We need to know our net environmental loss as well as our net material goods gain for all production and consumption decisions. The market mechanism does not provide us with this knowledge. It does not tell us the social value of environmental amenities, nor does it tell us what the damages are for environmental abuse. More specifically, it is subject to two biases: (1) underproduction of public goods; and (2) lack of consideration for pollution output, or negative externalities, to use the economist's term.[2]

1. Marshall I. Goldman (ed.), *Controlling Pollution,* Part IV, *The Soviet Parallel* (Englewood Cliffs, N.J.: Prentice Hall, 1967). It is not generally appreciated that markets are perforce important in Soviet society, nor that they can play an important role whether productive capital is privately or publicly owned. At the same time, this is not to gainsay the fact that a large part of Soviet production is not for the immediate benefit of the consumer and is insensitive to his preferences, whether for environmental quality or material goods.

2. A third bias is well known: the lack of correspondence between market-determined income and that which society deems equitable. This third bias has been widely recognized and needs no further comment here except perhaps to note that redistribution of income must be conducted in such a way as to minimize its obstructive effect on the efficiency of market operation, as described above. The task is not easy, but has received much attention in the professional literature. A good deal less attention has been given the implications of the first two biases, at least from the standpoint of environmental decision making.

The interesting thing about both biases is that social institutions filter human preferences in such a way as to give greater sway to those with adverse environmental effects. The environmental problem cannot be laid on the doorstep of native human crassness, incorrigibly short-sighted materialism, American exploitive traditions, or the Christian man-above-nature ethic without recognizing at the same time the difficulties inherent in obtaining an operational expression of true preferences.

True preferences include the desire to enjoy natural beauty and to be free of offense from waste products. The inadequacies in market expression of these preferences can be remedied to a significant degree, as will be seen below; but the need remains for expression of some environmental values through conventional political processes, or perhaps through institutional means yet to be devised. Nonmarket (political) channels have, of course, been employed to the present time. These channels do not have the efficiency of the market, but nonetheless environmental problems are so strongly felt that gains have been made using them.

Public Goods

Public goods include most of the traditional services of government: police and fire protection, the court system, public education, national defense, national parks, public recreation facilities, and others. They are distinguished from private goods in being inherently unsuitable for distribution through normal market channels. The reason lies in a failure of the exclusion principle. That is to say, consumption by one individual does not prevent consumption of the same public good by another. This means that rationing according to payment is an impossibility.

For example, the act of contemplating a work of art generates satisfaction and, in the relevant economic sense, is an act of consumption. Yet consumption of this sort does not prevent another person at another time from obtaining the same sort of satisfaction from the same work of art. Indeed, an endless stream of human satisfactions can be obtained by an endless stream of viewers of the same art piece. Similarly, the existence of police and fire protection and the court system serve all members of the community. Law and order cannot be consumed by one without being consumed by many others at the same time.

Contrast the situation with that of private goods. In order to consume an apple, an orange, or an automobile, that commodity must be removed from the market, and the very act of consumption by one individual precludes consumption of the same item by another. Markets are well adapted to the allocation of private goods because any would-be consumer cannot get the commodity unless he pays for it. If he does not pay for it, he can be excluded from consuming it.

Not so with public goods. Since consumption by one does not in itself prevent consumption by another, there is no automatic exclusion. In some cases barriers can be constructed to prevent consumption, such as by mounting the *Mona Lisa* in an enclosed area to which admission is charged. But this is not the same as automatic exclusion by consumption and, in any event, is not practicable for all public goods. Thus, it is not obvious that a part of the community can be excluded from law and order and still have law and order in the other part.

The crux of the difficulty appears in deciding who shall pay for public goods. If one cannot be automatically excluded from consumption—if he knows he will receive the public good anyway—then he has every incentive to try to avoid paying. This is an important part of our difficulty in financing public services. A clear matching of individual cost and benefit (supply and demand) is made impossible by the natural incentive of all who benefit to conceal their own desire for the public good (as part of a strategy to avoid paying for it) and to seek ways to shift the tax burden onto others. No one will be denied public education, national defense, police protection and so on. The unfavorable reception given tax increases at the local level is notorious. The situation is moderated somewhat by the complications and delegations that make political decision-making at the national level one step more remote. But the problem is hardly eliminated in moving to this level. As a result, our society produces luxury automobiles, television sets, apartments, and a host of conventional commodities in profusion while at the same time producing meager public services that have manifestly higher marginal utilities.

Public natural resource investments, such as in the acquisition of natural areas, suffer from the general malaise that besets the provision of public goods. The result, of course, is that public investment in natural areas has been constrained by the same institutional biases that work against public services in general. The problem is compounded by habits of thought. A large part of the population takes access to nature for granted. Individuals may wish to have natural areas available but think of them as a birthright furnished at someone else's expense. The traditional attitude is a carry-over from past natural abundance and adds to the difficulties already present as a result of public goods attributes.

Only the strongest, most persistent demands for public natural areas have been met, and these have benefited from the historic circumstance that a large part of the land now held in natural areas was already federally owned when its present status was determined. In the absence of this happenstance, less natural land would be preserved today. Examples abound of the increased costs of acquisition with present appropriations procedures.[3] To the extent that unique natural wonders are involved, there has been enough support manifested through political channels; otherwise, frequently not. The opportunity cost of private commercial uses forgone provides a continuing challenge to present natural areas. On the one side are the well-articulated values of natural resources for material benefits. On the other side are the poorly revealed preferences of the public for natural areas.

An alternative to the present decision-making mechanism for acquisition of natural areas would be to employ the exclusion principle. Access to natural areas can be limited through gate controls and in many cases is so limited at the present time. But admission fees, where used, are customarily quite nominal. If admission fees were set at levels that would maximize profits, then a decision as to whether and when to acquire additional natural areas could be made on the basis of expected revenue (properly discounted) and cost of site acquisition. Further, this approach would have the advantage of providing a test of the social utility of a given site for natural values or for exploitation of its potential in producing material goods. By application of the exclusion principle, alternative uses of the site would be reduced to a common basis.

As a first step in evaluating this proposal, it should be noted that just such applications of the exclusion principle are available in the private sector of the economy; and despite the importance of private outdoor recreation facilities, we do not consider them sufficient to meet the need for natural areas. There is, of course, the fact that a different pricing policy in the public sector would make more profitable private natural areas. But public acquisi-

3. Walter J. Hickel, "The Making of a Conservationist," *Saturday Review*, 2 October 1971.

tion of natural areas is justified by other public goods–type considerations that go beyond immediate uses of the areas. In particular, there are long-run conservation values. Once a natural area is thoroughly violated, it may not recover for several generations. Irreversibility in whole or in part means that a future option is lost or compromised. The market mechanism can, within limits, take account of future interests through time-discounted (interest rate) calculations. But market-determined interest rates do not adequately make comparisons over the periods of time here involved. The issue comes down to an ethical comparison across generations. We have good reason to think that the growth of human population over the next few generations will create congestion problems that greatly enhance the expected future utility to be gained from natural areas. But it is not necessary to argue for preservation on behalf of the unborn billions whose lives will be more barren in its absence. A public-goods demand for preservation exists today on the part of many, perhaps most, persons with standards of living above subsistence, to know that natural communities survive in sufficient abundance to assure their independent viability, whether or not those who hold this demand ever expect personally to visit these communities.

A similar consideration is the scientific value of natural areas. Since we are dealing with unknown increments to future knowledge, no more precision is possible here than in the preceding paragraph, and the conclusion is the same.

Third, there may be public gains over and above individual gains from recreation in natural areas. The argument is best understood by analogy with the case for public education in general. Education is both a public good and a private good. It is a private good in that the receiver benefits from received knowledge. It is a public good in that society benefits from learned patterns of social behavior and responsibility. A similar argument applies in the case of natural areas. Those who experience, appreciate, and carry with them a revised approach to life and their fellow men as a result of their sojourn in a natural area have gained in a way that benefits others as well as themselves. To the extent that others are benefited, we are talking about a gain that is collectively experienced, as for any other public good. Insofar as this argument can be applied, it supports the provision of natural areas as public goods.

The public-goods character of the demand stems from benefits to those who would not visit the sites and hence who would not pay admission fees. Because of this, it remains necessary to provide natural areas in greater abundance than could be justified on the basis of gate receipts. But the charging of admission fees that are not nominal is nevertheless desirable for a purpose not yet considered, i.e., to control crowding.

The point is sometimes overlooked that crowding imposes its own costs. If crowding is the alternative, some people would choose to pay the admission fee. An admission fee that replaces the disutility of crowding with a financial payment will cause each individual to recognize the costs he imposes on others by his presence and for this reason will cause him to use or not use the area according to a comparison of his and others' disutilities on the same basis. The result will be to bring an optimal level of crowding.

Other dimensions of the recreational experience need not interfere with the application of the preceding principles. Motorboating and certain kinds of camping may be more consistent with crowding. Wilderness backpacking may be more consistent with low density usage. Natural areas can be classified in such a way that they cannot be used for incompatible activities and within each class; the appropriate admission fee can establish the optimal level of crowding or lack of it.[4] Admission fees that are

4. An optimal admission fee is derived in the following way:

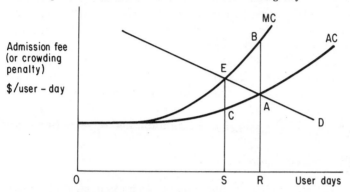

Curve D represents demand, with the price users are willing to pay measured in either dollars per user-day, or in disutility per unit of crowding. It is assumed that there is a monotonic mapping between these two measures.

Curve AC represents average cost to all users from crowding, i.e., each user creates more crowding as he joins in. The cost of crowding is experienced by all others, including himself.

Curve MC is the marginal cost of crowding, or the derivative of total cost at corresponding values of AC. MC lies above AC because the latter is assumed to be continuously increasing.

In the absence of a crowding toll or admission charge, equilibrium is reached at point A. The number of user-days is OR. The cost added by the marginal user is RB. The cost experienced by all users is RA.

The equilibrium at OR user-days is nonoptimal because costs imposed at the margin (RB) exceed the desire of users to pay (RA) at the same margin. Intuitively, individuals do not experience the marginal costs they impose. Optimization requires equalization of marginal costs and revenues (or payments, or disutilities). This is achieved at user-day output OS. Again, the crowding disutilities experienced at the margin are the average costs, in this case SC. An efficiency toll (admission fee) of CE is levied. The cost experienced at the margin and the disutility plus payment are equal at level SE.

To state the criterion in general: until marginal costs to society are recognized by individuals in their decision-making, they will behave in nonoptimal ways. Utility can be maximized by the introduction of admission fees geared to achieve an optimal trade-off in the individual recreationist's budget.

different at different sites of the same physical characteristics will permit visitors to select for themselves among
those that are crowded and those that are not, based on
their willingness to pay in order to avoid crowds. Whether
a high or a low payment would be required is another
question. If many people actually enjoy crowding, the
premium for the uncrowded areas would not be as high.

Revenues from crowding tolls should, of course, be used
to expand natural areas. But as previously noted, there
are additional social benefits that justify the acquisition
of natural areas beyond what is implied by crowding fees.

Pollution: A Negative Externality

The second bias of the market mechanism arises because
unwanted by-products create costs that are external to
its normal functioning. The disposal of wastes in public
waters and in the open air results in no assessment against
waste originators, though emission standards, where effective, constrain somewhat the use of this free service.
Charges are made for solid waste collection, e.g., from
residences in urban areas, but these charges cover only
the costs of waste transport from one site to another and
perhaps incineration. They do not cover environmental
damage from landfills or the adverse aesthetic effects of
the city dump. Similarly, sewage assessments cover only
the costs of collection and treatment, in various degrees,
by municipalities and, even then, seldom reflect the special
treatment costs created by certain industrial wastes. They
do not take account of the effects on the environment
of what comes from the municipal outfall.

Herein lies the second bias of the market mechanism:
there is no charge for the very large volume of waste
that continues to be released into the environment, whether
discharged directly by a waste originator or indirectly by
a waste collector, perhaps after partial treatment. The

environment is treated as a free remover of wastes when, in actual fact, it is removing wastes at the expense of those damaged by pollution.

As a society, we do not consider paying less than the full value of services used in producing any product. By the same token, we should not consider paying less than the full value of services of the environment used in removing any waste. Implicit in this point of view is an assumed right of all individuals to enjoy those services and amenities classed under the heading of "environment."

The fact that waste producers have paid nothing for environmental services and amenities destroyed means that pollution-generating products have not borne all their costs. If waste producers had been assessed sums that would in the case of each pollution output have compensated society for the environmental loss, then their products would have been more costly. Less of these products would have been produced, and less by-product pollution would have been released. Thus, the absence of a system for bringing environmental degradation into the market mechanism has produced an oversupply of pollution.

It is important to note that the case for assessing polluters an effluent charge is derived as much from society-wide efficiency as it is from equity considerations.

The equity argument is self-evident. It rests on the same ground as the legal principle of compensation for damages.

The efficiency argument is derived from the fact that environmental quality has value. If this value is to be reduced, then we had better be sure that, in accepting such a reduction, we receive in return at least equal value in the form of compensation. As long as the material products that gave rise to the pollution for which compensation is paid can be sold for a price that is high enough to comprehensively cover all environmental damages, then a trade off of environmental quality for these material products is desired by society. The market test, with effluent charges set at the level of the damages, tells us this. Otherwise, not.

Effluent charges are equally applicable to effluents generated from any source, whether by municipalities, business firms, mines, or other pollution-originating sources. Effluent charges play the same part in pollution control as wages do in the labor market. Both compensate for services rendered; both cause the producer to take account of something given up in the interest of production; and both provide the test by which a choice is made. In the case of labor the choice by the worker is between more leisure and more material goods purchased from earnings. In the case of the environment the choice by society is between environmental quality and more material goods. If environmental damages were incurred by a single identifiable individual, as leisure hours given up can be identified with individual workers, then the effluent charge could be paid to the damaged individual. Cases such as this do occur, as where brine from a given oil well infiltrates a neighbor's ground water supply. But if damages are to society at large, the only practical means of compensation is by payment to the public, represented in the form of a government agency. If the revenues from effluent charges are kept in a separate fund that is available only for financing environmental improvements, then expenditures from the fund are most likely to benefit those who were damaged by the pollution that gave rise to the effluent charges in the first place.

The best mode of operation is simply to give the pollution-originator the choice of the degree to which he should treat his wastes to remove pollutants. If treatment is less costly than dumping, he has the incentive to treat, up to the point where the costs of treatment exceed the public damages. Beyond this point, he will dump and pay the public damages. The state would be best advised to use the compensation received from such payments to help fund the development of better technologies rather than to turn these funds back into treating by existing technologies. It is known that the damages are not as costly as the treatment for the remaining amount of waste that is dumped.

The polluter himself will also have the incentive to seek and install better technologies because by doing so he can avoid the effluent charge he must pay if he dumps. Any amount dumped, however small, will result in an effluent charge as long as there are discernible damages. He will have a similar incentive to find by-product uses for his waste or to recycle it. Even though he might dispose of his wastes at a loss in some by-product use or recycle at a loss, this loss would be less than the loss he would incur by paying the damages associated with dumping into the environment.

The key information needed for the successful operation of an effluent charge system is a schedule of damages applicable for all possible pollution outputs of a given waste-discharger. The pollution-originator is then, in effect, comparing the value to society of two alternatives: (1) waste assimilation by the environment with attendant damages and (2) waste treatment, with the diversion of resources that it requires from other uses of these same resources. The choice, of course, will be made differently by different polluters.

Those with high cost of treatment will dump more and pay more. Their products will be priced higher as a result, and they will go out of business sooner. Those with low cost of treatment will dump less and pay less. Their products will not reflect as high a cost of treatment, and they are more likely to survive over the long run. The effluent charge system, in effect, adapts the workings of the marketplace to the ends of pollution control. It reconciles the environment and the market, which in the past have been working at odds.

A final fundamental point to note results from the philosophical base of effluent charges in the market system: effluent charges are based on economic considerations. The word *economic* is used here to include a wide range of phenomena: loss of material goods, damage to life, liberty, or property, recreation potential, aesthetic effects, and many others that go to make up the quality of life. Various ways have been, and will continue to be, found to impute economic values to associated losses of utility. At some point, however, noneconomic considerations enter. For example, a complete ban on the uses of DDT in the open environment might well be justified by the damages that have been done and are expected to be done to the large birds of prey, including the American eagle.

Such a ban is a political decision. It is presumably made with some knowledge of the social costs of doing without DDT, but is not made by price adjustments. The same is true of a ban on oil well–drilling in the Santa Barbara Channel or refusal to build a dam in the Grand Canyon. The use of the price system is abridged in these cases, just as it is when we draw a line between acceptable and unacceptable business practices in the normal operation of the economy. The need for noneconomic, or political, alternatives to pollution pricing should be recognized, but it does not change the case for bringing the price system into the service of environmental protection for the wide range of circumstances in which it can be applied.

Administration

As we look forward to pollution control over the decades immediately ahead, there is the question of whether practical means can and will be employed to integrate the instruments of control with the market mechanism. The advantages of so doing are clear from previous discussion.

First steps in the achievement of environmental protection have been taken at most levels of government by introducing quality standards. Ambient quality standards have been adopted to give targets for cleanup of the environment. They logically imply emission quality standards, and, in fact, the latter are in the process of being adopted. Undoubtedly, ambient standards reflect an implicit judgment of the severity of damages that would result in the absence of abatement, as compared with what can be reasonably achieved with present pollution control technologies. Emission standards can be expected to reflect even more the judgment of the standard-setters as to what is technologically feasible.

It is probably necessary for the immediate future to continue the control effort by use of quality standards simply because any fundamental change in criteria for control, such as would be necessary to put into effect comprehensive effluent charges, would require the reorientation of agency administration and enforcement practices. The prime consideration at the moment is to get on with the job of pollution control as rapidly as possible, to guard against the loss of momentum that a fundamental reorientation would probably entail.

Nevertheless, there are some disadvantages to quality standards. These disadvantages would be overcome by the use of effluent charges. First, the quasi-arbitrary nature of quality standards has been noted. Existing technologies condition the choice of standards. Once selected, the technology that gave rise to the standard becomes the means of meeting the standard. And progress stops there. To be sure, new technologies might be developed. But the waste-discharger has no incentive to do more than meet the standard. If the state, through a pollution control agency, wants to require an improved standard, it feels the necessity of finding or discovering the existence of a "practical" alternative to justify the improved standard.

Even if there is a publicly sponsored research program for new pollution control devices, it is a long step from the establishment of a basic concept to the application of that concept in a practical operating industrial process. The agency will have difficulty improving the standard.

Public agencies work at a disadvantage in selecting standards on technological grounds. The same is true in revising standards upward. Pollution control agencies typically are in no position to knowledgeably respond to arguments by a pollution-originator as to why a proposed standard is unreasonable. The latter knows far more about his technologies and plant operations than state or federal policy-makers and their advisers can reasonably be expected to know. Publicly employed engineers must deal with many pollution-originators. Public budgets are typically lean. The state is generally unable to support by closely reasoned engineering arguments a position much different from that advocated by the regulated industry.

Contrast the effluent charge. Effluent charges are based on expected damages. The state need not ask how or whether the pollution-originator will achieve abatement. Effluent charges are not adjusted by technology. They depend only on expected damages to the environment. The usual calculus of profit maximization will lead the waste-discharger to abate in the most efficient manner, given his existing plant. Further, he has the incentive to search for new technologies and adopt them if they will reduce his waste production. Again, this incentive results from damages he would otherwise have to pay.

A similar incentive, as previously noted, exists to develop by-product uses of wastes and to recycle wastes. With effluent charges, this incentive arises from the possibility of reducing the damage payments by using wastes in other ways rather than dumping. By-products and recycling might involve loss and hence be uneconomic to the producer unless he is forced to recognize the damages created by his alternative policy of dumping. No such damage payments and hence no such incentive is involved with quality standards, above and beyond the meeting of the standard.

Second, there is the case where no technology exists. With quality standards, public policy is in the position of having to choose between two untenable alternatives: (1) an impossible quality standard and (2) no abatement. With the effluent charge, the effluent-discharger simply pays the charge, which the state can use for improving the quality of the environment in other ways, while at the same time the waste-discharger has a strong incentive to find a new technology.

Third, the very uniformity across firms and industries that may appear to be an advantage of standards is, in fact, their principal disadvantage. The same total amount of pollution removed by any group of plants can be removed at least cost when those that are better equipped and more efficient do a larger part of the job. If all plants were required to remove the same fraction, the same pounds per pound of output, achieve the same quality of effluent, or meet some other fixed quality standard, the total cost to society would be higher for the same amount of pollution removed. Equity is achieved in the effluent charge system by submitting all to the same schedule of charges for the same damages. Plant operators are then in a position to treat intensively or not as their costs dictate. Group-wide efficiency is achieved at the same time since the amount treated will vary according to costs of treatment. Society-wide efficiency is achieved by adjusting effluent charge schedules to damages.

It is possible to introduce two limited applications of the effluent charge idea in the short run, even while there is principal reliance on quality standards. One such application is in a permit charge. Permit charges would apply during the planning and construction period for pollution control devices. They could be levied on a per unit time basis from the time a pollution-discharger has been directed to submit a plan for abatement to the time that plan is fully implemented. They would be payable annually or prorated over the year. They should be graduated in such a way as to take account of the quantity and quality of each pollutant in proportion to the standards for the same pollutant or, as more precise information is accumulated about damages, in proportion to the damages. Either way, they should be set high enough to provide an incentive for rapid development and implementation of a satisfactory plan for abatement.

The advantage of the permit charge is that it would speed the adoption of abatement processes. Just as the effluent charge provides a financial incentive for abatement, so the permit charge provides the same incentive for getting started. The pollution control enforcement agency need not get involved in evaluating claims by the pollution-originator as to causes for the latter's lack of progress. There is far less need for state review and critical evaluation. The polluter pays the permit charge per unit time until his pollution control devices are in final operation.

A second way of introducing an effluent charge is through a system of fines. These would be fines for not achieving the quality standards. The size of the fine makes a difference. To a large firm the fine means very little. To a small firm the fine means too much. The quantity of pollution dumped is important. A violation might involve a large dumping (generally from a large firm) or a small dumping. Similarly, the quality of the effluent is important. The more pernicious the effluent, the greater the downstream or downwind damages. Thus, there are good reasons to adjust fines in the same way that effluent charges are adjusted. As with permit charges, the fine can be adjusted in proportion to the standard; or if there is knowledge of damages, it can be adjusted in proportion to the damages.

As experience accumulates, there is every reason to expect that knowledge of damages will accumulate. When (1) enough knowledge of damages has accumulated and (2) the state has gained experience with permit charges and variable fines, it should be possible to consider a replacement of quality standards with effluent charges as the principal instrument of regulation.

It is desirable, as a general proposition, to shift from quality standards to effluent charges for most pollution-generating establishments all at the same time, rather than proceeding piecemeal. This is partly an administrative, partly an equity, consideration. The administrative advantages of carrying out all programs according to the same approach are obvious. Equity enters as a consideration to achieve a balance between different business firms in different industries producing substitute products. Similarly, municipalities would all face the introduction of effluent charges simultaneously.

Substitution of effluent charges for quality standards would consist in simultaneously introducing charges for whatever levels of effluent output are produced and relieving the pollution-originators of the requirement to maintain any fixed quality standard. The long-run effect might be to reduce the total expenditure of the pollution-originator on effluent control through technological progress, but the short-run effect is likely to be an increase in abatement costs. Such an increase is, however, fitting and proper. Until all of the damages from waste disposal are borne by the waste-originators, the total social costs of the wastes will not be taken into account.

With effluent charges, a system of fines would be unnecessary, at least for discharges. The charge itself, a legitimate business expense for tax purposes, would take the place of fines.

The validation of damage estimates for different effluents in different quantity under various circumstances is important to the success of the effluent charge system.

Much remains to be learned about the social damages of pollution, but the necessary knowledge is accumulating. Thus, the economics of recreation was the subject of several careful studies during the 1960s.[5] The effects of air pollution on urban property values have been established by econometric investigations.[6] The same is true of the health[7] and property deterioration effects of air pollution.[8]

If effluent charges are introduced in a second step, as described above, then information on damages can be gathered while quality standards are still in effect. It is anticipated that general indexes of damage might be developed for each effluent, depending on downstream population, population density, recreation potential, and other parameters. For practical administration it is probably best to treat in the same way all firms and municipalities in a given river basin or air shed. Any attempt

5. For a synthesis, see Marion Clawson and Jack L. Knetsch, *Economics of Outdoor Recreation* (Baltimore: Johns Hopkins, 1968).

6. R. J. Anderson, Jr., and T. D. Crocker, *Air Pollution and Housing: Some Findings,* Paper No. 264, Institute for Research in The Behavioral, Economic, and Management Sciences, Krannert Graduate School of Industrial Administration, Purdue University (January 1970). R. G. Ridker and J. A. Henning, "The Determinants of Residential Property Values with Special Reference to Air Pollution," *Review of Economics and Statistics* 49 (May 1967): 246–57. R. G. Ridker, *Economic Costs of Air Pollution* (New York: Frederick A. Praeger, 1967). R. O. Zerbe, Jr., *The Economics of Air Pollution: A Cost-Benefit Approach* (Toronto: Ontario Department of Public Health, 1969). K. F. Wieand, *Property Values and the Demand for Clean Air: Cross Section Study for St. Louis* (Ph.D. diss., Washington University, 1970). B. W. Peckham, *Air Pollution Damages to Residential Properties in Philadelphia* (unpublished manuscript, Raleigh, N.C.: Division of Economic Effects Research, National Air Pollution Control Administration, 1970).

7. Lester B. Lave and Eugene Seskin, "Air Pollution and Human Health," *Science* 169 (August 1970): 723–33.

8. L. B. Barrett and T. E. Waddell, *The Cost of Air Pollution Damages: A Status Report,* U.S. National Air Pollution Control Administration (July, 1970); and D. A. LeSourd et al., *Comprehensive Study of Specified Air Pollution Sources to Assess the Economic Effects of Air Quality Standards,* Research Triangle Institute (December, 1970).

to make distinctions on the basis of detailed imputations of waste transport from specific originators to specific receivers is likely to create more confusion than equity.

The need to gather information on damages and potential damages is explicitly recognized when effluent charges are used. This need is implicit in other control systems and is important for equitable criteria. If damage estimates are logically required whatever the control system, then the need for them does not create difficulties unique to effluent charges.

Summary

Two biases have been shown to prevent expression of environmental values in market processes. Conventional markets produce the preponderance of decisions that lead to environmental degradation but produce almost no decisions leading to environmental protection. To the extent that protection is achieved, political processes are the means. For the purposes of pollution control, market processes are abridged. Their replacement by regulation substitutes a mechanism markedly deficient in both concept and practice.

A more promising approach is to amend market processes. The one-sided efficiency of the market should be made two-sided through the introduction of congestion fees, effluent charges, and like surrogates for prices. That much can be done toward this end is implied by our analysis. That much should be done is implied by the combined effect of the two biases and the frustrations inherent in current policy.

W. Wesley Eckenfelder, Jr.

chapter fifteen

ECONOMIC ALTERNATIVES FOR
INDUSTRIAL WASTE TREATMENT

Industrial wastewaters have received varying degrees of treatment in the United States for the past fifty years. It has only been in the past few years, however, that increased water quality standards and resulting effluent requirements define levels of treatment for virtually all industrial categories. In the past, wastewater treatment was an expedient to eliminate immediate problems such as fish kills, but the future will require treatment to establish and maintain the defined water quality criteria. A recent projection by the Federal Water Quality Administration aims at 85 percent removal of contaminants (secondary treatment) and municipal pretreatment requirements by 1972, 95 percent removal of contaminants by 1974, and close to complete removal of contaminants by 1976. Such factors as plant location, expansion, and type and nature of product will be subject to these environmental constraints. Industrial water quality management in the future will be governed by several factors including economic alternatives, political considerations, and legal constraints, to name only the most obvious.

This paper will discuss some of the considerations relative to the economic alternatives for industrial waste treatment and how they might project to the future.

There are a number of factors that will exert a major influence on the cost of industrial waste treatment, both in the present and in the future. These include:

1. projected industrial growth and processing and product changes, considering the total and the geographical distribution of industrial complexes;

2. projected wastewater pollutional loads from various industrial categories;

3. projected wastewater treatment requirements and effluent quality criteria;

4. wastewater treatment technology.

The Impact of Projected Industrial Growth

A number of studies have recently been conducted projecting specific industrial growth in the United States. For example, the projected growth rate in the United States through 1975 in the organic chemicals industry is 9 to 10 percent per year with an increase in total production from 135.6×10^9 lbs/year in 1969 to 201.6×10^9 lbs/year in 1973.[1] This growth, however, shows marked regional trends varying from 5 percent in the northeast and Middle Atlantic states to 15 percent per year on the Gulf coast and 25 percent per year in Alaska and on the Pacific coast. The latter emphasizes the newfound petroleum deposits in Alaska. This growth distribution in turn will exert a profound effect on water quality management

1. *Projects of the Industrial Pollution Control Branch, July 1970,* Water Pollution Control Research Series 1200–07/70, U.S. Dept. of the Interior, FWQA (Washington, 1968).

problems in these respective geographical areas. For example, land-use planning could limit industrial growth in some geographical areas or impose exceptionally high effluent quality criteria.

Projecting to the future, it is a certainty that in some areas combined wastewater treatment will become common. Present examples of this are the Frendswood Treatment Facility in Clear Lake, Texas, which presently serves a number of industries on a prorated charge based on volume and strength of the wastewaters; the newly formed Gulf Coast Waste Disposal Authority in Houston, Texas, which is planning the development of a number of combined wastewater treatment facilities to service contiguous municipal and industrial areas.

The concentration of industrial growth in urban areas places increased emphasis on water quality management and projects increased levels of treatment in the future. This in turn will provide incentives for in-plant control, water reuse, and product recovery.

Projected Wastewater Pollutional Loads

At present, industry in the United States utilizes 15 trillion gallons of water per year and treats less than 5 trillion gallons prior to discharge. In terms of biodegradable organics (BOD) these wastewaters are equivalent to those generated by a population of 360 million people. Projections of industrial growth indicate a pollutional increase of about 4.5 percent per year, or three times faster than the increase in population.

The volume and strength of industrial pollution is about three times as great as the nations sewered population at the present time. Reduction of wastes prior to treatment and discharge to the receiving waters is a major industrial goal at present, and has a significant impact on the economics of water quality management. The alternatives in water quality management are shown in figure 1.

Volume and strength reduction of industrial wastes will be accomplished by in-plant education, better housekeeping, and so on. Modernization of plant equipment should yield lower wastewater loads. Waste reduction practices include: recirculation of relatively noncontaminated waters for process and other reuse; the segregation of cooling waters and other noncontaminated flows prior to treatment; the removal of concentrated residues in the semidry state for disposal, thus eliminating flushing to the sewer; the reduction of water volumes by the use of automatic cutoffs on hoses and the use of spray rinses; and the substitution of chemical additives of a lower pollutional effect in processing operations. Institution of these practices has resulted in substantial reductions of wastewater volumes and strengths in many industries. As a result, reductions in unit pollutional loads may in some cases reduce the total pollution prior to treatment level even considering projected increased production, as shown in figure 2.

Perhaps the most fruitful area for waste reduction results

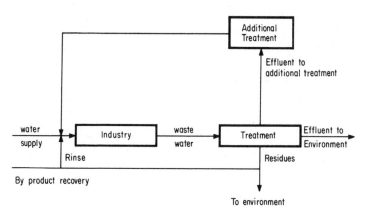

Fig. 1. Industrial water quality management alternatives

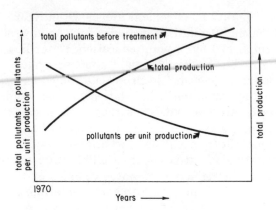

Fig. 2. Projected pollutional loads before treatment

from in-plant process changes. For example, changing the bleaching sequence in the pulp and paper industry and eliminating the caustic extraction stage results in a color reduction of 90 percent in the wastewaters. This process change results in a pulp of low strength and, therefore, has limited application.[2]

Substantial reductions in waste volume and strength have been achieved in the Timsfors Pulp Mill in Sweden.[3] Process modifications have included improved kraft pulp washing, reuse of the back water from the mechanical pulp mill in the kraft pulp washing. Waste constituents in this case are recovered in the kraft recovery system. Further waste reductions have been accomplished by the distillation and reuse of concentrated evaporator concentrates, the flocculation with alum of fibrous wastewaters

2. *The Cost of Clean Water and Its Economic Impact,* Vol. 4, *Projected Wastewater Treatment Costs in the Organic Chemicals Industry* (Pittsburgh: C. W. Rice & Co., 1969).

3. P. Ullman, *Planning a New Inland Kraft Pulp Mill* (Stockholm: International Congress on Industrial Wastewater, 1970).

and the reuse of the resulting sludge in the manufacture of low-grade papers. Wastes reductions in the pulp and paper industry in the United States in the order of 20 to 70 percent of paper machine wastewaters have been achieved by fiber recovery and wastewater reuse. Greater than 90 percent reduction has been achieved in wood preparation through water reuse.

Water reuse practices have markedly reduced the total wastewater effluent from the refining industry in the past twenty years.[4] For example, the total water used in petroleum refining from 1954 to 1964 increased 48.5 percent, for an average daily use of 16.8 billion gallons per day. The water intake, however, increased only 13.2 percent. This was accompanied by a crude capacity increase of 27 percent and a value added increase of 70 percent. Comparing the value added of 70 percent to a total water use increase of 48.5 percent shows that more product is being produced with less water use. This can be compared to statistics that show that, in 1955, 102 refineries used 324 gallons per barrel, which dropped in 1959 to 174 gallons per barrel. Projections would indicate that advanced technology could reduce this value still further to 50 gallons per barrel.

Since cooling is the major water use in refineries, advances in technology such as the use of air-cooled finned tube exchanges will substantially reduce water consumption and contaminant losses. Economic incentives are provided by the increased cost of wastewater treatment to high levels of water quality. Computer control of industrial processes should further reduce sewer losses.

The level of technology practiced in the industrial plant will have a profound effect on the volume and strength

4. *The Cost of Clean Water*, Vol. 3, Industrial Waste Profile No. 5, U.S. Dept. of the Interior, FWQA (Washington, 1968).

of wastewaters discharged from that plant. The flows and waste loading from pulp and paper and refining plants defined by three levels of technology, old, prevalent and new, are shown in table 1. The relative costs of achieving secondary treatment for each of these technologies for a kraft pulp and paper mill are shown in table 2. Comparisons of projected technology levels in the pulp and paper industry for 1963 and 1977 are shown in table 3. It is apparent that plant modernization will result in substantial savings in wastewater treatment costs. The comparison becomes more evident as higher levels of treatment are required.

From the foregoing it can be concluded that increases in industrial growth over the next decade may not substantially result in increased industrial wastewater loadings. Modernization of plant equipment should yield lower wastewater loads. Data relating wastewater flows and loadings to the level of industrial technology as shown above would indicate that the present loadings on a unit basis, i.e., gallons or pounds of BOD per unit production, would decrease in most industrial categories. In some cases

TABLE 1

COMPARATIVE WASTEWATER DISCHARGES FOR
VARIOUS LEVELS OF TECHNOLOGY

Type of Technology	Flow	B.O.D.
	gal/ton	*lbs/ton*
Bleached Kraft paper		
Prevalent	1.0	1.0
Older	2.45	1.65
Newer	0.56	0.75
Petroleum refineries	*gal/bbl*	*lbs/bbl*
Prevalent	1.0	1.0
Older	2.5	4.0
Newer	0.50	0.50

Source: *The Cost of Clean Water and Its Economic Impact*, vol. 3, Industrial Waste Profile Nos. 3 and 5, U.S. Dept. of the Interior, FWQA (Washington, D.C., 1968).

TABLE 2

RELATIVE COSTS OF TREATMENT (10 MGD)
OF PULP AND PAPER WASTES

Method	Cost
Primary	1.00
Aerated lagoon	1.84
Activated sludge without sludge disposal	3.20
Activated sludge with sludge disposal	4.90

Source: W. W. Eckenfelder and D. L. Ford, Economics of wastewater treatment, *Chemical Engineering*, 25 August 1969.

TABLE 3

PROJECTED NUMBER OF KRAFT PULP MILLS
AT VARIOUS LEVELS OF TECHNOLOGY

Technology Level	NUMBER OF MILLS 1963	NUMBER OF MILLS 1977
Older	24	6
Typical	68	48
Newer	8	46

Source: *The Cost of Clean Water and Its Economic Impact*, vol. 3, Industrial Waste Profile No. 3, U.S. Dept. of the Interior, FWQA (Washington, 1968).

the total waste load from an industry would show very little increase in spite of the projected growth of that industry. For example, in the pulp and paper industry, in 1968, the gross wastewater volume was 930×10^9 gallons and 2.71×10^9 lbs. of BOD, for an estimated annual production of 21,500,000 tons per year. Estimates for 1977 would indicate an increase in wastewater volume to $1,050 \times 10^9$ gallons per year and 3.21×10^9 lbs. of BOD per year, for an increased tonnage of 29,200,000 tons per year. This would indicate an increase in wastewater volume of 13 percent for an increase in tonnage of 35 percent. This reduction in unit wastewater quantity is shown in table 3.

Projections in the refining industry would indicate an increase in wastewater volume and BOD from 1968 to 1977 of 1.09×10^9 gallons per day to 1.18×10^9 gallons per day and 1.23×10^6 lbs. per day of BOD to 1.56×10^6 lbs. per day of BOD.

Wastewater Treatment Requirements

At the present time a majority of industrial plants have some form of primary treatment, a lesser number, some form of partial or complete secondary treatment. For example, in the pulp and paper industry, in 1967, 70 percent of the plants had some form of pre- or primary treatment and 35 percent of the plants, either partial or complete secondary treatment. Projections would indicate that, in 1977, 90 percent of the plants will have pretreatment or primary treatment and 85 percent of the plants, some form of secondary treatment.[5] In 1968 almost all of the petroleum refineries had gravity separators, with 5 to 10 percent having chemical treatment facilities. Approximately 25 percent of the plants had some form of biological treatment. It is estimated that, by 1977, virtually all refineries will have some form of biological treatment, including 55 percent with activated sludge plants. Through increased water quality restrictions it is estimated that 5 percent of the refineries will be employing tertiary treatment. The effluents attainable from present wastewater treatment processes are shown in table 4.

When considering projections for ten years it must be recognized that though present emphasis on wastewater treatment relates to BOD, suspended solids, and in some cases phosphorus and nitrogen (primary and secondary treatment), it is probable that in some parts of the United States higher degrees of treatment involving the removal of refractory organics and inorganic salts will be required. The former parameters are removed by conventional biological wastewater treatment processes, but the higher

5. Ibid.

TABLE 4

MAXIMUM EFFLUENT QUALITY
ATTAINABLE FROM WASTE TREATMENT PROCESSES
(MG / 1 UNLESS OTHERWISE NOTED)

Process	BOD	COD	SS	Nitrogen	Phosphorus	TDS
Sedimentation	10–30*	...	50–90*	...	...	...
Flotation	10–50*	...	70–95*	...	...	...
Activated sludge	<25	†	<20	‡	‡	...
Aerated lagoons	<50	...	>50	...	...	...
Anaerobic ponds	>100	...	<100	...	...	...
Carbon adsorption	<2	10	<1	...	...	...
Ammonia stripping	......	...	...	>95	...	...
Denitrification and nitrification	<10	...	...	<5	...	...
Chemical preparation	......	...	<10	...	<1	...
Ion exchange	......	...	<1	§	§	§

*Percent removal.
†(Influent COD) − (Ultimate BOD removed)/0.9
‡(Influent nitrogen) − (0.12 × excess biological sludge), lb.
(Influent phosphorus) − (.026 × excess biological sludge), lb.
§ Depends on resin used, molecular state, and efficiency desired.

levels of treatment projected require tertiary treatment
processes and marked modifications to existing wastewater
treatment technology, as indicated in table 4.

A number of studies have been reported relating the
cost of wastewater treatment to effluent quality. For
example, in the chemical industry the capital cost for a
3.2 mgd plant is estimated as $563,000 for primary treat-
ment, $2.24 million for secondary treatment, and $2.4
million to $5.3 million for tertiary treatment, depending
on the level of treatment desired. In projecting these figures
to the chemical industry it is estimated that in 1969, $82
million would be required to provide primary treatment,
$608 million to provide secondary treatment, and $650
to $1,370 million to provide tertiary treatment.[6] In 1973
these figures would increase to $253 million, $805 million,
and $860 million to $1,800 million respectively. The cost
of wastewater treatment as related to effluent quality

6. The Cost of Clean Water and Its Economic Impact.

for a kraft pulp and paper mill is shown in figure 3. It becomes apparent when considering these costs that water reuse must be considered in an economic optimization of the water quality management program. A study was conducted for a kraft pulp and paper mill relating water reuse to effluent quality and raw water costs. The resulting optimization is shown in figure 4. Effluent 1 in figure 4 employed primary sedimentation followed by an aerated lagoon. Effluent 2 employed activated sludge and Effluent

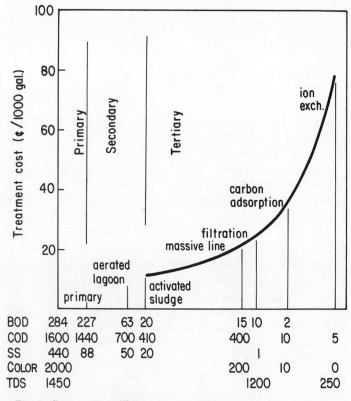

Fig. 3. Costs versus effluent characteristics

4 employed activated sludge followed by color reduction using chemical treatment. Since process water quality requirements dictate the degree of treatment that must be provided prior to reuse, the cost for fresh water can be directly compared to the cost required to achieve the degree of treatment required for reuse. Considering the multiple water uses in the mill, figure 4 makes an economic optimization of water use and reuse.

There is little doubt that water quality criteria will be upgraded in the future. Even if the existing water

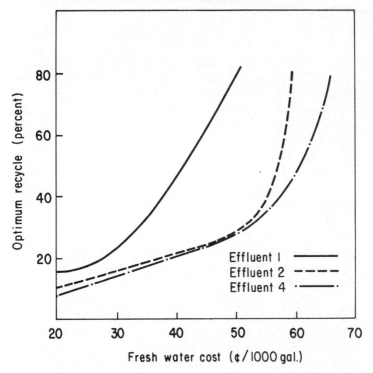

Fig. 4. Optimum recycle versus freshwater costs for varied effluent quality.

quality criteria are not upgraded, industrial and urban expansion in specific areas will require increased levels of treatment in order to maintain a specified water quality criteria. For example, one study in an urbanized area indicated that if an 85 percent treatment level were established for municipal and industrial wastewaters in 1967 resulting in a given water quality, to maintain this water quality industrial and municipal expansion would require a 95 percent level of treatment by 1980, and a 99 percent level of treatment by the year 2020. With regard to industrial wastewaters and the cost of wastewater treatment, it becomes apparent that the major emphasis in the future must be placed upon modifications and improvements in processing technology to reduce waste-water volumes and strength. Use of water and waste materials will become increasingly more attractive as the cost of disposal increases. As indicated in the pulp and paper example cited above, high levels of wastewater treatment appear increasingly advantageous for reuse of water and the recovery of by-products that it might not presently be economical to recover.

In many areas of the country there is an increasing emphasis on combined or joint wastewater treatment between industry and municipalities. Recent legislative changes provide for industry to pay a proportionate share of the capital and operating cost of the wastewater treat-ment facility. Most legislative bodies provide for pretreat-ment of industrial wastewaters to meet specified criteria acceptable to the combined wastewater treatment facility. The formula for charges is usually based both on the volume and characteristics of the wastewaters to be treated. Considering primary and secondary treatment, the primary criteria for costs are the volume, BOD, and suspended solids in the wastewater. In biological wastewater treat-ment facilities the reaction rate (the rate at which the wastewater is degraded in the treatment facility) is also an economic consideration. One formula that has been developed to define cost allocations for combined wastewater treatment facilities is:

$$\text{Cost}/\$1000 = 430\ Q^{0.84} + (110 + 37Q) \left(\frac{S_o}{200} - 1 \right)$$
$$+ (77 + 23Q) \left(\frac{SS}{200} - 1 \right)$$

in which Q is the wastewater flow in million gallons per day, S_o the wastewater BOD, and SS the wastewater suspended solids.

Consideration of the above equation indicates that wastewater volume reduction is the primary factor in reducing treatment costs and implies the economic advantages in industrial water reuse.

There is little doubt in the writer's mind that the next decade will see increased emphasis on combined treatment facilities in urban-metropolitan-industrial complexes. The newly formed Gulf Coast Waste Disposal Authority is an example of this type of organization.

Wastewater Treatment Technology

Although the majority of industrial plants have some form of pretreatment or primary treatment at present, a relatively small number provide secondary or tertiary treatment. The next five years will see emphasis placed on secondary treatment, with removal of suspended solids, biodegradable organics (BOD), oxidizable nitrogen, and phosphorus. Many states have already approved time schedules for completion of construction of secondary wastewater treatment in the next few years.

In cases where land area is available, lagoon systems, either aerated or unaerated, have been employed. These processes will provide a relatively high level of removal of BOD and suspended soilds (table 4) but are subject to a decrease in efficiency during the winter months. Nitrogen and phosphorus are not removed in these processes. The activated sludge process, with modifications, will effectively oxidize ammonia nitrogen and chemically precipitate phosphorus.

It is not economically feasible to achieve high effluent qualities from conventional biological treatment in cases where the organics in the wastewater are difficult to degrade or where the concentration of organics is high. A considerable research effort is presently being made to modify and improve biological processes with a view toward optimization of the process for specific applications. One example of this is multistaging of the process in order to take advantage of higher biological reaction rates in the initial stages. For example, in the treatment of a chemical wastewater with a requirement to reduce the BOD from 1,200 mg/l to 50 mg/l, a single-stage conventional process would require a residence period in the aeration basin of eighteen hours. By two-staging the process the residence time can be reduced to eight hours.

There have been several studies recently employing pure oxygen in the biological treatment process, thereby maintaining dissolved oxygen residuals in excess of 10 mg/l in the aeration basin. Some rather remarkable results have been achieved using this system treating high-strength organic industrial wastewaters. In one study treating a brewery waste, organic loadings to the process five to ten times higher than that obtainable with air have been successfully employed to yield the same effluent quality. Considerable research is still required to define the range of applicability of this process to industrial waste treatment. It would appear at this time that, depending on the cost of oxygen, the characteristics of the wastewater and the effluent quality desired that oxygen may provide substantial economic advantages and provide increased process stability in many cases.

It has previously been indicated that upgrading of water quality criteria in the future will require removal of constituents other than BOD, suspended solids, and nutrients. Color removal, particularly from pulp and paper mill wastewaters, refractory organics (COD), and inorganic salts will require partial or complete removal in many cases. The technology for effectively and economically removing these constituents is not well developed, and a major research effort by the federal government and industry is being expended in this direction. Color removal from pulp mill wastes can be accomplished by chemical precipitation with lime or alum; but the cost is high, and there are significant operating problems.[7] Absorption on carbon is feasible, and research efforts are being directed toward improving the economics of carbon use and regeneration. Recent studies by the Pulp and Paper Institute[8] on the use of reverse osmosis to concentrate the solids and recover water show some promise, but present projected costs are 75 cents to $1.00 per 1,000 gallons.

Physical-chemical treatment employing chemical coagulation followed by carbon adsorption is now being applied to the treatment of municipal wastewaters. Where biological treatment will reduce the BOD and suspended solids to 20 mg/1, the physical-chemical process will reduce the BOD to less than 5 mg/1 and the suspended solids to near zero. Economic projections would indicate that in many cases the cost of physical-chemical treatment compares favorably with biological treatment.

It is probably that physical chemical treatment or modifications such as a combination biological-physical chemical treatment for high strength wastewaters will prove

7. H. Gehn, *Color Reduction of Wastewater from Kraft Pulp Mills* (Stockholm: International Congress on Industrial Wastewater, 1970).

8. A. J. Wiley, *Progress in Developing Reverse Osmosis for Concentration of Pulp and Paper Effluents* (Stockholm: International Congress on Industrial Wastewater, 1970).

economically feasible for many industrial wastewaters, particularly if the effluent is reused in the industrial plant.

Summary

When one considers the cost of wastewater treatment as related to effluent quality coupled with the increasing effluent quality requirements, it becomes apparent that emphasis will be placed in the future on:

1. wastewater volume reduction and reuse;
2. by-product recovery;
3. modifications and improvements in processing technology to reduce wastewater volumes and strength.

Additional References

The Cost of Clean Water, Vol. 3, Industrial Waste Profile No. 3, U.S. Dept. of the Interior, FWQA (Washington, 1968).

W. W. Eckenfelder and D. L. Ford, Economics of wastewater treatment, *Chemical Engineering,* 25 August 1969.

S. Smith Griswold

chapter sixteen

CAN THE ENVIRONMENT BE PROTECTED UNDER CURRENT SOCIAL AND ETHICAL CODES?

The contamination of air, water, and land has occurred so gradually and the supply of these resources has seemed so inexhaustible that pollution has gone unnoticed and uncontrolled. Tremendous technological progress has been made in other parts of the economy, but until very recently, interest in pollution control has been largely theoretical and rhetorical. There has been little real action in the past half-century except for crash programs for the control of contagious diseases. The question that now concerns us is whether in the existing socioeconomic structure we can cope with the long-range complexities of a rapidly deteriorating natural environment in the face of continuously increasing population pressure.

Currently, with scarcely an exception, the quality of our air and water is progressively deteriorating in all urban areas, and in many cases at an accelerated rate. The cost of damage in the United States from air pollution alone is variously estimated, depending on the source, at 11 to 36 billion dollars.[1] This range of dollar estimates is wide because some estimates are based on strictly material elements alone and others give consideration to aesthetic values as well. To illustrate, let us say that a house with a view is worth more than the same house without a view. If the view or its natural beauty disappears, there is a deterioration of property value just as much as if there had been physical damage to the house. As another example, consider the case where one cannot work because of an attack of bronchial asthma or emphysema caused by air pollution. The disabling effects of air pollution could be evaluated in terms of a week-by-week payroll, but that is not considered by very many people as an adequate evaluation.

Set against the potential benefits of controlling pollution are the costs. The National Industrial Conference Board has estimated the industrial outlay for air and water pollution control equipment at about $300 million in 1969,[2] and this cost can be expected to rise each year along with the added operating and maintenance costs. Only in very rare instances can recovery of materials that pollute the air and water offset the cost of controls, or an appreciable part of that cost. However, these admittedly high costs are not prohibitive when considered in relation to final product output. Thus, the effect of adequate air pollution control for all of the emissions from steam electric power-plants together has been estimated by the National Air Pollution Control Administration to raise the cost of

1. Editor's note: L. B. Barrett and Thomas E. Waddell, "The Costs of Air Pollution Damages: A Status Report," U.S. National Air Pollution Control Administration, (July, 1970), p. 82, compute from a number of sources of damage a national total of approximately $16 billion.

2. Richard A. Hopkinson and Leonard Lund, "Growing Industrial Expenditures for Pollution Control," *The Conference Board Record*, Vol. 7, No. 2 (1970), pp. 53–56.

electric power by 1.3 mills per kilowatt-hour.[3] This should be compared with a national average production cost of 6 to 8 mills at the busbar for electric power production from large (over 300,000 kw) fossil fuel plants and a national average of 2 cents per kilowatt-hour for residential sales.[4] Thus, the 1.3 mills represents about a 6.5 percent increase in residential price. Basically, the thing I would like to bring out is that the cost of control in no way approaches the cost of air pollution, the cost of what it does, the cost that the public must pay without air pollution control.

Let us take a look at local situations. The air pollution problem in Los Angeles has been conceded to be the most serious in the nation. At least, it has been the most notorious. The county also has, in the opinion of those qualified to know, the most militant and sophisticated control program in the nation. It has very stringent air pollution regulations and strict enforcement in the courts, and it upgrades the regulations to keep pace with control technology. Since its inception in 1948 the control program has cost the taxpayers nearly $60 million.[5] Current expenditures are about 63 cents per capita annually.[6] However, the strictest regulation of industrial operations of the third-largest industrial complex in the country has over 22 years only required industry to spend $26 million in control equipment and $1.5 million in new basic equipment.[7] Today, industrial sources in Los Angeles are clean up to the limit of control technology, and industries are

3. "The Cost of Clean Air," Second Report of the Secretary of Health, Education, and Welfare to the Congress of the United States, U.S. Sen. Doc. 91–65, 91st Cong., 2d Sess. (April, 1970), p. 4.

4. "The Economy, Energy and the Environment," Joint Economic Committee, 91st Cong., 2d Sess. (September, 1970), Table 32.

5. Personal information.

6. Personal information.

7. Personal information.

still healthy, and industrial operations are continually expanding.

On the other hand, Steubenville, Ohio, for example, had spent little or nothing on air pollution control prior to a federal study in the mid-sixties to determine the comparative living costs in heavily populated Steubenville with those in relatively pollution-free Uniontown, Pennsylvania. In particulate matter, which is dirt in the air, Steubenville was twice as dirty as Uniontown, and the added per capita cleaning costs alone were $84 annually per family of four.[8] Other similar studies of other areas that take into account added health and other costs show an even greater differential.

We ask, then, why? If the effects of pollution are so much more expensive than the cost of control, why is not more being done to control it? The answers are reasonably apparent. Control of pollution upsets custom and usage. It requires extensive effort on the part of industry, the payoff from which is not immediately discernible. It requires an informed public demanding remedial action and willing to pay the price, because undoubtedly they are going to pay it through product prices and not in the very long run. It requires pressure by the mass media and those in the field of medicine. It requires government responsive to the public rather than to vested interests. It requires knowledge of complex, technical, socioeconomic, medical, and legal problems. It competes for funds to alleviate crime, poverty, and other much more visible urban ailments.

These answers raise the question I have been asked to discuss, "Can the environment be protected under current social and ethical codes?" Held to a yes or no answer I am mindful of twenty years of discussion on

8. I. Michelson and B. Tourin, U.S. Public Health Service Report, Vol. 81, No. 6 (1966), p. 505.

pollution of land, water, and air, of progress being made in technological applications, public interest, and financing. My answer is an unequivocal "No."

To evaluate the question and my answer, we must examine attitudes of three major sectors: the public, industry, and government. They are all polluters, and at the same time, they all share the responsibility for the control of pollution. Let us take the public first; that is all of us.

There is a general lack of knowledge and sustained interest that inhibits the public determination of its own needs and desires, the establishment of priorities, and the support of legislative and administrative officials. All too often the public does not know what it wants. Should pollution be reduced to levels that would assure the right of every individual to enjoy life, or is something less than this adequate? Additionally, public ardor for environmental enhancement tends to cool before the specter of expenditures in the multiple millions, which is to a degree understandable in the face of spiraling living costs. The public tends to react only to the purely personal nuisance—smoke from a backyard barbecue, incinerators next door or down the block, beer cans cast on the lawn, or filth in the favorite trout stream.

In other words, pollution in the public mind is almost always caused by someone else and is a part-time problem that someone else should do something about. Rarely do people understand that by actively pressing pollution control in their own activities, they enhance their power to control other sources of pollution. Participation in pollution control with its attendant inconvenience creates understanding of the problems and rights of others, which hopefully will in turn engender a desire to participate on a broader scope. One of the most effective directions this urge can take is the application of pressure upon legislators and control officials.

The kind of pressure that is necessary is illustrated by one organization that had more effect than any other in cleaning up Los Angeles. This was a group known as S.O.S., which means "Stamp Out Smog." It was made up largely of housewives. They went to every woman's club in town and said, "We know you ladies have too much to do to get involved in smog and air pollution, but we'd like to be your spokesmen on smog; just smog alone"; and they said, "We'll advise you what's going on and we'll send one of our members to every one of your meetings no matter when they happen. All we want is the right to say, when we appear before the Board of Supervisors, 'We are the Stamp Out Smog group of Los Angeles and we represent 535,000 women.'" That is impressive.

The private individual is at a very practical disadvantage in competing effectively with industry on environmental programs. Although there is political machinery to assure his right as an individual, more often than not he cannot afford the time and effort required to properly present his views. Real gains are made through concerned political leadership at the national, state, and local levels backed by the militant, sustained effort of service organizations such as the PTA, medical associations, women's clubs, veterans and labor groups, conservation groups, and the like. It is only when the public is informed, motivated, and organized, and aided by the mass media in exercising sustained pressure for pollution control that environmental problems can be resolved.

The importance to the public in electing legislative or administrative officials also cannot be overestimated. No person is elected to office without support either in money or in other campaign activities and at the polls, and he feels justified in voting with this support. He has little potential for becoming a potent source in environmental control unless he has been elected primarily by constituents who want an improved environment. The successful candidate who owes his election to office mainly to the financial support of corporate executives is likely to give little more than lip service to environmental problems. In the political arena money is always available to speak for the large industrial polluter.

Even if the finest legislation is enacted, a good law may be ineffectively implemented to a point where its accomplishment is less than that of a comparatively poor law diligently administered with imagination, incentive, and enthusiasm. Some jurisdictions in the United States that have promulgated the most stringent control laws and regulations have not experienced improvement in air quality because their legal tools are inept or they are inadequate as used by the control officials.

The potential of industry to design, fabricate, install, and operate control equipment or to clean up basic fuels is practically limitless. The question is one of desire and cost. Industry ordinarily abhors regulation and is thoroughly imbued with a theory of laissez faire. It feels a complete ability to cope with any problem as the need arises but, unfortunately, is not yet convinced that the hour of environmental need has come, nor is this conviction apt to be triggered by less than an environmental disaster in one or more major metropolitan areas.

Environmental control programs based on voluntary compliance do not work and will not work as long as the industrial sector is profit-motivated exclusively. A good example of this occurred in the area of Los Angeles. In one large area in the San Fernando Valley there were about twenty hot asphalt plants. Most of them would turn off the water at night in their hot asphalt scrubbers and would cut every corner; therefore, it was necessary to be policing them continuously. I mention this in connection with the ethics of industry. Industrial leaders like to talk about ethics, they often offer generosity in connection with welfare, but in their business life, for the most part, where air pollution is concerned, they are not really ready to evidence it.

In all fairness to industry, however, it should be pointed out that regulations should be equitable and uniform. Even those industrial organizations that recognize the increasing seriousness of environmental problems want assurance that the cost of their compliance will not place them at a competitive disadvantage with other businesses in their area or with areas bordering their markets. And willing compliance can hardly be expected if regulation is subject to such frequent change that expensive control equipment purchased to meet today's requirements will not meet those of tomorrow.

In saying this, I do not support industry's practice of, in effect, setting its own schedule for compliance with environmental regulation. This is managed through the structure of large national trade associations. National trade associations would not be in business if they did not reflect, and reflect militantly, the philosophy of their most recalcitrant member, the one that does not want to do a thing. They want him in the trade association; otherwise, they cannot watch him for other equally obnoxious practices.

Further, industry's leadership selection practices are tailored toward evading and postponing indefinitely the necessity for complying with environmental regulation. It is worth describing current management procedures for the new recruit. Typically, he is given a three- to six-months intensive orientation in the principles and philosophy of the industry. Then they take him, as a promising young man, out to a plant. This plant may be of many kinds, but one I remember most clearly was a recovery plant of a large aluminum firm, where they took old aluminum pots and pans and cigarette wrappers and oily industrial waste from threading screws and all that sort of thing, and melted it down in the furnace. They told him when he came in, "John Hitchcock was here before you for three years; he has a very fine record. We've sent him on up the line. We're sure he'll succeed in his next plant, and we're equally sure that you're going to succeed in our plant."

They had about ten reverbatory furnaces. There were no hoods on them, and all of the firebrick was falling out of them. But they gave him this thing to run, and he was to take care of his own problems. If he could not take care of his problems, the expense came out of his maintenance funds; and he was given a pitiful amount of maintenance funds each year. The plant was known as a profit center, and on this profit center depended the new recruit's future.

With this kind of a selection process, it is not surprising that plant managers stall and stall. Nothing ever happens unless there is legal action, and only then after several threats to move the plant out of town. I have been in the air pollution field for twenty years, and so far I have not seen one plant, except a business that burned the grease off old engine parts or the insulation off of copper cable, that would move anywhere, and they moved to the next town. They moved from there out to the desert, and finally they closed down on the desert.

Current trends will not be easy to reverse. There is general agreement in industry, and in the public and government sectors, that steps must be taken to improve the environment. The only question is when. Those who feel that a costly program cannot be undertaken during wartime and periods of inflation also feel it cannot be initiated during peacetime recession. And it cannot be initiated during periods of combined recession and inflation.

One thing is axiomatic. A bird cannot foul his nest indefinitely, and we have paid far too little attention to ours. We cannot afford to make the earth unlivable until we have somewhere else to go. Nothing but a team effort based on mutual understanding in all three sectors will reverse the current trend. Moderate sacrifice rather than unlimited selfishness must be the order of the day.

Michael McCloskey

chapter seventeen

REORGANIZING THE FEDERAL ENVIRONMENTAL EFFORT

The rhetoric of recent years has driven home a new awareness: that the earth's ecology cannot endure endless insult from man's technology and industry. If heedless abuse continues, the habitability of the planet may be jeopardized, and in any event, the quality of life will decline. This realization raises an obvious question: what do we do to forestall these dangers, particularly in the United States?

The dawning of the environmental decade has come with few helpful suggestions being put forward about what can be done in the immediate future, though many fundamental changes have been suggested, ranging from changes in life style, to lowering the standard of living, to abolishing capitalism, to overthrowing the industrial revolution. Those who want to move now to try to cope pragmatically with the problem are left wondering where their energies can be most usefully employed.

Federal Focus for Reorganization

Despite a growing skepticism about the efficacy of federal action, I would like to argue that the federal government should be a prime target in any program of environmental action, though not an exclusive one. The federal government must be a focus for remedial action because so many environmental problems are national in scope, reflecting as they do the integrated nature of the nation's economy. Federal pressure, for instance, on detergent formulas can produce quick results, whereas no state can have a comparable effect, and consumer boycotts may take years to generate sufficient market pressure. Moreover, often only the federal government has the power, as a huge institution, to cope effectively with huge industries. In seeking remedies, it is vital to employ institutions which have the inherent power to prevail. In addition, many environmentally objectionable programs emanate from the federal government, programs such as the SST. Remedial efforts must be directed at the federal government to curb and redirect these programs. Finally, while it is no easy task to move the federal government, effort invested in this task may yield the greatest results in terms of time and energy expended. It is often just as hard, if not harder, to persuade state and local government and private industry to act as it is the federal government. For the effort expended, a success at the federal level can yield far greater results, inasmuch as national patterns, rather than limited, local ones, are affected. Also, the obstacles in the way of success at the federal level are usually fewer: the power of commercial opponents is more diluted at the national level; a nationally organized media tends to be sympathetic; and there are many forces at the federal level that welcome additions to their power.

Complaints about the inefficiency and obstinacy of the federal bureaucracy often overlook certain facts. The federal performance often leaves something to be desired because contradictory instructions are given the bureaucracy. For instance, Congress has asked the Corps of Engineers to dredge wetlands, the Soil Conservation Service to fill them, and the Bureau of Sport Fisheries to preserve them.[1] It is no wonder that progress seems slow. There is no agreement on the goal. Moreover, the bureaucracy often fails to move forcefully because different administrations keep shifting emphasis between moving cautiously and quickly, and Congress often fails to provide the funding to carry out instructions.[2] In short, the public is often not clear in its resolve and expectations when it establishes bureaucracies. Finally, many problems which are given to agencies to solve are inherently intractable. Quite often no consensus exists about what should be done, and much of the knowledge and expertise that is needed simply does not exist. Often an agency is simply directed to gather data, to make grants to have the problem studied, and to develop demonstration projects. This is particularly true in the environmental field, and is also a characteristic pattern in dealing with social problems. On the other hand, when clear goals are assigned, adequate funding is provided, and sufficient expertise is available, bureaucracies can be very efficient. We become acutely aware of this when we oppose the program of an agency, as with much of what the Corps of Engineers does. We tend then to complain about its excessive efficiency and call it "narrow

1. Cf. 16 U.S.C. §§ 590h, 715a to k-3 (1970); 33 U.S.C. §§ 540–41(1970).

2. In fiscal year 1969, for instance, appropriations fell $974.2 million short of authorized levels for solid waste disposal ($15.3 million), air pollution control ($96.3 million), land acquisition through the Land and Water Fund ($95.5 million), highway beautification ($26.1 million), sewage treatment plants ($468 million), and water and sewage grants ($225 million). See Citizens Advisory Committee on Environmental Quality, Report to the President and to the President's Council on Environmental Quality, August 1969, Appendix B.

and mission-oriented." The problems, thus, with the federal government often are not inherent, but reflect public confusion, indecision, and at times, impossibly high hopes.

In continuing to look to the federal government for solutions many environmentalists are fully aware of the pitfalls and the disappointments that are inevitable. They are not expecting miracles or instant solutions. They are, however, determined to make progress. They know some efforts will fail, while others will succeed in varying degrees. Just as reformers working on previous problems have been pragmatic in being willing to try various approaches, so also are many environmentalists. They have promoted a multitude of programs and agencies, which are as confusing in their own way as the alphabet of agencies of the 1930's.

Some feel this confusion suggests that environmentalists should be more concerned with questions of reorganization among agencies. The question is often asked: How should the federal government best be reorganized to meet the environmental crisis? What institutions are needed to maintain a tolerable balance between nature and man's works, and how should they be organized? To date, environmentalists have shown little interest in these concerns. For the past decade they have been more interested in developing basic programs and agencies than they have been in ideal arrangements of agencies. In a pragmatic manner, they have been trying to fashion effective new instruments from the materials at hand, which often are older agencies being given broader assignments, such as the Public Health Service, which initially was given the task of abating both air and water pollution.

Until recently, environmentalists have been somewhat skeptical of massive reorganization proposals for a number of reasons. For one thing, these proposals often were suspected of being offered as a panacea that they could not be. In promising to rearrange agencies, they offered the illusion of forceful action but often the benefits were hard to detect. Quite typically the problem has been more lack of authority and funding than the departmental location of an agency. A reshuffling of agencies might disrupt efficiency as much as it would improve it. Moreover, some of the talk about reorganization seemed to come from those who had a vested interest. One of the most outspoken advocates of a Department of Natural Resources made it clear that his motive was to get the Corps of Engineers and the Bureau of Reclamation together so they could build bigger water projects. He wanted to engraft the budget of the Corps onto that of the Bureau so that it could acquire the financing needed to build the North American Water and Power Alliance aqueduct from Canada.[3] Clearly, too, the Secretary of Interior has a vested interest in seeking to expand his department, but such expansions do not necessarily work in the best interests of the environment. Finally, environmentalists have not been too interested in the proposals of political scientists who have approached reorganization on a mechanistic basis, devoid of commitments to policy goals. Considerations of symmetry in structure and functionally related grouping have not seemed compelling enough to be worth pursuing for their own sake. In short, until recently there has been no real constituency for reorganization.

A number of factors are now causing environmentalists to take a closer look at questions of governmental organization. Foremost among these factors is the heightened sense of urgency with which the environmental movement has been imbued by the basic questions of survival that have surfaced in the last few years (this heightening is evident in the progression of phrases that have been the watchwords for the movement during the past decade:

3. Senator Frank Moss of Utah has long been advocating reorganization for this purpose; see S. 27, 93d Cong., 1st Sess. (1973).

it began with emphasis on outdoor recreation, shifted in the mid-sixties to natural beauty, shifted again a few years later to environmental quality, and now focuses on survival and ecology). Concern with survival demands that all useful reforms should be pursued, including reorganization. Moreover, enough experience has been accumulated with various agencies and programs to suggest that reorganization may be more helpful than previously thought. First, more environmental agencies exist now than before, and problems of interrelationships are becoming more intricate. Second, as some agencies have grown, the problems of inappropriate departmental location have become more acute, as in the case of the Federal Water Quality Administration, which has been moved three times in five years, and is now in the Environmental Protection Agency. Third, as progress has been made in solving problems of authority and funding, environmentalists are now better able to turn their attention to questions of organization. Fourth, new agencies are coming into existence that cannot find logical and hospitable housing within any existing department. The Environmental Protection Agency is an example; it was finally established as an independent agency. As more new agencies come along, it will become increasingly critical that problems of organizational structure be solved. The new agencies have to be put somewhere where they can thrive.

Recommendations

While there has been a modicum of interest in environmental restructuring throughout the 1960's, interest began to quicken in 1969. A number of major reorganizational bills were introduced in Congress at that time, the principal ones by Senator Henry Jackson, Senator Edmund Muskie, and Representative John Dingell. One close observor identified three main focal points of attention at that time:

"(1) declaration of a national policy for the environment; (2) establishment of a high-level council for surveillance, review, and reporting on the state of the environment; (3) reorganization of the executive departments for more effective coordination and administration of environmental policy."[4] These concerns were supplemented by interest in improving the tools of Congressional action also, and in widening the opportunities for action in the courts.

In just a few years considerable progress has been made on this agenda. With the passage of the National Environmental Policy Act of 1969,[5] a comprehensive statement of environmental policy has been set forth for all federal activity. While this policy is not self-executing, it is important in setting a goal to which all other efforts can in theory relate. The question of compatibility of goals, however, is ducked; it remains to be seen, for instance, whether the Full Employment Act of 1946[6] can be compatible in practice with the National Environmental Policy Act of 1969. Under the National Environmental Policy Act, the goal is stated to be establishing a state of productive harmony between man and nature.[7] Among other things, this state includes achieving a balance between population numbers and resources, preserving diversity in the environment and key elements in our national heritage, and assuring that people's surroundings are safe, healthful, productive, and pleasing.[8] Moreover, the Act declares that it is the policy of the federal government to secure such an environment for our citizens,

4. L. Caldwell, *Environment: A Challenge for Modern Society* (1970), p. 217.

5. 42 U.S.C.A. § 4332 (Supp. 1973).

6. 15 U.S.C. §§ 1021–25 (1970).

7. 42 U.S.C.A. §§ 4331(a) (Supp. 1973).

8. Id. § 4331 (b).

and that they in turn have a responsibility to contribute to its maintenance.[9] Further national goals are defined as the wide sharing of amenities, the avoidance of actions with undesirable and unintended consequences, recycling of depletable resources, and acceptance of the obligations of trusteeship for future generations.[10] While it is still too early to ascertain ultimately how much effect this policy will have on federal programs, agencies are having to take notice of it because of an action-forcing mechanism joined to it. This mechanism[11] consists of a requirement that all agencies proposing legislation, or contemplating major action significantly affecting the quality of the human environment, must file an advance statement furnishing information on environmental impact. This statement is to include data on unavoidable adverse effects, alternatives, comparison of local impact, short-term and long-term effects, and irreversible or irretrievable commitments being made. A flood of lawsuits has been brought by citizen groups to force dilatory agencies to file these statements,[12] and many are now being criticized for their self-serving and conclusionary character.[13] Many of these statements attempt to comply with the statute by merely asserting that the adverse effects are minimal, that no reasonable alternatives exist, that no long-term drawbacks will develop, and that similarly no irreversible commitments are being made.

This action-forcing mechanism will fail to achieve its

9. Id. § 4331 (c).

10. Id. §§ 4331 (a)-(b).

11. Id. § 4332 (c).

12. See, e.g., Sierra Club v. Froehlke, 345 F. Supp. 440 (W.D. Wis. 1972).

13. See 1 *Environmental L. Digest* 52.0 (1970). A discussion of current problems in securing full compliance with § 102(2)(c) of the Act can be found in chapter 1 of the Third Annual Report of the Council on Environmental Quality, August 1972.

purpose unless federal agencies are required to comply fully and thoughtfully. While federal agencies are not required in their reports to show that adverse impacts will be minimal, they are required to comply with the general policy of the Act, to the extent permitted under their present statutory authorities. To the extent they cannot, they were required to notify the President no later than July 1, 1971.[14]

Oversight of this policy was vested by the National Environment Quality Act in the Council on Environmental Quality, a three-man Council housed in the Executive Office of the President.[15] This Council was given the surveillance and review functions.[16] It assesses the state of the environment and the adequacy of federal programs.[17] It is also to foster ecological research.[18] Already it is evident that this Council does not have the powers necessary to perform its work. When legislation to establish this Council was being considered, environmentalists proposed that the Council be given authority to veto federal actions inconsistent with the policy of the Act. This was regarded as too large a step to be taken at once. It was said that the Council would have to prove itself first, and that in any event it would have the ear of the President, who instead could be persuaded to veto the action. Nevertheless, the lack of any rejection authority is turning the requirement of environmental impact reports into a hollow gesture. The Council must be given clear authority, at the very least, to reject inadequately prepared reports. It is now relying on persuasion alone to have poor reports redone, and it is not even willing to let the public see

14. 42 U.S.C.A. § 433 (Supp. 1973).
15. Id. § 4342.
16. Id. § 4344.
17. Id.
18. Id.

many of these.[19] The Council was given a clearer mandate to coorinate federal environmental programs by the Environmental Quality Improvement Act of 1970,[20] but it still does not have authority to keep agencies from violating the National Environmental Policy Act.[21] These violations are not an academic possibility. In the second session of the 91st Congress, the Corps of Engineers forwarded requests for authorization of 45 projects for which no environmental reports were prepared.[22] The Council was not able to stop the Corps.

Not only does the Council lack sufficient authority, it also has been denied the funding and staffing it is authorized. Ultimately, many environmentalists would like to see the Council become the traffic regulator of federal environmental activity. In the environmental field, it should perform functions analogous to those of the Office of Management and Budget. Moreover, some feel it should assume ombudsman functions. It could have a division which hears public complaints and tries to find the source of a problem and develop solutions through a combination of persuasion and statutory power. In an Executive Order implementing the Policy Act,[23] the President gave the Council authority to hold public hearings. This power might be used to begin to develop functions of this sort.

In the summer of 1970, the President, following sugges-

19. In mid-November 1970 the Council took the position that only "final" reports were public documents and announced that it was reserving the right to keep reports that were being revised from being released. Environmentalists protested this action on the grounds that the Act makes no distinction between preliminary and final reports and that the public ought to be able to participate in the process of critiquing reports when they are first submitted.

20. 42 U.S.C.A. §§ 4371–74 (Supp. 1973).

21. Id. § 4372.

22. See, e.g., Tupling, "Washington Report," *Sierra Club Bulletin* 31 (October 1970).

23. 3 C.F.R. 903 (Comp. 1966–1970).

tions of his Advisory Council on Executive Organization (the Ash Council), acted under his reorganization powers to effect a massive reshuffling in the Executive Branch of agencies with environmental responsibilities. Two new super agencies were created: the Environmental Protection Agency,[24] which was made an independent agency, and the National Oceanic and Atmospheric Agency,[25] which was placed within the Department of Commerce. While there was some congressional opposition to placing the National Oceanic and Atmospheric Agency in the Commerce Department, no congressional veto was asserted, and both reorganization plans went into effect.[26]

The National Environmental Protection Agency, a comprehensive pollution control agency, is charged with identifying harmful pollutants, setting allowable exposures and devising programs of prevention and abatement.[27] Thus, its activities include research, monitoring, standard-setting, and enforcement. It drew together pollution control activities from many departments: water pollution control from the Department of the Interior, air pollution control from Health, Education, and Welfare, and radiological control from the Atomic Energy Commission and the Federal Radiation Council.

In contrast to the Council on Environmental Quality, which is an oversight agency, the Environmental Protection Agency is an operating agency. It is to actually perform the work of combatting pollution.

While most environmentalists applauded the creation of the Environmental Protection Agency, it is too early

24. Id. at 1072.

25. Id. at 1076.

26. See Council on Environmental Quality, *Environmental Quality: The First Annual Report of the Council on Environmental Quality*, August 1970, Appendixes H, I, and J.

27. 3 C.F.R. 1072 (Comp. 1966–1970).

to assess its success. Some of the Environmental Protection Agency's arms have only recently received the operating authority they need. It took action by the 91st and 92d Congresses to complete action on a package of legislation to overhaul basic water and air pollution statutes to give both its air and water pollution control agencies authority to set federal standards on intrastate as well as interstate activities, and to set emission and effluent standards, with stricter enforcement.[28] Also, basic legislation to control noise pollution has just been enacted.[29] Moreover, no real programs yet exist to deal with pollution caused by heavy metals and other toxic substances, though legislation in this subject will undoubtedly be before the 93d Congress.[30] Finally, it remains to be seen whether the Environmental Protection Agency will be successful in coordinating its constituent agencies. For instance, the Environmental Protection Agency must assure that an industrial plant that is prevented from passing its effluents into the air does not instead put them in nearby waters.[31] However, establishment of the Environmental Protection Agency does put the agencies with related purposes in closer proximity to each other, and the top leadership of the agency will have only one purpose—pollution control—and will not be diverted by other programs.

While establishment of the National Oceanic and Atmospheric Agency was regarded as a logical step by environmentalists, many objected to it being placed in the Commerce Department. The ostensible reason for housing it there was that its largest component agency

28. 33 U.S.C. § 1151 (1970); 42 U.S.C. §§ 1857–58 (1970); 49 U.S.C. §§ 1421, 1430 (1970).

29. 49 U.S.C. § 1301 (1970).

30. See S. 1187, 92d Cong., 2d Sess. (1972); H.R. 5267, 92d Cong., 2d Sess. (1972); H.R. 5390, 92d Cong., 2d Sess. (1972).

31. 3 C.F.R. 1072 (Comp. 1966–1970).

already was in Commerce, the Environmental Services Administration, which includes the Weather Bureau and the Coast and Geodetic Survey among its better known bureaus. Other agencies which have gone into the National Oceanic and Atmospheric Agency include the Bureau of Commercial Fisheries from Interior, parts of Interior's Bureau of Sport Fisheries (marine sport fish program), the marine minerals program of the Bureau of Mines, and various research bodies in the Department of the Navy and Army. For the most part, the National Oceanic and Atmospheric Agency's functions are research and data collection.[32] Environmentalists believe the real purpose of this is to promote commerce, accelerate offshore mineral production, and exploitation of fishery stocks. While the President has directed[33] that the National Oceanic and Atmospheric Agency maintain close liaison with the Environmental Protection Agency and the Council on Environmental Quality, environmentalists fear that ecological constraints will be largely absent from the National Oceanic and Atmospheric Agency's outlook. They feel prime attention should be given to conserving the ocean's productivity and quality, rather than to promoting its development. The present placement of the National Oceanic and Atmospheric Agency, thus, cannot be regarded as a final solution.

Remaining Action

In light of the President's major re-organizational actions in 1970, it is now logical to ask: what remains to be done? Actually, a great deal still remains to be accomplished, though major steps have been taken. In broad outline,

32. Id. at 1076.
33. Address by Richard M. Nixon, Joint Session of Congress, 15 February 1973.

the following probably constitutes an agenda for further reform in the executive branch and related areas: (1) environmentally irresponsible agencies need to be controlled; (2) regulatory commissions need to be reconstituted; (3) more new control agencies need to be created; and (4) a new super-department probably should be established.

In bringing new agencies into existence, one does worry about a top-heavy bureaucracy. Less new bureaucracy might be needed if some of the older agencies were disbanded, or had their programs curtailed. This is particularly true with respect to agencies such as the Corps of Engineers, the Bureau of Reclamation, the Bureau of Public Roads, the Federal Aviation Administration, and others whose programs produce the most traumatic impacts on America's ecosystems. Some of these agencies should just have their appropriations trimmed back, while others should have major programs abolished, such as the channelization program of the Corps of Engineers and the Soil Conservation Service.[34] Perhaps the Corps could be usefully redirected to build sewage treatment plants, and the Bureau of Public Roads could be assigned the task of constructing rapid transit systems. In any event, care should be exercised in trying to reassign these agencies to other departments. This should only be done in such a manner that a new mission is given the agency. Otherwise, the reassignment may merely create the illusion of reform without any real change in statutory direction.

One of the saddest results of reform efforts that began almost a century ago is that regulatory commissions have failed largely to protect the public interest. Whether by happenstance or design, these commissions have tended, on the whole, to be lethargic at best, and at worst to be instruments of those very interests the commissions

34. See Report of the National Water Commission, November 1972 (recommends curtailments).

are supposed to regulate. The Federal Power Commission, the Federal Trade Commission, and the Atomic Energy Commission all exhibit these symptoms, as Ralph Nader's investigations[35] have revealed. Not only are the commissions afflicted with a fatal sympathy for promoting the business of their charges, but the judicial stance they have adopted has caused them to avoid taking affirmative and aggressive action to protect the public interest. Rather than seeking to be the advocate of the public, they wait for the public to show up to plead its case. If these commissions are to be reformed, some way must be found to make it difficult for commercial interests to capture control of them. One way may be to expand the size of the commissions and to disperse the power to appoint their members among so many elements in society that the commercial interests involved cannot possibly capture all these elements. One of the great innovations of the new approach to conservation embodied in the San Francisco Bay Conservation and Development Commission was the dispersal of the appointing power: some of the seats are appointed by federal agencies, some come from state agencies; some are appointed by the Legislature; some by the Governor; and some by the affected cities and counties. This approach might be tried at the federal level.

The creation of the National Environmental Protection Agency has raised a basic question about environmental responsibility in this country. If we are to achieve the goals set forth in the Act, all elements in society will have to conform to acceptable modes of conduct. Yet, the Act only sets standards of conduct, and weak ones at that, for federal agencies. Why should these same standards

35. See, e.g., R. Fellmeth, *Nader Report on the Federal Trade Commission* (1971); J. Turner, *The Chemical Feast: The Ralph Nader Study Group Report on Food Protection and the Food and Drug Administration* (1970).

not be applicable to the states and to all private parties? The environment can be equally damaged by a facility built by the federal government, state government, or private industry. Ultimately, it will be necessary that all activity having a significant impact on the environment be regulated. Legislation should be enacted to make the National Environmental Policy Act applicable to all industries that send products into interstate commerce or pollutants across state lines. A new regulatory agency should be established to license plants, products, and advertising to assure that they are environmentally safe. To get a license, a firm should have to show that the place it wants to put its factory is suitable—that no rare or indigenous species will be destroyed, for example; that its products will not have side effects, nor release ubiquitous substances such as polychlorinated biphenals into the atmosphere. Presently, utility plants are licensed by many states. Why shouldn't chemical plants also be licensed, to cite just one example? Presently, foodstuffs and drugs are tested for safety. Why should other products not also have to pass standards of environmental safety?

If such a new agency is brought into being to regulate industrial operations, one immediately faces the question of where it should be put. Certainly, it should not be put in the Commerce Department, as its purposes are inimical to those of Commerce. Clearly, it is related in general purpose to the Environmental Protection Agency, yet its functions go beyond pollution prevention. It would be concerned with questions of siting, land use, and consumer safety as well. In addition, a number of proposals have been made to establish an agency to prepare and coordinate energy planning in the United States. Inasmuch as energy planning must be keyed to environmental constraints, such as pollution controls, land planning, and conservation of scarce resources, this agency would appear to be linked with the others.[36] This same problem will arise if other new environmental agencies, which are under discussion, also are created. Senator Henry Jackson is advocating a bill to establish a national land use policy.[37] It would set federal standards in this field and require states to prepare statewide land use plans. The plans would have to designate areas to be reserved as open space and hopefully would identify areas of fragile ecology. A new federal agency would be needed to oversee the adequacy of these plans. Senator Jackson has proposed establishment of an office of Land Use Policy Administration in the Department of the Interior as a new agency that would take on this work. Similarly, Senator Philip Hart is proposing legislation[38] to provide greater federal control over the generation of electrical power and the location of plants and transmission lines. Under his bill, a new agency would be created to certify that state plans for siting power plants are in conformance with federal standards. It is not clear where this new agency would be housed, though the Nixon administration has proposed that it be in the Interior Department. A whole division for energy and mineral resources has been proposed there under the Ash Commission's reorganization scheme.[39]

The best answer to the question of where these new agencies should be housed would appear to be establishment of a new Department of Environmental Affairs. In the past, many proposals have been advanced for a Depart-

36. See S. 3802, 92d Cong., 2d Sess. (1972). See also S. 70, 93d Cong., 1st Sess. (1973).

37. See S. Rep. No. 92–809, 92d Cong., 2d Sess. (1972). See also S. 3600, 92d Cong., 2d Sess. (1972).

38. S. 363, 92d Cong., 2d Sess. (1972).

39. See Second Annual Report of the Council on Environmental Quality, August 1971, p. 7.

ment of Conservation, a Department of Natural Resources, a Department of Environment and Population, and the like.[40] These proposals have all met with an apathetic response because they did not respond to any clear need. Most of these involved relabeling the Department of the Interior and giving it additional agencies. Basically, the Interior Department is designed to house agencies managing federal lands and promoting development of natural resources. No important function is served by changing its name, though some agencies might be logically relocated there, such as the Forest Service and the Soil Conservation Service from the Department of Agriculture, and the Corps of Engineers.[41] However, enough problems arise out of these shifts to make it questionable as to whether there is any net environmental gain. In any event, the Interior Department's scope and traditions are clearly too limited to make it a logical base for broader environmental activity.

A Department of Environmental Affairs could be built around the Environmental Protection Agency. In addition to the Environmental Protection Agency, it could also include the National Oceanic and Atmospheric Agency, and the four new agencies I have just discussed: those dealing with land planning, power plant siting, energy planning, and environmental control of industrial operations. The latter agency might also be put in charge of recycling programs. In addition to these, some of the population control functions of the Department of Health, Education, and Welfare, which Congress extended in the 91st Congress, might be better located in the new Depart-

40. For a discussion of the case for such a department, see Moss, "Wilderness and the Proposed Federal Department of Natural Resources," in M. McCloskey and J. Gilligan, eds., *Wilderness and the Quality of Life* (1969), p. 170.

41. It now appears the president may try to establish such a department through executive action under the Executive Reorganization Act. See *Washington Star and Daily News*, 15 December 1972, at A-14, col. 1.

ment.[42] While research and instruction on family planning might stay in the Department of Health, Education, and Welfare, research on population levels and general education on the relationship of population to environment might be better housed with other environmental programs.

In addition to the agencies just mentioned, another new agency might be established to aid all of those in the department. This would be a branch of field legal services, similar to the Rural Legal Assistance effort in the poverty program. This branch could provide lawyers at public expense who would act as public defenders to make sure environmental concerns are not slighted by public and private interest alike.

Creation of a Department of Environmental Affairs would serve a number of real needs. It would encourage the formation of needed new agencies by offering a logical place to house them. It would provide an impetus for moving the National Oceanic and Atmospheric Agency out of the Commerce Department, where it is likely to be given undesirable direction. It would provide an improved mechanism for coordinating environmental programs in an hospitable atmosphere. And it would provide a strengthened and unified influence for sound environmental policy in the federal government.

Congressional Reorganization

If many environmental programs are unified in one department, this would argue strongly for also restructuring the manner in which Congress oversees these programs. Presently, environmental legislation is handled by a plethora of committees: Interior, Commerce, Public Works, Government Operations, and Labor and Welfare in the Senate; Public Works, Interior, Merchant and Marine

42. Act of 16 March 1970, Pub. L. No. 91–213, §§ 2–9, 84 Stat. 67.

Fisheries, Interstate and Foreign Commerce, Government Operations, and Science and Astronautics in the House. The Joint Committee on Atomic Energy is also involved, and of course the Appropriations Committees in both houses fund all operating programs. The picture is further complicated by a variety of subcommittees.[43] Legislation[44] has been passed twice but never reported from conferences to establish a Joint Congressional Committee on Environment and Technology to bring key members of both houses together to oversee this burgeoning field of concern. While this committee will afford a better look at the whole picture, it cannot initiate legislation. This will remain the prerogative of the standing subject committees. It seems increasingly doubtful that these subject committees can continue to provide the kind of leadership and support that strong environmental programs will need. In each instance, the committee's main work is in other areas, with the possible exception of the Interior Committees. Environmental legislation should not be the step-child of all of Congress's committees. As environmental programs in the executive branch become increasingly complex and inter-related, Congress will find itself under growing pressure to establish major standing committees on the environment. Such committees would provide a parallel structure to the Department of Environmental Affairs that I have suggested and could oversee all programs connected with it.

Improved Redress in the Courts

Even if all the restructuring I have just described should take place, environmental problems are not likely to be

43. See Muskie, "Environmental Jurisdiction in the Congress and the Executive," 1 *Environment L. Rev.* 141, 146 (1970). See also R. Cooley and G. Wandesforde-Smith, eds., *Congress and the Environment* (1970), pp. 229–33.

44. S.J. Res. 17, 92d Cong., 1st Sess. (1971); H.R.J. Res. 3, 92d Cong., 1st Sess. (1971); H.J.R. Res. 1117, 91st Cong., 2d Sess. (1970).

completely solved. Some agencies will fail to perform as directed, and some polluters will escape governmental detection. A strong role remains for private action, and particularly private action in the courts. In the field of public law, the standing of private groups to act as private attorneys general needs to be clearly affirmed. While this novel doctrine—which permits private citizens to seek judicial help in holding agencies to standards of lawful conduct—has been growing in recent years, it is under a cloud of sorts as a result of a recent holding of the Supreme Court in *Sierra Club v. Morton*.[45] While the Supreme Court did make it clear that non-pecuniary interests provide a sufficient basis for standing in litigation, it continued the requirement that litigants in fact suffer a direct injury. Thus, it turned away from adopting a full doctrine of private attorneys general that would have set forth a clear basis for citizen access to the courts.[46] For only with such access can citizens hold agencies to the intent of the statutes that they can persuade Congress to pass. Legislation, moreover, is pending to give citizens a new cause of action against polluters. The Hart-McGovern Bill[47] would allow citizens to file actions against polluters without having to show personal injury, and they could obtain injunctive relief. Citizens' right to an environment free of unreasonable impairment would be affirmed, and they would have clear standing to sue in a representative capacity in a new type of class action. Similar legislation has already been enacted in the state of Michigan.[48]

Finally, many believe the kinds of goals embodied in the National Environmental Policy Agency and the Hart-McGovern Bill should be clearly established as basic rights.

45. 405 U.S. 727 (1972).
46. Id.
47. S. 1032, 92d Cong., 2d Sess. (1972).
48. See Mich. Stat. Ann.§ 14.528 (202) (1971).

They are calling for amendment of the Constitution to provide a Bill of Environmental Rights that will give birth to a new body of protective case law. Without such a new Bill of Rights, they point to the following paradox:

> Our old freedoms are being eroded without due process. Without any court order, any finding of fact, or any weighing of values, our health, our security, our freedom, and our privacy are being taken. These unauthorized takings of singleminded technologists are unilateral, arbitrary, and private usurpations. If society should in some instance decide that any taking is warranted, that decision should be made by open, fair, and public processes.
>
> And society should also draw lines around the nucleus of environmental rights. Certain rights should be invulnerable—inalienable. Just as nature's law of limits fixes the tolerances needed for life, our laws also should set environmental limits beyond which society cannot intrude, no matter what the excuse. While it may take time for the courts to find and fix those limits, clearly there must come a point where mass institutions are to be restrained from poisoning people any further with effluents, additives, insecticides, and smog.
>
> We may be able to discover the seeds of the new rights we need within the meaning of our old Bill of Rights. But the important thing is that they be set forth and established now: the right to be free from uninvited assault by noxious and annoying substances; the right to be undisturbed by uninvited sounds; the right to be unregimented and uncrowded; the right to have nature's presence accessible and to have its most vivid and vital expressions undefiled; the right to have representative biological communities survive and to have the best soils conserved; the right to live as part of a healthy ecosystem.
>
> In short, we need a Bill of Environmental Rights that will make continued life possible.[49]

Such a Bill of Rights could be an inspiration for all our environmental institutions and would assure that the

49. McCloskey, "A Bill of Environmental Rights," in *No Deposit No Return*, ed. H. Johnson (1970), p. 269.

high purpose that brought them into existence could not be neglected with impunity. Our citizens would know their rights and would demand that they be guaranteed.

Index to Authors Cited

Subject Index

Academic role: in environmental affairs, 2–4, 53–54, 57–58
Administrative problems: in pollution control, 252–59
Air pollution: damage estimates of, 277–78; experience with control of, in Los Angeles, 279–85; meteorological effects of, 70–90; policy for control of, 208–10
Air Quality Act of 1967, 115. *See also* Clean Air Act of 1970
Amishland: as example of congestion, 100–101
Ash Council (Advisory Council on Executive Organization), 297, 303
Atmosphere: man's impact on, 70–90

Bill of Environmental Rights, 308
Biological necessities, 21
Biological systems, 17, 28–37. *See also* Ecosystems
Birth control techniques, 107–10, 231–34

Birthrate. *See* Population
Birth tickets: as means of population control, 231–32

Cities of the future: location of, 145; man and nature in, 197–202; social environment in, 192–97. *See also* Urban areas; Environment
Clean Air Act of 1970, 116
Cloud formation: affected by pollution, 76–88
Clouds, artificial, 70–72; produced by power plants, 83
Cloud seeding, 71–74
Commons: problems of, 63–64, 67–68
Congestion: control of, 246–48; as ecological problem, 33–34; examples of, 101–3; and psychic stress, 192–95
Congress (U.S.): proposed reorganization of, for environmental oversight, 305–6